STRANGE GODS

STRANGE GODS

The Great American Cult Scare

David G. Bromley and
Anson D. Shupe, Jr.

Beacon Press   Boston

Beacon Press books are published under the auspices
of the Unitarian Universalist Association, 25 Beacon Street,
Boston, Massachusetts 02116

Published simultaneously in Canada by
Fitzhenry & Whiteside Limited, Toronto

Printed in the United States of America

(hardcover) 9 8 7 6 5 4 3 2

(paperback) 9 8 7 6 5 4 3 2 1

Library of Congress Cataloging in Publication Data

Bromley, David G.
    Strange gods.

    Bibliography: p.
    Includes index.
    1. United States—Religion—1960-
2. Christian sects—United States.   3. Cults—
United States. I. Shupe, Anson D. II. Title.
BL2530.U6B76   1981   291'.O973   81-65763
ISBN 0-8070-3256-5   AACR2
ISBN 0-8070-1109-6

To Donna and Janet

Thou shalt have no other gods before me.

Exodus 20: 3

And Jesus answered and said unto them, Take heed that no man deceive you.

For many shall come in my name, saying, I am Christ; and shall deceive many.

. . . For there shall arise false Christs, and false prophets, and shall show great signs and wonders; insomuch that, if it were possible, they shall deceive the very elect.

The Gospel According to Saint Matthew
24: 4-5, 24
The Holy Bible (Authorized King James Version)

Preface

Since 1976, when we first began collaborating on studies of the current controversy over new religions, a great many magazine articles and books aimed at the general public have been published. Ex-"cult" members have piously reported how they lost their psychological innocence at the hands of powermad gurus, deprogrammers have inflated themselves to the level of heroes, and others have capitalized on the general concern about the dangers and abuses possible in new religions, producing sensational exposés. Little of this literature has merit as nonfiction, and, after a brief stay on bookstore shelves, has been returned to the overstock rooms of publishers' warehouses.

Yet it is on the basis of such reports, articles, and books, and from the TV testimonies of persons who write them, that in the 1970s and 1980s laws restricting religion have been proposed by state legislators. These laws have ranged from the moderate to the ludicrous, including, on the one hand, bills for stricter control of charitable fund-raising by religious groups, and, on the other, a bill (voted down by the New York State Assembly) to make it a felony offense to start a "pseudoreligion."

In all this controversy remarkably little attention has been paid to the actual research that social scientists, psychiatrists, and others have conducted on the new religions. When partisans have seized on a finding or conclusion useful to their own purposes, they have publicized it. Otherwise, the substantial amount of research findings have been ignored. One of our purposes in writing this book is to correct the impression that the so-called cults are mysterious, or that very little is known about them, or that only their critics *really* understand them. Two advocates of such a mistaken view recently wrote:

> The cult experience and its accompanying state of mind defies all legal precedents. It has also taken the mental-health profession by surprise: The conceptual models and diagnostic tools of psychiatry and psychology have proved inadequate to explain or treat the condition.[1]

Here we will argue the reverse. There is not the vacuum of understanding about the new religions and their members that such authors portray. Nor are controversies over new religions without precedent in American history. If readers come away feeling that scholarly research has made the whole issue much more complex than it appears at first, we will have achieved one goal. (In the struggle to understand complex issues, we should not settle for simplistic solutions.)

A larger purpose, however, is to offer an independent assessment of the cult controversy and claims made against unconventional groups. Undoubtedly this effort will not please either side in the debate. We have friends (and critics) in both camps and are promoters of neither. We are not impressed by religiously minded persons in the new religions who would, for the best of motives, save us from ourselves. Nor are we ready to enlist in the ranks of those who have a personal ax to grind against the new religions and who seek to interpret their own immediate grievances as everyone's problem. Be forewarned: we are suspicious of zealots, whoever they may be. If at times our arguments seem to come down more heavily against the opponents of the new religions, or anticultists, it is because statements by these people have saturated the media and thus the public mind. When we debunk, therefore, we are forced to pay more attention to anticult claims. If our assessment clarifies the conflict, however, and provides the average noninvolved reader with a basis for making a more informed decision responsive to the entire controversy, then the book's larger purpose will be fulfilled.

David G. Bromley
Hartford, Connecticut

Anson D. Shupe, Jr.
Arlington, Texas

Introduction

Harvey Cox

Despite all the elegant rhetoric about the Pilgrim fathers and the smiling exchanges at interfaith banquets, America has not set an exemplary record in the area of religious freedom. The English Calvinists who settled in Plymouth and Massachusetts Bay did not come to found a society where spiritual liberty would reign supreme. They came to found a theocracy, as the four Quakers, including Mary Dyer, who were hanged on Boston Common between 1659 and 1661 soon found out. Unpopular and unconventional religious beliefs and practices were not only unwelcome, they were not tolerated. Roger Williams, a Baptist, was hounded into the frozen wilderness. When Henry Dunster, the president of Harvard College, decided not to have his fourth infant baptized because he had come to accept adult baptism, he was forced to retire. Later on, in other parts of the country, Mormons, Jews, Masons, Jesuits, and ordinary Roman Catholics felt the hard edge of harassment and discrimination because of their religious convictions. A couple of generations ago, Jehovah's Witnesses were the main target of prejudice. Now we have the "cults." It seems Americans are never really happy unless there is some unfamiliar religious group to abuse. The spirit of theocracy lingers on.

The authors of this solid study of the cults wisely refuse to become partisans on either side of the current fray. Rather they render a considerably more valuable service by summarizing in one readable volume the best available research on what I prefer to call the "new religious movements in America" and the organized opposition that has arisen against them. Since no single book has done this before, their accomplishment is a significant one for all students of religion and social issues. No one seriously interested in the new religious movements and what they say to us about the larger society in which they have emerged can avoid dealing with the material the authors have assembled or with the careful assessments made. This book is required, not just elective reading for anyone who wants to understand the current controversies about "brainwashing," coercive persuasion, "pseudo-religions," deprogramming, conversion, the allegedly hypnotic power of charismatic leaders, and all the rest.

The authors present the evidence impartially. However, since our nation has such a tarnished record in the area of religious freedom, I feel free in this introduction to become a bit more partisan. Frankly, I found that the record spread before the reader in the pages that follow is a shocking and upsetting one. The hanging of the Quakers and the hounding of the Mormons is over, but the fear and suspicion that built the gallows and fired the hatred are still there. We have learned, it seems, very little. And that is disappointing.

The basic issue is still that of religious freedom. As bizarre as some of the new religious movements may seem to us (and some of them appear bizarre indeed), it is hard for people to see that oddness or distastefulness has nothing to do with a religious movement's claim to religious freedom. It is precisely unpopular movements that most need due process of law, the supposition of innocence until proven otherwise, and the protection guaranteed by the Constitution.

Yes, many people will say, but what about?...and they will name a group that seems to call existing restraints on religious persecution into question. To their credit, the authors have not avoided the hard cases. They discuss Moonies and Scientologists and Jim Jones's People's Temple, among others. They do not try to make any of the unpopular movements seem more attractive or acceptable. They do no whitewashing. But it is just because they have not sidestepped the difficult issues that the implicit moral of their careful exposition seems so undeniable. Although the currently popular sport of cult-chasing may be understandable, it is still wrong. It is not only unethical and illegal, it is also useless and counterproductive. In addition it is stupid, since the religious movements in question differ from each other so fundamentally that stuffing them all in the cult basket makes no sense whatever.

A glance at some of the groups usually included in the cult category should raise questions right away about the category itself. The Hare Krishnas represent the coming to America of Vaishnavite "bhakti," a centuries-old Indian devotional tradition. The Reverend Moon's Unification Church blends elements of East Asian folk religion with entreprenurial energy, American civil religion, and latter-day Calvinism. Scientology is the imaginative invention of an ingenious science fiction writer. People's Temple had almost nothing in common with any of the above. All the so-called cults seem to share is that someone finds them a menace or objects to their teachings, their methods of recruitment or fund-raising, or finds the way their leaders treat their adherents malicious. The result is that the word cult has now lost its technical significance in the study of religion and has become a term of opprobrium used to refer to a religious movement one does not like. Mary Dyer and Henry Dunster were, by this definition, among our first "cultists."

There is much to dislike, disagree with, and even to oppose in some religious (and political and therapeutic and other) movements today. There are certainly dishonest and scheming individuals operating in religious movements and in many other kinds of movements as well. The "cult scare," however, goes far beyond any legitimate cause for concern. It conjures up a general specter, a Godzilla from the depths that must be destroyed by any means available. The fact is, however, that legislation already exists to countermand all the illegal acts attributed to the religious movements and leaders who violate such laws without making the cults themselves a target. It is already against the law in the United States to kidnap people, to hold them against their will, to extort their money and to prevent them from eating red meat if they want to (and can afford it). No advocate of religious freedom defends the right of someone to deprive people of their freedom or to falsify income taxes just because he or she is a religious leader. Being a religious leader does not exempt anyone from criminal liability.

Anyone is free to oppose the teaching of any religious group, criticize its ideas, question its practices, and argue against the claims it makes. I have done my share of this polemicizing in the past and will continue to do so in the future. But those who have created the great cult scare are not satisfied with these forms of protection and of refutation. They want to marshal the power of the state, the churches, the mental health profession, and other sectors of the society in rooting out something they see as an unprecedented threat, and they are perfectly willing to sacrifice legal guarantees, established scholarly procedures, and accepted boundaries of civil discourse to do so. They want us to believe the cults pose an unprecedented and extraordinary threat so that the use of unprecedented and extraordinary means to uproot them can be justified.

As a partisan in these matters, not just an interested student (which I also am), I appreciate the way the authors of this book have shown that there is no Godzilla, that the cult menace is largely a fabrication or an illusion. Their documentation makes it clear, to me at least, that this is not the time to discard our hard-won religious liberties because something utterly new and lethally dangerous is about to overwhelm us.

Reading this book strengthened my belief that the anticult movement will only succeed in creating a new armory of repressive techniques that an increasingly repressive society will inevitably apply to more and more unpopular groups and individuals. "Deprogramming" has already been used against political deviants, and in a widely reported case where there was no suggestion of religious affiliation at all, a Cincinnati mother recently engaged a deprogrammer to un-brainwash a daughter whose lifestyle she did not approve of. If there is a menace abroad, it is probably the growing power of the alliance between government and mental health sectors to keep people thinking and acting the way those in charge think they should.

As the scion of generations of Baptists and Quakers, perhaps I am touchier than some others might be to the threat the "anticult" movement poses to freedoms I cherish deeply. Still, because our record in this country on these matters has been so tawdry, it is surely better to sound the alarm now than to wait until the damage is done. Like our other freedoms, our freedom of religion could disapper. If it did, it would not happen by a single stroke, like the revocation of the Edict of Nantes, but by slow erosion and gradual attrition. I want to protect that liberty because, theologically considered, it is the essential basis for all the others. Unless rooted in a transcendent source, all rights become arbitrary, something governments can bestow or take away at will.

I hope readers will pardon me for writing a "partisan" introduction to such a balanced, impartial, and scholarly work. I do not want to impose the conclusions it helped lead me to on others. Some may reach different conclusions or even opposite ones. Still, it is difficult to see how the oftentimes heated discussion on this perplexing topic can proceed productively unless all sides understand the material that is so well presented in the lively pages that follow.

HARVEY COX
Thomas Professor of Divinity
Harvard University

Contents

STRANGE GODS

1

The Heart of
the Issue

Anyone who has followed the newspapers for the past decade, or even for the past few years, knows that America is presently preoccupied with one of the bitterest and most significant religious conflicts of the twentieth century. Involved are a number of unconventional "new" religious and quasi-religious groups, often referred to as "cults," such as the Unification Church, Transcendental Meditation, Hare Krishna, the Church of Scientology, and the People's Temple. At stake may not only be their fates but also the shape of religious freedom and civil liberties in the future.

Set against the new religions is a coalition of groups known as the "anticult" movement. Like the new religions (which as we shall show make up a diverse lot), the anticultists are divided into a number of organizations. Best known to the public are groups composed primarily of family members of converts to the new religions with names such as Individual Freedom Foundation, Love Our Children, and Citizens Freedom Foundation. Closely related to these family-based groups is a loosely organized network of deprogrammers who act as agents of parents to remove converts from new religions, by force if necessary. Finally, there is a rather autonomous set of fundamentalist Christian organizations with names such as Spiritual Counterfeits Project, Cult Exodus for Christ, and Christians Helping Resist Insidious Satanic Teachings (CHRIST) that condemn the new religions on a variety of theological grounds. While they rarely condone deprogrammings, they and the other groups are nevertheless united in their opposition to cults.

Since the conflict began, the air has been filled with emotional charges and countercharges. Consider just a small sampling of recent new items:

> "Moses" David Berg, spiritual leader of the Children of God, condemns Christianity as corrupt and impotent and proclaims that the day of divine reckoning is at hand. A group of fundamentalist ministers angrily responds to Berg by denouncing the Children of God as a fraudulent pseudoreligion and Berg as a charlatan and pervert.

> Fishermen in Gloucester, Massachusetts, charge that the Unification Church is attempting to monopolize the fish-processing industry and uses unpaid labor to gain an unfair competitive advantage. Church spokesmen in turn charge local residents with harassment.

> A youthful member of Hare Krishna is physically abducted by deprogrammer extraordinaire Ted Patrick and eventually renounces his faith, thanking Patrick. Another Krishna member escapes, rejoins the group following the bungled deprogramming, and has Patrick charged with kidnapping and false imprisonment.

> Local communities pass ordinances designed to impede the efforts of Moonie mobile fund-raising teams. An appellate judge strikes down such ordinances as an infringement of religious freedom.

> State legislators introduce a bill attempting to define and suppress "pseudoreligions." Civil libertarians warn of the dangers of trampling on precious religious liberties and predict the emergence of a 1950s-style witch hunt.

> Syndicated talk show host Phil Donahue, like his dozens of imitators at local television stations, organizes a stormy live session in which distraught parents and bitter ex-members of the Unification Church trade accusations with fervent devotees of Reverend Sun Myung Moon. Nothing is resolved.

The lines of battle could hardly be more clearly drawn. Speaking for the anticultists, Ted Patrick steadfastly asserted, "What I have done and will continue to do till I can no longer draw breath is to fight for an honorable cause, the freeing of the minds of men and women who have been victims of enslavement and psychological kidnapping perpetrated by thousands of cults now prospering in our country and around the world." In defense of the new religions, civil libertarian Dean M. Kelley countered: "Let us not forget the anguish of parents is not the only anguish involved here. Let us give equal consideration to the feelings—and rights—of young people who go about in daily dread of being physically seized and subjected to protracted spiritual gang-rape until they yield their most cherished religious commitments."[1]

The rhetoric of speechmaking aside, this conflict has raised a number of significant questions that some have ignored and that others would prefer not to raise. What is a church, and is there any basis or practical means of distinguishing legitimate from fraudulent churches? When does a religious group committed to promoting fundamental changes in society breach church-state boundaries? To what extent should pluralistic societies tolerate the growth and development of groups that exploit constitutional safeguards and try to construct an alternative society that would dissolve those very liberties? Do parents' rights to protect their children from "bad influences" extend into adulthood? Should we demand greater financial accountability from churches and other organizations enjoying tax-free status? Is there a point at which individuals become so enmeshed in a religious group that they become incapable of autonomous action and outside intervention becomes needed? Such issues transcend the present conflict, and the ways in which we resolve or fail to resolve them will have long-term consequences for us all.

THE CULT HOAX

In this book we insist, on the basis of hard, reliable evidence, that much of the controversy over so-called cults is a hoax, a "scare" in the truest sense of the word. *There is no avalanche of rapidly growing cults.* In fact, there probably are no more such groups existing today than there have been at any other time in our recent history. Furthermore, the size of these groups has been grossly exaggerated and almost all have long since passed their peak periods of growth. Much of the "cult explosion" has been pure media hype. *There is no mysterious brainwashing process used to trap and enslave millions of young Americans.* Few young adults have found these new religions attractive enough even to experiment with membership, and the vast majority of those who have tried them have walked away after only a brief stay. *There is no convincing evidence that all new religions are out merely to rip off every available dollar from the American public.* Some have shown relatively little interest in accumulating large sums of money or in being the recipients of public donations. *There is no compelling reason to believe that all modern gurus and spiritual leaders are complete charlatans.* Finally, *there is no bona fide mental health therapy called deprogramming that works as its practitioners and promoters claim.* If anything, the logic behind deprogramming smacks of the same medieval thinking behind the seventeenth-century Salem witch trials in colonial America.

Yet this cult hoax is not the result of hallucination. Nor is it sheer fabrication by the people who have been most anxious to promote it. It is not a deliberate fraud, but it *is* a deliberate attempt to horrify and anger us. Stories are spread by a number of Americans who sincerely believe them and genuinely feel they have been victimized. At least some of their complaints are not groundless. These new religions are at odds with the values, lifestyles, and aspiration of the majority of contemporary Americans. Virtually all of the groups do condemn and reject the way most of us live. They do seek to recruit and reshape anyone who will listen to them. In general, they do show limited concern for individual members' past ties and obligations to families, friends, and personal careers. Many of the new religions do act unscrupulously and do treat us with some mixture of pity and contempt. Like other zealots, they presume they know what is best for us better than we ourselves do. New religions do take advantage of laws and constitutional protections to further their own ends. These facts are naturally disquieting since most of these groups, if successful, would create worlds in which few of us would wish to live.

What we obviously have in this controversy is more than just a simple case of right and wrong. The issues, in fact, are relatively complex. Real people's lives and emotions are being seriously disrupted, and all of us are being forced to deal with a series of larger issues that have profound implications. Unfortunately, the average informed citizen seems to be increasingly barraged daily with complex emotional issues from abortion to women's rights. Sorting out fact from exaggeration is no easy task. In the cult controversy the basic question confronting that citizen is this: How can one best make sense of the issues and claims to arrive at a reasonable, realistic understanding of them?

Together as social scientists we have spent the past six years trying to come to grips with the claims and counterclaims of partisans on both sides of this conflict. We have been accused, alternately, of being "procult" and "anticult." We have concluded that the most hardheaded but ultimately insightful way to understand the entire cult controversy is to see it fundamentally as a conflict of interest, which occurs when two parties desire very different outcomes in the same situation but one of them gains only at the expense of the other. When people find themselves in this kind of predicament, they want to control their opponents so they can maximize their gains and minimize their losses. Parties in conflict attempt to do this by enlisting powerful allies, by using propaganda to try to discredit their opposition's motives and actions, and by pulling their own ranks together for the ensuing fight. As conflict continues, differences tend to sharpen and deepen until a point is reached where the mentality becomes: "If you're not for us, you're against us." While this is normal behavior for antagonists in a conflict, it is not very helpful to onlookers who must decide if they have any stake in the conflict outcome.

Most Americans are in precisely this "onlooker" situation in the cult/anticult conflict. The partisans in both camps confront us with terrible allegations about their opponents and at the same time hasten to assure us of the justness of *their* cause. We have concluded that what would be most useful to those who are being called to join the conflict by one or both sides is to ask the questions that neither side seems to want to discuss frankly. What are the *real* interests of the new religions and of their opponents? To what extent do the interests of either side overlap with most citizens', and to what extent can any of us allow either side to achieve total victory without endangering our own interests? We shall attempt to answer such questions by looking at what the partisans do rather than simply listening to what they say, by following what the real implications of their actions are for us rather than accepting what they claim will happen if their goals are realized, and by asking ourselves how willing we would be to live in a world created by either one of them. It is our purpose in this book to provide the kind of information that will help readers make such decisions for themselves.

NEW RELIGIONS IN AMERICAN HISTORY AND CONFLICTS OF INTEREST

We may begin to unravel the meaning of the cult challenge to America by examining this country's history, for this is not the first time that America has been confronted by "strange gods." The major churches and denominations, such as Baptists, Methodists, Presbyterians, Roman Catholics, and Congregationalists, coexist so peacefully that we often forget just how much religious conflict has occurred in the past. American religious pluralism is something our textbooks take pride in *now*. It was not always the case. For many religious minorities, simply winning the right to coexist and survive came only after persecution and conflict. As we shall show, many of America's former new religions in other eras generated just as much controversy and hostility as their contemporary counterparts do today.

In the past, three common threads have run through the various controversies surrounding the appearance of new religious groups. First, we can identify a basic conflict of interests between these new religions and one or more established groups. Second, not long after the clash there follows an outpouring of allegations of wrongs, often of crimes, against the groups. Finally, counterorganizations have predictably sprung up to oppose these new religions. If not always ultimately victorious, such countermovements have been surprisingly effective. By briefly glancing at just a few past controversies we may gain a better perspective on the current conflict.

Conflicts of Interest

Historically, when new religious movements have appeared they have created confrontations with groups seeking to preserve the status quo. Virtually every new religious group of any size that has sought major change in traditional values and established institutions has also been the target of severe persecution. In each such case some other group in society that perceived this intended change to be a threat took the lead in mobilizing opposition. Whether or not these perceptions of threat were justified, opposition groups determined that these new religions would subvert the social order if left unchallenged. There have been few features shared by the groups we describe, i.e., Quakers, Mormons, Roman Catholics, Christian Scientists, Seventh Day Adventists. They have differed widely in their beliefs, their organizations, and their memberships. The common element of such persecuted groups has not been any specific characteristics as much as others' fears that they would have some detrimental effect on American society.[2] A few prominent examples will illustrate this point.

The Mennonites. The Mennonite Church, which dates from the Protestant Reformation in the sixteenth century, suffered violent persecution in Europe and eventually sought refuge in America, first settling in Germantown, Pennsylvania, in 1683. The Mennonites believed that all existing churches had been corrupted and compromised spiritually. They therefore wanted to create a spiritually pure church. For example, one unique practice they emphasized was the baptism of adult converts after a voluntary confession of faith. Members were expected to follow the dictates of discipleship as laid down (presumably) by

Jesus. They interpreted this to mean a strict separation from the "corrupt" world, a condemnation of existing churches, and a refusal to accede to governmental control in such matters as conscription into the army. In an era when church and state were united, such acts were tantamount to treason as well as heresy, an obvious threat to both political and religious power-holders. It was this total rejection of established churches, withdrawal from the larger society, and refusal to acknowledge the authority of the state that led to Mennonite persecution. The Mennonites' stubborn refusal to serve in the armed forces or to accept the legitimacy of local draft boards later brought them into confrontation with the United States government in this century.

The Shakers.   Like the Mennonites, the Shakers (their formal name was the United Society of Believers in Christ's Second Appearing) were European transplants, arriving in North America in 1774. Ann Lee, the group's founder and spiritual leader, claimed to have received a revelation of Christ's second appearance and of the visitations of disease and famine on the wicked of the world. She and her followers wished to withdraw from what they also viewed as a corrupt world. The objective of life in communally organized Shaker "families" was to live perfect lives in preparation for the perfect state they believed awaited them. Lee's followers eventually became convinced that she was, in fact, the second appearance of Christ. It was both the Shakers' separation from conventional society and their conscientious objection to participation in the American Revolution that led to their severe persecution by other colonists.

The Mormons.   Another example can be found in the Mormon Church (formally the Church of Jesus Christ of Latter-Day Saints), which was established in the United States in 1830, a decade after founder Joseph Smith's first spiritual vision. Smith claimed to have been visited by God and Jesus Christ and chosen as a prophet commissioned to reveal the "error" of existing churches and to reveal God's full truth. He was ordered to establish a new line of apostles and a new Christian tradition. Mormonism departed dramatically from orthodox Christian theology in a number of respects. However, it was Smith's goal of gathering together a chosen people to actually build a new nation of Zion within the United States in anticipation of Christ's return and the practice of polygyny that provoked the most animosity. In accordance with their anticipation of Christ's return, Mormons isolated themselves in a theocratically organized society based on communal principles. It was the combination of segregation into such communities, which often became laws unto themselves, along with the growing economic prosperity and local political influence, that Mormons achieved wherever they settled, which created fear and mistrust of them.

The Jehovah's Witnesses. The Jehovah's Witnesses group was founded by Charles Russell in 1884. The Witnesses' theology taught that a conspiracy of religious, political, and commercial institutions in America wielded Satan's inspired power and worked together to oppress the righteous and exploit the poor. The Jehovah's Witnesses predicted an imminent restoration of the divinely ordained order when Jesus would return with the forces of Jehovah and destroy the forces of Satan. The Witnesses' strident beliefs led them to clash openly with the United States government as a result of their persistent refusal to salute the flag, register for the military draft, or allow their children to receive blood transfusions.

The Roman Catholics. Roman Catholicism is perhaps the classic case of conflict generated by a new religious group that eventually became an entrenched part of the religious establishment. At one time Catholics experienced some of the most severe discrimination and violent persecution in American history. Their sometimes vicious treatment at the hands of Protestants is particularly ironic considering that today they have become the largest single Christian denomination in the United States. Their persecution began during the colonial era when the Catholic population was still quite small. Catholics were accorded few political rights, and in many areas they were even denied the right to hold public office. It was only after the American Revolution that Catholics began to gain the full rights of other Americans. Much of this early mistrust and persecution unquestionably stemmed from the long history of Catholic-Protestant conflict in Europe, an antagonism transplanted to the New World from the Old. Since Catholic persecution is now virtually a thing of the past and contrasts so sharply with their acceptance today (some 130 years later), it is worth considering the Roman Catholic case in greater detail.

Rapid growth of the Roman Catholic population beginning in the 1820s and 1830s, largely an influx of Irish immigrants, provoked the century's major anti-Catholic crusade. A combination of overpopulation, English politics, and later a devastating potato famine drove tens of thousands of Irish to migrate to both Canada and New England over the next few decades. By 1850 there were almost one million Irish Catholics in the United States, especially clustered in New York and Massachusetts.[3] As largely unskilled, poor, illiterate Catholic immigrants began flooding into urban centers where the Industrial Revolution was operating in full swing, apprehensions among the Protestant majority began to grow. One reason was that the immigrants competed with the native population for jobs, largely as unskilled or semiskilled laborers. Another reason was the traditional Protestant fear and distrust of popery, by which Protestants meant an alleged blind obedience of all Catholics to the Pope. Many Protestants, among them the outspoken Samuel F. B. Morse, inventor of the telegraph, feared that if sufficient numbers of the Irish could form voting blocs in cities (a possibility that eventually proved true), they could then subvert the political sovereignty of the United States. Historian James S. Olson has written:

> In New England especially, many Americans thought the Irish threatened Anglo-Saxon civilization. Irish immigration coincided with the democratic, antiauthoritarian worship of the common man popular during the era of President Andrew Jackson, and Roman Catholicism seemed contradictory because it gave authoritarian power to the pope. Some Yankees questioned Irish allegiance, doubting that they could become "true Americans" because dual loyalty to a religious monarchy and a liberal democracy seemed im-

possible. . . . With their devotion to the liberation of the old country (Northern Ireland), their religion and their communities, they defied Anglo-American conformity. Many Americans resented such pride.[4]

Particularly in view of traditional Catholic emphasis on integration of church and state, suspicion of Catholicism found fertile soil in the United States, where there existed an equally strong Protestant commitment to church-state separation. Certain policies and decrees from the Catholic Church hierarchy during this period (such as warnings against "corrupt" [i.e., Protestant] translations of the Bible, plans for building Catholic parochial schools for the purpose of "saving" children from the "perversion" of public education, and advocating a campaign to convert Protestants) only aggravated anti-Catholic feelings further. To make matters worse, nineteenth-century America seemed caught up generally in a foul mood of extreme nationalism, and Catholics (as well as other groups that did not closely mirror Anglo-Saxon Protestant culture) were viewed as subversive. Thus, as has been the case with many other new religious groups past and present, the perceived threat to cherished values and institutions triggered persecution of the Catholic Church.

Allegations of Danger

One of the common features of human conflict is the flood of self-righteous accusations each side hurls against the other. Wartime provides the most vivid example of the use of such propaganda. In wartime, adversaries routinely claim atrocities committed by the other side, such as bombings of civilians and hospitals, rape and looting, and murdering of prisoners of war. Horror stories of this kind can be more effective than bullets. If constructed and used convincingly, they can serve to rally one's own supporters and demoralize the enemy. Each individual story reinforces the stereotype of the enemy, and the overall stereotype in turn makes each story believable.[5]

Returning to our example of Roman Catholicism, we can see that the conflict between Catholics and New England Protestants was marked by exactly this kind of gross stereotyping and recounting of horror stories. In fact, the atrocities of which the Catholics and other "new" religions of the nineteenth century were accused were so much alike that if the name of the alleged perpetrator were omitted, it would be impossible to identify which new religion was under attack. As we shall see, the horror stories spread about Catholics also are remarkably similar to those currently being circulated about the six new religions discussed in this book. The themes that we have found to be common to both old and new controversies include (1) deception and coercion used to recruit and hold members, (2) illegitimacy of beliefs, (3) sexual perversion, (4) political subversion, and (5) financial exploitation.

Deception and Coercion.   Individual Catholics usually were not blamed by Protestant critics for professing their faith, but were seen as the unwitting dupes of priests, Jesuits, and papal authorities. Ordinary Catholics, it was claimed, had their minds controlled by confession, which gave priests access to their innermost secrets and thoughts. (The term "brainwashing" had not yet been coined.) Another purported means of clerical manipulation were fraudulent miracles by which gullible members were easily impressed. More sinister measures were supposedly used to lure young women into convents. Nuns were portrayed as enslaved either by physical coercion or by fear. As one individual (alleged to be an ex-nun and escapee from a convent) recalled:

> I have often reflected how grievously I had been deceived in my opinions of a nun's condition. All the holiness of their lives, I saw now, was merely pretended. The appearance of sanctity and heavenly mindedness, which they had shown among us novices, I found was only a disguise to conceal such practices as would not be tolerated in any decent society in the world.[6]

If deception was not enough to maintain nuns' subservience, then humiliation, beatings, and even murder were used (so claimed ex-nuns) in order to prevent nuns from escaping and revealing the full scope of Catholic brutality to the outside world.

Illegitimacy of Beliefs. Given its long, majestic history, the Catholic Church hardly seems vulnerable to charges of heresy or illegitimacy as a church. It is hardly a pseudochurch. Incredibly enough, however, this is precisely what anti-Catholic groups contended. They literally turned history on its head, claiming that Protestantism began with Christ's birth and not with the sixteenth-century Protestant Reformation and Martin Luther. The Reformation simply represented the reemergence of Protestant religion (presumably the *true* Christianity), which had been suppressed for centuries by ruthless, absolutist papal power. So it was Protestantism, not Catholicism, that critics said was the original legacy of Christ. In arguing the fraudulent nature of Catholicism, Protestant critics used a time-honored technique of comparing biblical text with Catholic theology and practice. Naturally Catholicism—like any fallible enterprise of mortals—failed to measure up completely to the ideals of Christian teachings. The Catholic doctrine of papal infallibility was denounced as a biblically unsupported ploy to ensure papal control over Catholic parishioners. The veneration of the Virgin Mary, for example, was condemned as nothing less than sheer paganism.

Sexual Perversion. Victorian critics of Catholicism dwelt extensively on the alleged perverted sexual practices priests and nuns who, they claimed, were forced to live unnaturally under celibate conditions until they could stand the strain no longer. Celibacy corrupted natural sexual instincts, critics charged, and rather than producing the abstinence intended it created a legion of priests filled with frustration and lust. There were lurid tales of innocent parish women and young nuns seduced by designing priests:

> Imagine a beautiful young woman kneeling before an ardent young priest in a deserted room. As she confesses, he leans over, looking into her eyes, until their heads are nearly touching. Day after day, she reveals to him her innermost secrets, secrets she would not think of unveiling to her parents, her dearest friends or even her suitor. By skillful ques-

tioning the priest fills her mind with immodest ideas "until this wretch has worked up her passions to a tension almost snapping and then becomes his easy prey."[7]

Convents were thus referred to as slave factories, priests' harems, and baptized brothels. It was alleged that sexually starved priests were using nuns to satisfy their frustrated desires. Of course, pregnancies frequently resulted from these illicit unions, and in what were certainly the most grotesque allegations of all, priests were accused of having newborn (illegitimate) babies murdered and their bodies dissolved in lime pits.

Political Subversion. If ordinary Catholics were viewed as victims, Catholic leadership was depicted as power-hungry and ruthless. This theme was evident in the accusations of sexual manipulation made against priests. It was not, however, these individual acts of coercion and brutality that concerned Protestants most. There were many who were convinced that Catholicism was a colossal conspiracy bent on the destruction of democratic institutions. Catholicism, it was argued, was inherently authoritarian and hostile to democracy. The Pope was elevated to a Godlike position and his reach extended presumably all the way down to local parishioners through a network of bishops, priests, and Jesuits. Bloc voting by Catholic immigrants was seized upon as evidence of papal control. The Inquisition was pointed to as evidence of papal brutality. Protestant spokesmen warned that should papal power gain a foothold in the United States, freedoms of speech, press, religion, and even thought itself were doomed. As one writer put it:

All knees would bend, or be broken before "His Holiness" of Rome; all tongues would sing paeans to the tenant of the Vatican, or be plucked out by the roots; the crosier and the sword would beat the bones of heresy to dust; daring Galileos would sup in dungeons of horrors.[8]

Sometimes specific plots were laid at the door of the Catholic Church. For example, the Pope was alleged to have schemed to take over the United States. The strategy involved sending waves of immigrants to the American West. Once Catholics had settled that region in sufficient numbers to gain control over it, they would launch an armed revolt against the nation on papal order. The objectives of this conspiracy were twofold. First, the Pope simply wished to expand his dominance. Second, papal authorities feared the free, open political climate in America. Should those Europeans under papal control gain a glimpse of freedom, the church's unchallenged power would be endangered.

Financial Exploitation. Given the depiction of Catholic leadership as self-serving and ruthless, it is not surprising to find allegations of greed as well. Various Catholic doctrines and practices supposedly lined the pockets of priests and officials. The elaborate ceremony of the mass, for example, was dismissed by Protestant critics as a tactic for creating awe in the naïve minds of parishioners so that large donations could be obtained more easily. Confession and penances were seen as thinly disguised coercion to fill church coffers. Extreme unction (the sacrament administered by a priest to one in danger of death through the application of holy oil and prayers) and purgatory were derisively labeled as tricks by which to extort the life savings of individuals on the brink of death. There was no doubt in the minds of many anti-Catholics that the church was merely a cover for greedy and ambitious men whose root desire for wealth and power was insatiable.

Sources of Horror Stories

Allegations leveled against various new religions in American history have come from many sources. In most cases, however, the most important and influential source has been disillusioned or disgruntled ex-members of the religious groups (or at least individuals who claimed to have been members). Such persons, we have found in our research, make a predictable entrance into antimovements. Antimovements call for radical action against new religious groups and must justify such extreme measures. They are faced with a problem, however, since they must provide convincing, credible evidence that the groups in question really do deserve harsh, punitive measures.

These ex-members, or defectors, provide the perfect solution to this problem. In the past, whether claiming to be ex-Mormons, ex-Catholics, or ex-whatevers, these individuals have been able to sway audiences and actually incite mobs with their inflammatory accusations and lurid claims of "I was there, I saw it happen!" As a result, American religious history has a rich literature of "exposés" that carry such titles as *Secrets of Nunneries Disclosed*, and *Rosamond; or, A Narrative of the Captivity and Sufferings of an American Female Under the Popish Priests in the Island of Cuba, with a Full Disclosure of Their Manners and Customs.*

These purported firsthand accounts were extremely effective in arousing public opinion and by and large seem to have been accepted uncritically. Many of the individuals who wrote these exposés, however, undoubtedly had their own private motives for joining the ranks of opponents of, in this instance, Roman Catholicism. Certainly the most celebrated cases of individuals with private grudges who were extremely successful in gaining public support were those of Maria Monk and Rebecca Reed. Both women wrote books, *Awful Disclosures of the Hotel Dieu Nunnery* and *Six Months in a Convent*, in which they claimed to be escaped nuns who had witnessed horrible atrocities during their convent captivities.[9] Actually, neither woman had ever been a nun, a fact well known to the Protestant groups that used them to whip up anti-Catholic hatreds. The two books were largely ghostwritten by leaders of the anti-Catholic movement. According to historians who have investigated both cases, Reed worked in a convent for a short time and Monk's only contact with a convent came when she was confined by her mother to a Catholic-run mental asylum for incorrigible behavior. According to one historical account of the Reed case:

> In order to escape censure as a failure, she put her imagination to work instead of her muscles and thereby found a way to get out of her intolerable position with honor. She decided to flee the convent and spread the story that she was being forced to take orders against her will. Once out, she quickly got into the clutches of the Beecher (Protestant) group . . . [10]

Monk, on the other hand, was about to give birth to an illegitimate child (the father was a notorious anti-Catholic activist) and sought to escape her obvious dishonorable state by blaming the whole affair on forcible seduction by a Catholic priest. While the Reed and Monk cases are extreme, they illustrate the operation of private motives in such conflicts and warn against uncritical acceptance of unverifiable accounts.

Organized Opposition to New Religions

Antigroups that opposed new religions have traditionally come from established churches, various levels of government, and groups of individuals who have come into direct, personal conflict with the new religions. For established churches the issue has been the new religions' belligerent rejection of them. In each of the cases we have described, the new religion claimed special revelations or spiritual authority that had the effect of elevating it to a superior position both morally and spiritually. The established churches could not allow such claims to pass unchallenged. If there were a truth higher than traditional Christianity, what would be the basis of the established churches' authority and what was the worth of moral decisions and personal sacrifice made in the name of their teachings? Naturally clergy and parishioners alike reacted defensively to the claims of new religions with anger and alarm.

Leaders of established churches usually warned their parishioners of the spiritual dangers posed by the new religions and tried to discredit their teachings. Often they were not averse to rallying public opinion and stimulating government action wherever possible. Organizations formed with the avowed purpose of exposing and attacking one or more of the new religions. In the campaign against Catholics, for example, there were a number of organizations, such as the American Protestant Association, the Protestant Reformation Society, and the American Protestant Union, which were led by Protestant clergy. Other organizations emerged later to combat the Mormons and Jehovah's Witnesses, and many of these (such as Ex-Mormons for Jesus, Saints Alive!, Mission to Mormons, Ex-Jehovah's Witnesses for Jesus, Help Jesus, and Jesus Loves the Lost) are still active today in the United States.

Government action against new religions has taken place when political interests have been directly threatened. Refusals to acknowledge the legitimacy or supremacy of the United States government (such as by refusing induction into the armed forces and refusing to salute the American flag) have brought swift, harsh punishment. The Mennonites, Jehovah's Witnesses, and Quakers have all paid a heavy price for such beliefs. Indeed, at one time a number of Quakers were sentenced to death for refusing military induction, although their sentences were later commuted. Jehovah's Witnesses not so long ago were beaten and lynched for the same reason. The nineteenth-century campaign against Catholics led to the formation in the 1840s of the American Republican Party, which enjoyed considerable electoral success on a platform attacking foreigners and Catholics. Although the new party was not able to muster enough support to pass the kind of repressive legislation it sought, a distinctly anti-Catholic flavor permeated the policies of several state governments as well as the federal government during this era. One cannot read the history of the times without coming away convinced that those new religions had been afforded less legal protection than established churches.

Large-scale public reaction to new religions has been most likely when some segment of the population has sensed a direct threat from their activities. Popular uprisings have been most successful when the government has been unwilling or unable to enforce the religious liberties of minority groups by protecting them. Certainly the classic example is the anti-Catholic campaign during the 1830s and 1840s, when public opinion was inflamed by traditional Protestant fears about papal power and the economic competition and clash of lifestyles that the large wave of Irish immigrants brought to New England. Protestant leaders further stirred up public sentiments by playing on public fears. In 1834, the Ursuline Convent in Charleston, Massachusetts, was burned to the ground by a mob incited by rumors that a young woman was being held there against her will. There were numerous instances of anti-Catholic rioting during these decades; mobs destroyed homes, churches, and convents, causing numerous lives to be lost. Probably the worst rioting occurred in Kensington, a suburb of Philadelphia, in 1844. A series of rumors sent a mob into Catholic neighborhoods. Thirteen people died and two churches were burned to the ground. The rioting was halted only after the militia had been called out and finally forced to fire pointblank into the crowd. There were similar vigilante-style actions against the Mormons and Shakers that kept driving these groups from place to place seeking refuge. The Mormons were ultimately forced to seek sanctuary in the then-remote reaches of Utah after having been persecuted across more than half the United States.

THE LESSONS OF HISTORY

We began this chapter by presenting a thumbnail sketch of the contemporary conflict between new religions and their opponents. While some genuine conflicts of interest exist between the two sides, much of the controversy surrounding new religions is really based on a hoax, a mythology of misinformation. The purpose of this book is to document that claim. We repeat our view: if we are to grasp the real meaning of the present controversy, it will be more helpful to view it in terms of conflicts of interest rather than as a conspiratorial plot against Christianity, America, or innocent youth.

This chapter's brief review of the appearance of new religions throughout American history has revealed some real conflicts of interest and some issues that stubbornly keep reappearing during such conflicts. There have been clashes over which religious tradition would have supremacy: the degree of separation of church and state, the right of the federal government to compel military service, the kind of marriage arrangements that would be treated as legitimate, and decisions about employment and housing. Looking backward, we can appreciate that Protestants became concerned with the advent of large-scale Catholic immigration, that native workers resented immigrant competition in the labor market, that the Puritan heritage made the

Mormons' plural marriages look like a thin disguise for promiscuity, and that in time of war pacifism could easily be interpreted as cowardice or treason.

Granting that there were real conflicts of interest, today one can see many of the claims made with passionate conviction as pseudoissues or as outright preposterous. Was it ever plausible that the Pope was masterminding a plot to foment revolution in the United States? Were convents actually prisons in which priests kept innocent young women to satisfy their frustrated sexual desires? Did Catholic priests and Mormon leaders possess strange powers through which they were able to ensnare unwitting parishioners or enslave women or make them concubines? Was Quaker and Jehovah's Witness opposition to military service a treasonous act that would undermine America's capability to defend itsel. against foreign enemies? Were leaders of each of these new religions merely greedy, power-hungry despots who exploited their followers to further their own ends?

From a modern vantage point, such past accusations range from exaggerated to ludicrous. However, the pattern of persecution that we have documented indicates the very real fear and hatred felt by individuals who were caught up in those conflicts. Some of those who led the opposition to the earlier new religions no doubt fervently believed that disaster was at hand. Others exploited the conflict for their own purposes. Whatever their motives, few of us today would be likely to join a crusade against one of these groups, yet we find ourselves in much the same position as citizens in nineteenth-century America. On one hand, we are being asked to side with those opposed to the contemporary new religions, and, on the other, these groups are requesting our help. The accusations, the fear, and the warnings of dire consequences are all there—once again. The question we must answer is whether it is in our best interest to take sides. Is it really different this time? Is there a clear and present danger? Or are we still failing to learn the lessons of history? Let us consider the groups and the issues before we answer hastily.

2

Who Are the Cults?

Most Americans have heard the label cult applied to a wide range of groups claiming their inspiration from the gurus of the Orient, the charismatic fringes of Judeo-Christianity, and even flying saucers. The word's frequent use leaves the impression that there is a specific category of religions universally recognized as cults and that these groups can be treated as if they were all basically alike. As deprogrammer Ted Patrick has claimed:

> You name 'em. Hare Krishna. The Divine Light Mission. Guru Maharaj Ji. Brother Julius. Love Israel. The Children of God. Not a brown penny's worth of difference between any of 'em.[1]

Articles about cults have appeared frequently in such popular magazines as *McCall's, Good Housekeeping, Seventeen,* and *Reader's Digest,* as well as in virtually every American newspaper until the public has come to feel, perhaps intuitively at least, that it knows what cults are.

In actuality, however, cult is a fashionable buzz word thrown about haphazardly by the media, anticultists, establishment ministers (who no longer worry about the label being applied to *them*), and even some social scientists who should know better. Although the term has a fairly precise technical meaning, it has been run into the ground by persons who indiscriminately attach it to any group not conforming to a narrow range of so-called normal middle-class religions. Cults are thus touted as new, expanding at alarming rates, and potentially dangerous both to their members and to larger society. They are allegedly the products of a breakdown in modern American institutions.

In chapter three we will examine the roots of this stereotype, which, as chapter one suggested, is an example of history again repeating itself in the time-honored American tradition of receiving new religious groups with suspicion, fear, and even violence. In this chapter we lay the groundwork for our later analysis by describing six of the most prominent, controversial groups called cults: the Children of God, the Unification Church of Sun Myung Moon, the International Society for Krishna Consciousness, the Divine Light Mission of Guru Maharaj Ji, the Church of Scientology, and Jim Jones' People's Temple. In describing the origins, beliefs, and organization of these groups, we will challenge certain myths that claim American society is in imminent danger of being overwhelmed by a cult explosion or that all new religions can accurately be described by the term cult. Moreover, through our references to the growing body of scientific research, we will try to correct the mistaken idea that the current rash of new religions is totally beyond the experience and understanding of professional observers. Such groups are not mysterious, but the public's lack of any but superficial firsthand encounters with them has made them appear incomprehensible. Ironically, the very groups condemned as cults have in some ways unwittingly contributed to the stereotypes about themselves, and where this has occurred we need to ask why.

Before turning to a look at the new religions themselves, however, it will be useful to consider briefly just what a cult is. The term, as we noted, has been terribly overused, so if an effort is made at the outset to insist on a consistent definition, the problem of sloppy overgeneralization will be avoided later in our discussion.

A DEFINITION OF CULT

The word cult is obviously the nucleus of the word *culture*. It has been used in the past by anthropologists and religious scholars to mean an organized set of beliefs and rituals surrounding some object of worship. Thus within modern Roman Catholicism there exists a cult of the Virgin Mary (referred to as Mariolatry, the purpose of which is to venerate her role in Christianity) just as in ancient Egypt certain gods, such as Isis and Osiris, were singled out for particular adoration. Outside of religion, similar cultlike followings surround Elvis Presley, the Beatles, and the television series *Star Trek*.

However, the most consistent use of the term by modern scholars, in particular sociologists, is organizational.[2] Sociologically, a cult is the starting point of every religion. Its organization is extremely simple. There is no bureaucracy or priesthood. In fact, there is barely any structure at all except for the single charismatic leader and his or her small band of devoted followers. Jesus and his twelve disciples offer a classic example of a cult. Nor are there scriptures, not only because the cult rejects all or part of society's dominant religious traditions but also because it is simultaneously engaged in the act of creating its own traditions out of which later generations will record "gospel" truths. The cult is thus nonconformist for two reasons. First, it struggles to start a radically new religious tradition, and, second, it exists in tension and conflict with what it regards as a corrupt, troubled world.

Most cults are short-lived. They either take seed, thrive, and go on to become what we know as larger religious traditions, such as Islam, Buddhism, or Christianity, or they disintegrate and fade away. Successful cults are relatively few in number. The majority fail, for any number of reasons. Perhaps the cult is persecuted into extinction, or the leader dies before provision for a successor can be worked out (thus shattering the fragile bonds among the followers), or the leader is discredited in the followers' eyes. At any rate, the odds of any one group encountering the right combination of circumstances and surviving are slim at best.

As details on the beliefs, organizations, and activities of various new religions unfold throughout this chapter, readers will want to keep in mind the definition of cult as a religious starting point. It should soon become apparent that many highly publicized groups only remotely resemble cults.

None of the groups described in this book are small. Indeed, with the exception of the now defunct People's Temple, all have well-developed organizations. Some, like the Unification Church and the Church of Scientology, even have bureaucracies with budgets running into the tens of millions of dollars and memberships in the thousands. Far from being primitive, these groups possess elaborate theologies and sometimes even separate scriptures. Moreover, with the exception of Scientology, all can be located within major world religious traditions. Jones's People's Temple was even part of a conventional Christian denomination, the Disciples of Christ. Thus the term cult, applied indiscriminately to a host of different groups, from which we will only sample a few better known examples, can be very misleading.

SIX CONTROVERSIAL RELIGIOUS MOVEMENTS

The public has been confronted with some imposing, even alarming, claims about the number of so-called religious cults and "cultists" in the United States. James and Marcia Rudin, two outspoken anticultist authors, cite various estimates that between two and three million Americans have become involved as members in anywhere from one to three thousand such groups.[3] The Citizens Freedom Foundation–Information Services, the largest national coalition of anticult associations, frequently offers the figure of over 3000 "destructive cults" operating in this country. Deprogrammer Ted Patrick, not to be outdone in the numbers' race, has stated that at least 20 million

Americans have been victimized by dangerous "cultic" groups masquerading as bona fide religions.[4]

Yet the actual number of unconventional religious groups currently in the United States is unknown. Determining a fixed number depends on where one draws the line between "conventional" and "unconventional." This surprisingly simple observation is frequently forgotten or ignored in the rush to obtain cult statistics. For example, one list of cults circulated among anticult associations in 1977 listed such well-known groups as the Unification Church and the Hare Krishnas, but it also included the Worldwide Church of God (led by Herbert Armstrong and—at one time—his son Garner Ted) and the Jehovah's Witnesses, neither very threatening to public order by reasonable standards. Evangelical Christian writers have long lambasted as cults such religions as the Mormons, Christian Scientists, Seventh Day Adventists, and such relatively obscure groups as the Swedenborgians and Rosicrucians.[5] Frequently these writers incorporate such religions with the "Moonies" and the Krishnas. Some also mention groups as diverse as modern tree-worshipping Druids and any Christians who speak in tongues. One evangelical tract included the Oriental martial arts of kung fu and aikido as well as various forms of yoga under the "cultic" label.[6] In a 1979 interview in *Playboy* magazine, Ted Patrick accused Billy Graham and Ruth Carter Stapleton, former President Jimmy Carter's evangelist sister, of being cult leaders employing hypnotic techniques.[7]

The range of groups termed cults is quite arbitrary, depending on how one defines "normal" religion. Many definitions of cults tell you more about the critics than about the groups in question. It is next to impossible to determine any reliable final figure of just how many cults exist in this country, particularly if we rely on the anticult movement and hostile Christian critics for our numbers. Nevertheless, a small cluster of groups generally acknowledged as unconventional by most observers has raised the ire of anticultists and has been specifically marked for vigorous opposition.

The Children of God

Origins. The Children of God organization recently changed its name to the Family of Love, no doubt partly because of the enormous negative publicity it has received in the United States and Europe. It began as the innocuous Teens for Christ, a coffeehouse ministry in Huntington Beach, California, which evangelist David Berg reorganized in 1968. For 13 years Berg (himself the son of evangelist parents) had been the booking agent for West Coast media evangelist Fred Jordan. When Berg left Jordan and, at his mother's direction, took over management of the Huntington Beach Teen Challenge Coffee House, the Jesus Movement of the late 1960s was in full swing. The Coffee House ministry, however, had made little inroad into the local countercultural community, so Berg changed its name to Teens for Christ and adopted long hair and the more laid-back language and lifestyle of the hippies. He directed his ministry at street people, many of whom were burned out or disillusioned with the hedonistic limits of the drug culture. Converts were encouraged to move in and live communally, and many did.

Berg's group soon became a local controversy in its own right, however. Berg had earlier in his life been an ordained minister of the fundamentalist Christian and Missionary Alliance but left that organization after a heated disagreement. Apparently this parting left Berg with a bitter dislike of all organized religion, for the Teens for Christ began "demonstrating" in local churches, disrupting services and enraging parishioners and ministers in the process. As one sociologist described their activities:

> Berg and thirty or forty of his followers would arrive at respectable middle-class churches attired in hippie garb, troop down to the front of the church, and sit on the floor in front of the pews. Berg was to refer to these later as "goodwill visitations to local churches to help them get better acquainted with us . . . " but this description is perhaps more than a little self-serving. The hostility felt by the group toward organized religion led its members on occasion to challenge the minister or shout abuse at worshippers. Their radical

enthusiasms led them to loud praising and prayer to which the church members were unaccustomed.[8]

Berg's group also refused to comply with certain rules for distributing pamphlets on local college campuses and was accused of discouraging teenagers from attending public schools. Amid growing public scrutiny and hostility, Berg and approximately 75 to 100 followers left Los Angeles, heading east, first to Tucson, Arizona, then breaking up into smaller mission units that canvassed the country, selling their literature and recruiting new members, finally making their way to a rendezvous in Canada. There Berg began being referred to as "Moses," "David," and later "King David" (many of his followers also adopted biblical names), and he initially organized members into a dozen groups representing the twelve tribes of the Old Testament. Scattering across the North American continent in small clusters once more, the group developed a reputation as nomads, picking up young, disaffected, college-age middle-class youths and living off the sale of its pamphlet literature. The media nicknamed Berg's loose movement the Children of God. He apparently liked the name, and it stuck.

In 1970 Berg asked his former boss Fred Jordan if the COG could use Jordan's Old Texas Soul Clinic Missionary Ranch in Thurber, Texas, as a semipermanent base. Jordan agreed, seeing the COG as useful for public relations purposes. COG members appeared on his television programs, praising Jesus and eager to contrast their former sordid drug- and sex-filled lives with their newfound faith. While Berg's group remained in Texas, he drew up plans for missionary units, or colonies, to spread worldwide. By 1971, when the radical *prophet* "Moses" Berg began to emerge and had a falling out with the more conservative Jordan, COG had almost 2100 members worldwide, many having joined when other similar fundamentalist Jesus Movement groups merged with COG.

In 1972 "Moses" David Berg led his own exodus of COG members out of Egypt, i.e., the United States, dispatching small COG colonies to England, Scandinavia and Northern Europe,

South America, Australia, Asia, and Africa. Berg was no doubt keenly aware of the great hostility he had aroused nationwide from the press, parents of young COG members, and some officials, and felt the time was right for departure. (He had, as we shall see, theological reasons as well.) COG's nomadic, communal, authoritarian lifestyle often made communication between youthful members and their families difficult at best, and parents were frequently confused at their offsprings' sudden conversions and seemingly fanatical commitment. FREECOG (its official name was "The Parents' Committee to Free Our Sons and Daughters From the Children of God Organization") was the first American anticult association, formed in 1972 by concerned families of COG members. Soon it began seeking legal means to investigate and urge legislation directed against COG. In 1973, for example, so much public concern had been created that the New York Attorney General, Louis J. Lefkowitz, began an investigation (with Governor Nelson Rockefeller's encouragement) into COG's operations. Meanwhile, Ted Patrick found a steadily increasing stream of paying clients for the deprogramming service he began promoting in 1971.

At present there are between 4000 and 5000 Children of God scattered worldwide in approximately 600 colonies.[9] The majority do not live in the United States (there are probably only several hundred persons still affiliated with the group here), and after a decade of COG operating almost exclusively overseas it is questionable as to how many are even American.

Beliefs.   No systematic statement of COG theology exists. The Bible is the group's main scripture, but it is supplemented by Berg's prophecies strewn through the hundreds of "Mo" newsletters he has published, making it difficult to contrast briefly COG beliefs with those of other Christian religions. Like most groups with highly charismatic leaders who believe they periodically receive divine revelation, parts of the theology can change drastically within a short time. Nevertheless, we can say enough about COG beliefs and how they are acted out to give readers a general picture of the group's ideology.

Above all else, COG is millennial, which means it expects the imminent Second Coming of Jesus Christ who will rule for 1000 years, after which the faithful forces of God will line up against the armies of Satan for the final battle of Armageddon and the Last Judgment of all sinners. Those who harken to Berg's prophetic warnings (those who join the Children of God, that is) will be saved. "Systemites" (Berg's term for nonbelievers, members of other churches, and even most other Jesus People) will not. Berg has repeatedly prophesied that current events, real or imaginary, are evidence that mankind is living in the final days of the world as we know it. For example, when Berg and his band of followers left California in 1969, he prophesied that Los Angeles would soon be struck by a massive earthquake. In 1971, as negative public reaction against the group grew and Berg made plans for COG to move into Europe and Third World countries, he again prophesied, this time that the comet Kahoutek would destroy the "hopelessly fallen" United States.

Berg has divided up the last half of the twentieth century into four critical time periods:

1. In 1968, Berg revealed, the "End of Time of the Gentiles" and the beginning of the "Restoration of the Remnant of Israel in the Children of God" occurred. COG's special function since then has been to spread this message, cut members' ties to the Whore of Babylon (i.e., larger society), and gather the faithful, who will survive the coming troubles.

2. The "Time of the Great Confusion" will occur in the late 1970s or early 1980s. Sociologist Roy Wallis, who has made one of the best analyses of COG doctrines, describes the Time in this way:

> . . . the Children of God expect a progressive worsening of the world situation, rampaging inflation, increased pollution, civil strife, political chaos, and economic disaster. Berg believes that the United States, being the nation most objectionable to God, will suffer particularly. He believed that Nixon would establish a dictatorship of the radical right, leading in turn to revolution by the left. The time-scale here is not altogether clear, but more or less simultaneously Berg believed that the Arab-Israeli War would

> intensify, drawing invasion of Israel by Russia, World War
> III, and the virtual destruction of America.[10]

During this time the Anti-Christ is supposed to emerge as an important world leader who wins support of the masses by pledges of peace and international stability.

3. By 1985–1986, when the Anti-Christ has assumed supreme international power, the preparations for the battle of Armageddon foretold in the Book of Revelations will take place. During the first three and one-half years of the final seven-year period, international communism will spread in relatively conflict-free fashion. The latter three and one-half years, however, will be known as the Great Tribulation. The masses will be required to worship the Anti-Christ as God, and all who resist will be persecuted.

4. Around 1993 "The Rapture of the Saints" will occur. The returning Christ and his defenders will do battle with the followers of Anti-Christ, achieve victory, and establish a throne in Jerusalem with COG members serving as important rulers and officials during Christ's 1000-year reign.

After a millennium's rule, however, Satan will rise again with what remains of the unrepentant and unconverted and engage in a final confrontation. Following Christ's ultimate victory at Armageddon, the "Great White Throne Judgment" will take place, at which all those who remained faithful to the Anti-Christ will be judged and banished from the newly remade heaven and earth.

Thus the Children of God expect an end soon to the social and political worlds in which we (and they) live. Things will get much worse before they get better. Members seek to withdraw into their communes, taking a few more worthy individuals with them while they wait out the coming sequence of disasters and wars until they may reemerge to assume important positions in the new reign of Christ. All this is prophesied in the Bible, says Berg, or newly clarified in revelations he has received from God.

Organization.   When the Children of God was only a modest-sized operation in the late 1960s, David Berg assumed that the members could remain self-sufficient, growing their own food, pooling member's cash and salable possessions, "spoiling Egypt" (e.g., shoplifting or soliciting contributions under false identification), and in other ways remaining independent of regular work in the outside world. But in the early 1970s Berg began to envision COG colonies of no more than a dozen members spreading throughout the world, then splitting into other colonies as membership grew. A new means of economic survival had to be found, and, like such groups as the Unification Church and the Hare Krishnas, COG turned to soliciting donations on a large scale from the very "corrupt" society it condemned. COG members began "litnessing," i.e., begging donations from passers-by in the streets in exchange for their pamphlets and newsletters.

Street solicitation became common and bankrolled the rapid proliferation of COG units. By the late 1970s, COG had evolved into a complex pyramidal structure, starting with the basic local unit of the colony and moving up through ever larger levels of districts, regions, bishoprics, archbishoprics, prime ministries, and the final elevated level just beneath prophet Berg, the King's Councillorship. Decisions came to be made through meetings of officers at each level who ratify policy suggestions from above rather than arbitrarily ordered by Berg alone. As a result, the modern Children of God has become a much looser, decentralized, and more complex organization than most people, including its enemies, wish to admit. This has caused the prophet Berg continual headaches, as he has had to resist the tendency of individual colonies to grow too large and assume more power than his visions dictate. The facts that COG's colonies are so far-flung, that Berg himself keeps on the move and has no permanent base, and that all the while he must keep alive the expectation of the Second Coming have made the prospect of COG's larger colonies splitting off into factions a very real possibility. Yet to bureaucratize the movement will transform it into the very sort of thing (i.e., just another religious group) that Berg and COG despise. All expanding religious movements face this dilemma, and COG is no exception.

The Unification Church

Origins. The Unification Church of America is simply one local affiliate of a larger multinational conglomerate whose formal name is the Holy Spirit Association for the Unification of World Christianity. The public is frequently unfamiliar with either name, however, and knows the group only from its nickname — the Moonies. South Korean evangelist-industrialist Sun Myung Moon's movement to unify world religions and build a world family that will usher in the Kingdom of God on earth is undoubtedly the best-publicized modern religious movement in this country. Certainly it has been at the heart of the cult controversy almost from the beginning, quickly replacing the Children of God as anticultists' "public enemy number one."

Most Americans have the impression that the Unification Church sprang forth out of nowhere in the early 1970s, or that it was suddenly imported about the same time the home-grown Children of God emerged. Actually the reverse is the case. The movement formally began in 1954 when Sun Myung Moon, a former political prisoner of the North Korean communists and self-ordained charismatic evangelist, took out a charter with the South Korean government for the Holy Spirit Association for the Unification of World Christianity. Moon was acting on a vision he said he received at the age of 16 in which Jesus Christ appeared to him and commissioned him to attempt the restoration of God's Kingdom on earth. He struggled with a handful of early followers against the poverty and political turmoil of post–Korean War society to build a movement that would eventually aim to transform every society, government, and economy on earth.

The Reverend Moon's first missionaries arrived on the West Coast of the United States in 1959 and spent the 1960s languishing in almost total obscurity, with only a few hundred members to show for their efforts. The sixties, as we shall see in the next chapter, were not receptive to millennial religious movements.

It was only after disillusionment with the failure of the sixties' social movements to remake a more just, equitable society that a movement such as Moon's (and not only Moon's) gained appeal.[11]

Beliefs. Like the Children of God, the Unification Church claims to be uniquely Christian, the only modern group truly in tune with the will of God. Unlike COG's loosely formulated theology, however, the Unification Church has a complex, sophisticated theology that is laid out in *Divine Principle*, the movement's main scripture, which offers an updated interpretation of the Bible (both Old and New Testaments) based on Moon's revelations, and in other church publications. Though there is much more to Unificationist beliefs than simply the theology in *Divine Principle*, it is nevertheless the primary document used to interpret America's role in what Moon claims is God's providence, or plan, for human history. What follows is a rough scenario based on its contents.

Moon claims, through direct revelation from God, Jesus, and other biblical personages, to be able to interpret biblical history correctly for the first time. The Bible according to Moon is a "cryptogram," a source of wisdom written in code and secret meanings that must be deciphered. In one speech to followers, Moon said:

> Unless you truly know the meaning behind it, the Bible can reveal very little . . . The Divine Principle gives the true meaning of the secret behind the verse.[12]

Moon traces all problems of human history back to the Garden of Eden. There Adam and Eve failed to obey God and form a sinless family that would have served as a God-centered prototype for succeeding generations. The archangel Lucifer, jealous of God's attention to the primal pair and filled with lust for Eve, literally seduced her (making him the Spiritual Parent of all mankind). Her fornication with Lucifer, made all the worse by her own later seduction of Adam in an attempt to erase her sin, was the original sin that caused God to cast the first family out of Eden. Since that vaguely defined time, all human history has been a succession of unsuccessful attempts by various biblical figures such as Noah, Abraham, Moses, and Jesus to marry and raise an ideal or model family as God originally had intended Adam and Eve to do.

Unificationist theology pays lip service to Christian theology by referring to Jesus as the Son of God and admitting that He did achieve spiritual salvation for mankind by His sacrificial death on the cross. Jesus, however, is not regarded as part of the Trinity (i.e., as part of the triune Godhead of Father, Son, and Holy Ghost)—indeed, the Church ignores the concept of the Trinity that is so basic to orthodox Christianity—and spiritual salvation is clearly inadequate in Moon's scheme of things. God purportedly intended a single socialist theocracy to rule the world, and until such a goal is attained the coming of a second messiah, or Christ, is necessary to end the vicious chain of war, inequality, poverty, and misery. Thus Christhood is perceived as a role to be earned, and anyone may aspire to it.

Moon's movement is millennial because he claims we live in "the last days," when the opportunity to usher in the Kingdom of God is at hand. Such opportunities have come before, but each time they were bungled and mankind subsequently paid for its mistakes in untold suffering. For example, the last lost opportunity (i.e., he had not yet married and formed a God-centered model family) occurred when Jesus failed to win acceptance from the ancient Israelites and was prematurely killed. As a result mankind suffered two thousand years of needless misery. The *Divine Principle* estimates that this century presents yet another opportunity for restoration and that the messiah will likely be a South Korean (no direct reference is made to Moon) since South Korea is interpreted as the "new Israel." The second half of the twentieth century is seen as a unique period of history in which to concentrate efforts on building the foundation—in terms of finances, political power, and converts—for God's Kingdom on earth.

In the 1950s and early 1960s Moon boldly prophesied 1967 as the year of achieving the Kingdom. Later he revised his figure so that three seven-year "courses" or sequences, beginning in 1960 and ending in 1981, would be required. In 1980, however, when the movement still fell far short of achieving spectacular changes in the world, Moon again revised his figures. The current postponement extends to the year 2001, after which time Moon will presumably no longer be around to make further postponements. In the past Unificationist members and theologians have disagreed as to what precisely would be accomplished by each date, but at least pushing the date into the next century will presumably take members' minds off the immediate problem of contrasting their ambitious, world-transforming goals with their relatively modest accomplishments.

Though most Moonies, and indeed Moon himself, hedge on admitting publicly that he is the messiah or Lord of the Second Advent, there is little doubt that most members see him in that role. The Unification Church is a millennial Christian movement with the interesting twist that the anticipated Second Coming of Christ will have little to do with Jesus of Nazareth.

Organization. In late 1971 Moon shifted the focus of his international movement to the United States. Like a general personally come to lead his troops, Moon arranged for several speaking tours across the nation during 1972–1974 and called on American Unificationist members to perform public relations functions. Moon's presence in this country galvanized the American Church into action. The messiah was *here*, and suddenly for hundreds of members, and later several thousand, the last days seemed considerably closer.

Moon's presence in the United States streamlined and invigorated a stagnating movement. Instead of members working at conventional nine-to-five jobs and pooling their wages while they lived communally, as they had done during the sixties, they were encouraged to quit their jobs and solicit contributions or members full time for the Church. This required a "bridge-burning" decision for many members and weeded out the half-hearted. Publicity was aggressively sought. Moon's legions sought honorary keys to cities, citizenship decrees of special state, and pictures of Moon taken with influential politicians at local, state, and federal levels. The Reverend Moon became an honorary Kentucky Colonel and received good wishes from such officials as Los Angeles Mayor Tom Bradley, Alabama Governor George Wallace, Georgia Governor Jimmy Carter, and President Richard Nixon. Moon's speaking entourage rented convention rooms in expensive hotels in cities and wooed local bigwigs to fill audiences from Chicago to San Francisco to Boston.

Membership and finances climbed in the early 1970s. There was a high turnover of members but also the need for only a relatively small corps of dedicated full-time members to bring in enormous cash flows. As a result, it is not surprising that the more psychologically sophisticated Unificationist leaders employed high-pressure recruitment techniques that "converted" young adults for a temporary period but left them emotionally burned out after a year or so. Realistic (as opposed to exaggerated anticult and purely sensationalistic media) estimates of Unification Church membership put the total "core" number at no more than two to three thousand members in the 1970s. The Church has officially released figures of 5000 to 7000 core members and 23,000 "associate" members, but the first figure is grossly inflated and the associate category can be dismissed as fictive. The Unification Church is a world-transforming, communal movement with few places for hangers-on, who will not pledge their full time and energies to the cause. There are, for all practical purposes, no associate members, and the impression that many thousands of core members exist is created by the much smaller group's ability to be deployed on a moment's notice to virtually anywhere, for any task, in the United States. The Church, like many other religious groups, has an obvious interest in padding its membership figures to appear popular and growing (just as anticultists have an interest in portraying it as a growing menace so as to mobilize official concern), but in reality it is neither. By 1974–1975 the Unification Church's heyday of growth was over. Young adults no longer joined the Church in significant numbers, and dropouts continued.

The modern Unification Church is not one monolithic organization, but an extremely complex conglomerate of loosely related incorporated enterprises that seek to accomplish different goals, that answer to the same executive board of trustees, and that (whatever the church's enemies think) frequently operate in ignorance of each other's activities. The Church is administered by two groups: a formal board of trustees, composed mostly of the oldest and earliest church missionaries in this country, and a more informal board of elder statesmen in the movement who advise on Church operations. Below these two groups are specific task-oriented committees, companies, and operations such as the Church's New York City daily newspaper, *The News World*, the Barrytown, New York, Seminary, and individual state-level churches. Such task-oriented committees and subgroups are rapidly formed to accomplish immediate individual projects, such as the Bicentennial God Bless America Committee, which was created when the Church wanted to capitalize on America's two-hundredth birthday to publicize its own mission, and the National Prayer and Fast for the Watergate Crisis Committee. These projects are just as rapidly dissolved when their time is over, and the members are reassigned to others, so a minimum of bureaucracy is required to coordinate the Church's bewildering maze of operations.

The Reverend Moon's role in all of this appears to be mixed. On the one hand he often suggests only the broadest outlines or direction for a task (his sudden inspiration "We must turn to the sea," for example, was translated by followers into the recent acquisition of numerous fleets of fishing boats and canneries). On the other hand, however, he has been known to pay particularly close attention to personal matters, even to the point of buying church officials' clothes or picking who among his seminary graduates should go on for further graduate study at other universities. As the House Subcommittee on International Organizations found in investigating the possible role played by the Unification Church in the "Koreagate" scandal, Moon's personal signature endorsed numerous Church checks and bank drafts, indicating that he also keeps close tabs on the financial health of his movement.[13] The Unification Church is thus a curious mix of bureaucracy and charismatic leadership, as if Jesus were still alive and leading a first-century Christian movement that had enormous size and wealth.

The International Society for Krishna Consciousness

Origins. ISKCON's members are usually known by their nickname, the Hare Krishnas or simply the Krishnas. Few Americans, especially if they travel by air but even if they only walk in city parks or streets, have not seen the orange-robed, shaved-headed devotees of this Hindu sect. Most encounters are of two fleeting kinds. Either people are approached and requested to give donations (usually in exchange for a carnation, lapel pin, or book about the group's teachings), or they stroll past a group of dancing members and hear the rhythmic chanting of their devotional mantra "Hare Krishna" as they beat drums and shake tambourines. Since the Krishnas now wear wigs and conventional street clothes when they seek donations, people may not recognize them.

The imported Orientalism of ISKCON has attracted a great deal of media attention in this country since 1965, when a sixty-seven-year-old retired Indian businessman came to New York City and one year later founded the movement. However, founder A. C. Bhaktivedanta Swami Prabhupada, who died in 1977, was part of a Hindu religious tradition that had its roots in fifteenth-century India. The worship of Lord Krishna as the highest manifestation of God was vigorously promoted by Chaitanya Mahaprabha, a Hindu saint born in 1486 (Krishna followers view him as an avatar, or living incarnation of Krishna). Chaitanya taught that *bhakti* (love) for Krishna rather than worship of other manifestations of God would overcome bad *karma* (accumulated spiritual demerit) and provide ultimate *mukti* (liberation). Over the past four and one-half centuries, a succession of swamis (literally "one who controls his senses," or enlightened teacher) have carried on Chaitanya's creed. Bhaktivedanta's own swami charged him with the mission of carrying Krishna-worship to the Western world.

Bhaktivedanta, a University of Calcutta graduate and an official in a pharmaceutical firm, became interested in the Krishna sect as an adult. His commitment grew, and in 1944 he began the *Back to Godhead* magazine, which continues to be a regular publication of the movement. In 1959, at the age of 58, he followed the time-honored Hindu custom of forsaking all previous ties to the material world and devoting himself exclusively to religious matters. He renounced his wife and five children, left his job, and became an ascetic Hindu monk. In 1965 he fulfilled his teacher's charge, arriving in the United States to spread the message of Krishna-worship.

Sociologist Gregory Johnson states that Bhaktivedanta believed young persons were more open to conviction than his contemporaries, and there is good evidence that the swami was right. He opened his mission on New York's East Side in 1966 (with modest results) and a year later moved to San Francisco's Haight-Ashbury district, where he attracted large numbers of hippies and other countercultural youths with the promise that one could "Stay High All the Time and Discover Eternal Bliss."[14] For a while he also attracted Beatle George Harrison, musicians in such rock groups as the Grateful Dead, and poet Allen Ginsberg, thereby gaining ISKCON further publicity. Like David Berg's Children of God, ISKCON was able to benefit from the large numbers of young adults dissatisfied with the drug subculture of the 1960s but who were unwilling to turn back to conventional middle-class religion.

Beliefs. Classical Hindu theology is monistic, claiming there is one Eternal Absolute in terms of which our own egos and our individual consciousnesses are simply illusions. Ideally, therefore, the goal is ultimately to lose one's sense of distinctiveness and merge back into the Absolute. Since the pressures and demands of the material world work against such realization, true religious devotees customarily withdraw from it.

The Hare Krishnas are monotheistic, however. In classical Hinduism there are three manifestations of the Absolute Godhead known as Brahman (the creator), Siva (the destroyer), and Vishnu (the preserver). Krishna is a manifestation of Vishnu, whose philosophy and deeds are recorded in the *Bhagavad-Gita*, or Song of God, India's most famous and sacred text. ISKCON theology turns this scheme upside-down. Members regard Krishna as the highest manifestation of the Godhead, and his personality's separateness is emphasized, not downplayed in favor of an impersonal Eternal Absolute behind everything else. The basic requirement for human happiness and humanity's highest religious duty is therefore *bhakti* — love, or devotion to Krishna. As anthropologist Francine Daner observed,

> Bhakti is the only means of gaining the right relationship with Krishna. The paths of work, ritual, and knowledge lead to lesser pleasures unless they are sanctified by bhakti. Bhakti is a state of active worship of the deity, not a state of inaction. The love and pleasure are reciprocal. Whatever the devotee gives to his Lord is returned with love many times over.[15]

The Krishnas' most famous trademark, their chant (or *Sankirtana*) of "Hare Krishna," is their primary ritual of devotion. Each member is supposed to say the chant daily for sixteen rounds (one round equals completing the chant once for each of 108 prayer beads on a string). They believe that this mantra "tunes in" the chanter to Krishna's divine energy, erases karma, and generally improves the world. When they rise, anywhere from 3:00 to 3:45 A.M. each morning, they pray and chant before eating and beginning the day's work and continue chanting during spare moments throughout the day. While the group practices other rituals, such as eating their elaborate 10 to 15-course vegetarian meals, repetition of the "Hare Krishna" mantra still remains their most distinctive practice.

Organization. Precise estimates vary, but we know that ISKCON is composed of approximately 3000 to 4000 members living in 50 or more temples throughout the United States. One problem in claiming precisely what the membership size is, as anthropologist Daner notes,[16] is the high turnover. Statistical estimates of membership for the Children of God and the Unification Church suffer from the same weakness. Membership is in such a state of flux, with many new members trying the lifestyle and deciding it is not for them, that knowing with any certainty at any given time how many members there are becomes next to impossible. Journalists Carroll Stoner and Jo Ann Parke in their anticult book, *All Gods Children: The Cult Experience,* reinforce a false stereotype in their sweeping generalization that "barely a soul is immune to the pleas and promises of the 'new' religions."[17] Indeed, a substantial number of curious young people may inquire into what a demanding ascetic group like the Hare Krishnas has to offer, but they reject it in droves. (As we shall see in chapter four, on conversion, the feeling is mutual. The Krishnas have a lengthy experimental period of candidacy during which they filter out the people *they* do not want. The Krishnas, like the Marines, are only "looking for a few good men.")

Knowing that he would not live to exercise his personal charismatic authority for very many years, in 1970 Bhaktivedanta organized the Governing Body Commission for ISKCON. Under it the world was divided into twelve zones or regions, six in the United States and six for the remainder of the planet. Bhaktivedanta personally appointed these commissioners. While he lived they served as his liaisons to the movement, helping to plan and establish new temples and to oversee the faithful following of the movement lifestyle. Since his death, the temple presidents have the responsibility to elect the dozen commission members for three-year terms, as he planned. (The temple presidents convene at least annually.) Temple presidents emerge as local leaders somewhat less predictably. They are frequently those talented, charismatic individuals who stand out in any organization. Bhaktivedanta used to appoint them personally when the movement was smaller and he knew most members by name. Now a temple president may designate his own successor upon retiring.

In addition to Governing Body Commissioners and temple presidents, there is one final leadership group: the *sannyasis,* or preachers. Their job is to study scriptures, promote theology, and lecture. They are not assigned to any specific temple but function as an elite corps of scholars who perform something similar to old-fashioned revivals—only Krishna-style—when they visit local temples. The commissioners and temple presidents preserve some stability in the daily affairs of ISKON; the *sannyasis* retain the more charismatic flavor of the movement's founder.

The Divine Light Mission

Origins.   Guru Maharaj Ji, the central figure in the Divine Light Mission, is the son of a family of gurus. His father, Sri Hans Maharaj Ji, was regarded as a *satguru*, or Perfect Master, and young Ji and his three brothers grew up in India with the expectation that they too would demonstrate spiritual gifts. James V. Downton, Jr., who has made an in-depth study of Ji's movement, reports:

> Guru Maharaj Ji, like his brothers, was treated like a divine being by the many Mahatmas and premies who served his father in the ashram. Thus, he received the attention and affection of his father's devotees, who happily responded to his every wish. Luxury and service were his birthright and later became his personal lifestyle when he was elevated to his father's position as Perfect Master at the age of eight.[18]

Early on Ji supposedly revealed unique talents, extraordinary spiritual sensitivity, and superb discipline. Thus at the age of eight Guru Maharaj Ji, not his eldest brother, was named *satguru* and became (at least symbolically) the head of the Divine Light Mission.

Guru Maharaj Ji first came to the United States in 1971 at the invitation of several American "premies," or followers, who had received the Knowledge (enlightenment) from the movement in India. Ji has always demonstrated a great deal of independence throughout his life, and even though his mother (referred to by followers as the "Holy Mother") disapproved he came anyway. He was thirteen years old when he arrived in Colorado and settled on Denver as the location for his national and international headquarters. Apparently he caused considerable interest among the hippies and college-age youth of the area. His premie missionaries aggressively spread the word of this adolescent holy man's existence, the local counterculture responded enthusiastically, and soon the movement began its rapid growth phase. By the end of 1973 an estimated 50,000 persons received the Knowledge and then moved on elsewhere in their spiritual quest, or simply returned to the counterculture. Certainly most dropped out of the movement soon after experimenting in it. Membership size in the mid-1970s was closer to the more realistic figures of between 500 and 1200 members, estimates of the actual number of persons living in the movement's two dozen or so *ashrams* (communal centers).[19]

Nevertheless, the much larger number of persons who at least received the core of Guru Maharaj Ji's spiritual message or who lived in conventional lifestyles but occasionally dropped in at a Divine Light Mission center suggest his wide appeal to religiously dissatisfied young adults.

Beliefs. Whereas the Hare Krishnas are monotheistic, worshipping Krishna as God, Guru Maharaj Ji's theology is monistic. There is One Reality of which we are all part. All distinctions are therefore illusory. Ji's theology has also been described as syncretic, individualistic, and "loose." The main emphasis is on receiving the Knowledge, i.e., understanding "the primordial energy or source of life,"[20] which is also the Divine Light. The Knowledge is provided by a special Initiator, or movement teacher, and afterward its full implications are to be explored in daily meditation and in *satsang*—spiritual discourses or lectures on the Knowledge given by Ji or other teachers. According to sociologist Thomas Pilarzyk,

> The mystical experience among DLM premies was considered the basis for all world religious scriptures. Continual meditation on the "Divine Light" and its effects guaranteed salvation for the individual and became a theme reinforced through the selective use and interpretation of various scriptural references. Little devotional ritualism developed and although verbal lip-service was paid to the illusory nature of the external world (maya), greater emphasis was placed

upon the "practicality of meditation for daily living."[21]

Other than the Knowledge, however, the Divine Light Mission never cultivated a really systematic theology or developed its own scriptures. The Knowledge is believed to be the basis for all major religions, hence all are "true," a belief that blurs the differences between the Mission and all other groups. At one point Ji was referred to by members as Lord of the Universe and was regarded as a living avatar. There was also a vague millennial expectation among premies that Ji's presence portended some sort of imminent change in the Universe. Little development in the beliefs occurred, however. This lack of a sophisticated or complex theology may be one reason that so many young people were initially attracted to the movement, but paradoxically it may also explain why they found so little there to hold their commitment.

Organization.   In the first few years of his American residence, Ji's movement had a fairly simple structure and not many rules for ashram lifestyles other than prescribed celibacy and vegetarianism and taboos on alcohol, tobacco, and drugs. In 1973 the movement's headquarters in Denver was run by 125 full-time employees, but each ashram was fairly autonomous and not very separate from the non-premie world. In 1974, for example, an estimated two thirds of all members had outside jobs from which they contributed some of their wages to the movement. Members caught up in the heady overnight popularity of their guru probably saw no need for further organization. There had been no significant problems so far, and they seem to have expected the guru's continued acceptance by more and more people. Says Downton:

> Within the Mission a belief was developing among premies that the day was approaching when the masses would recognize the virtues of their guru, receive the Knowledge, and join them in their mission of peace.[22]

The disastrous Millennium 1973 rally changed the situation. The Divine Light Mission rented the Houston Astrodome in

1973 for what was billed as "the most significant event in human history." Guru Maharaj Ji gave *satsang* and members expected the rally would usher in everything from the Age of Aquarius to UFO landings. Attendance fell far below expectations, however, and what Millennium 1973 did most certainly usher in was a debt of over half a million dollars. To meet this obligation, some fairly drastic measures were taken to reform the Mission operations. First, ashrams were encouraged to become economically self-sufficient by developing businesses run by members (such as bakeries and health food stores) instead of depending solely on members' donations from other jobs. Second, stricter membership requirements and rules for ashram living came down from the Guru, which, with pressures for ashram residents to leave their outside jobs and work full time in ashram businesses, cleared out the deadwood and left only the more committed members.

These changes did tighten up the loose movement, at the same time reducing its mass appeal to young persons. Events in 1974, however, had a dramatic impact on the Divine Light Movement from which it may never recover. Guru Maharaj Ji, then seventeen years old, married his older Caucasian secretary against his mother's wishes. Since Ji had earlier advocated strict celibacy for his followers, his marriage obviously came as a shock to them. Thomas Pilarzyk estimates that between 40 and 80 percent of the ashram premies (the core of the movement) defected over this issue.[23] Some ashrams closed down altogether.

The marriage also brought to a climax the rift between Ji and his mother in India. In his years in the United States, Ji had begun to undergo changes she did not approve, including a fashionable hairstyle, Western clothes, a luxurious lifestyle complete with mansion and limousines, and hippie vocabulary. At the same time he deemphasized the more Hindu elements of the Mission. When he was photographed embracing his bride-to-be with a huge smile on his face, his mother announced that his title of *satguru* was revoked, to which he replied, in essence, that Perfect Masters are born, not made. While the remaining American premies may have lined up loyally in support of their guru, the Divine Light Mission of Guru Maharaj Ji was suddenly cut off from the much larger international movement.

Since 1974 the movement has abandoned much of its Hindu flavor. Ji is no longer referred to as Lord of the Universe, and the earlier millennial expectations have been totally removed. The Divine Light Mission has become more decentralized than it was immediately following Ji's reforms in 1974, when he wanted to weed out the parasites and hangers-on. In the late 1970s, the movement experienced a brief internal revival with Ji once again regarded as a quasi-divine personality, and some former premies apparently did return to ashrams. But the growth period was clearly over. The movement had peaked in 1974 and has never approached its former size and wealth.

The Church of Scientology

Origins.   The Church of Scientology in all its aspects — origins, doctrines, and organization — bears the unmistakable stamp of its prolific, indefatigable founder, Lafayette Ronald Hubbard. Hubbard was and is a talented, charismatic individual. Born in Tilden, Nebraska, in 1911, he has been a world traveler most of his life and is a legitimate member of the Explorers Club in New York. In World War II he served in the Pacific as a naval officer, including a brief stint with naval intelligence. At times Hubbard has claimed exaggerated accomplishments, such as a Ph.D. from a renowned quack diploma mill and an expertise in nuclear engineering in spite of the fact that he failed (spectacularly) to obtain even a bachelor's degree in physics.[24] Before he became involved in Scientology and its predecessor, Dianetics, however, he did achieve modest fame as a science fiction writer (a recent visit to B. Dalton's bookstore in San Francisco revealed several of his books still on the shelves).

The roots of Scientology can be traced back to the Dianetics movement, but exactly how Hubbard arrived at Dianetic theory can only be surmised. Obviously Hubbard had some passing familiarity with Freudian psychoanalytic ideas, such as the concept of the unconscious' influence on adult behavior and the effects of repressing traumatic events. Somewhere in his physical science background he also came to think of the mind as a machine analogous to a computer. What *is* definitely known is his cultivation in the late 1940s of a friendship with John Campbell, Jr., another writer and editor of the popular *Astounding Science Fiction* magazine. Campbell was impressed with the ideas that Hubbard had put together on the origin of psychological disorders and the workings of the mind. Hubbard claimed that his new science of Dianetics could deliver people from a host of problems and demonstrated this to Campbell's satisfaction by "curing" the latter's chronic sinusitis—at least temporarily. Campbell became for a time an intense promoter of Dianetics and featured an article on the subject by Hubbard, with much fanfare, in the May 1950 issue of *Astounding Science Fiction.* Dianetics' claims had instant appeal, not surprisingly, to many persons suspicious of or disillusioned with the conventional medical establishment. As one writer described these claims:

> So effective were these techniques, all of which were bundled under the term Dianetics, that individuals could with a few hours of "auditing" (the name for the actual running of the treatment, which was later also given the somewhat unfortunate title of "processing") be rid of illnesses which had steadfastly resisted years and years of orthodox medical or psychiatric treatment.[25]

Demand for more information about Dianetics mushroomed almost immediately, so much so that Hubbard's book published that same year, *Dianetics: The Modern Science of Mental Health,* became a best-seller. Critic and psychologist Christopher Evans chalks up its success to the wish of many armchair psychologists among the readers of science fiction to short-circuit conventional lengthy and expensive graduate training by latching onto this self-help, inexpensive therapy that they could apply to themselves and try out on others. In late 1950, to satisfy the public demand for his new alternative therapy, Hubbard founded the Hubbard Dianetic Research Foundation and became a sought-after lecturer.

As British sociologist Roy Wallis has described in meticulous detail,[26] the Dianetics movement quickly spread but with very little control by Hubbard. After all, purchasers of his book could become instant Dianetics therapists and, organized in local groups, practice it on each other and on "clients." Soon, various individuals began to introduce their own idiosyncratic twists and variations into Hubbard's original "science." Also, as with most fads, popular interest in Dianetics began to wane about the same time.

Hubbard met these trends head-on in two ways. First, through a prolonged struggle during the 1950s that involved much correspondence and eventually bitter feelings, he purged his movement of "amateurs," "heretics," and "revisionists," consolidating control over the "licensing" of persons who could formally claim expertise in Dianetic therapy. In other words, Hubbard tightened up supervision of just *who* would practice Dianetics and *how* Dianetics would be practiced. Second, seeing that Dianetics' quasi-psychotherapeutic theme had run its course, he livened it up with a number of new elements. Hubbard went beyond Dianetics and in 1952 created Scientology, a new therapeutic system that incorporated notions of reincarnation, extraterrestrial life, and (ultimately) a spiritual dimension missing from the more purely psychological Dianetics. In Scientology Hubbard established considerably more complex levels of emotional/spiritual health and definite criteria for the persons administering techniques. Both changes consolidated the authority of Scientology in the hands of its founder. In 1955, convinced that Scientology now possessed a spiritual element that moved it from the category of psychic science into the category of religion, Hubbard's organization applied for and received official recognition as the Founding Church of Scientology, a tax-exempt status it has retained ever since.

Beliefs. Christopher Evans calls Scientology "The Science Fiction Religion."[27] Indeed, Hubbard's literary background as a science fiction writer and the cosmic scale of his Scientological doctrines have usually been linked by critics. The obvious implication, sometimes blatantly suggested, is that in Scientology

Hubbard has consciously or unconsciously concocted science fiction to supplement Dianetics' neopsychoanalysis and is selling it as psychospiritual snake oil to the gullible.

Dianetics' original concern was with *engrams*, psychic scars that inhibit full adult potential and operate much the same as Sigmund Freud's repressed desires that result in neuroses and psychoses or Carl Jung's complexes. Hubbard distinguished between the *analytic* and *reactive* "minds." The *analytic* mind is analogous to the Freudian "ego," i.e., consciousness, normally processing in computerlike fashion data inputs and making cost-benefit decisions about actions. The *reactive* mind is similar to Freud's unconscious. In times of enormous stress, or sleeplike states, the analytic mind breaks down, halts, or lapses into dysfunction. The reactive mind, however,

> which has been brooding away cloddishly without much to do, momentarily comes into play. It immediately begins to record details of the experience — generally alarming — which have caused the analytic mind's loss of consciousness.[28]

Engrams contain specific sensory details of the traumatic experience: sounds, sights, smells, and tactile sensations on the skin. These must be relived, through the process of "auditing," a question-answer therapy process that operates pretty much by a questioner's random throwing out of adjectives and a respondent's subtle reaction to key words, and which, after exposing an engram, clears up its current negative effects. Unlike psychoanalysis, however, Dianetics takes auditees back beyond early childhood into experiences of the fetus in the womb:

> The peace which we normally feel is associated with foetal development turns out, according to the practitioners of Dianetics, to be a pretty illusory one. The wretched baby, it seems, is more or less continually being knocked unconscious, either by thumps, kicks, violent sexual intercourse, or the mother bumping against furniture — all these incidents of course storing engrams in the receptive mind.[29]

The goal of Dianetic therapy was for an individual to reach the level of "clear," named after the button on a calculator that erases all previous calculations. Few clear individuals manifested themselves during the early 1950s, however. These few claimed superhuman (and incredible) abilities ranging from extraordinary longevity (into the centuries), to the regeneration of pulled teeth in the gums, to exceptional resistance to viruses such as the common cold. But supporting evidence proved meager. Thus, clear as an end state soon disappeared, perhaps because it was too abrupt a final goal for believers and one that delivered less than its lofty promises.

The creation of Scientology added a cosmic dimension, involving trillions of years, that elevated Dianetics from (in its critics' view) a bastardized psychoanalysis to a candidate for religious status. In 1952 Hubbard, through his own auditing of his life and past lives, fortuitously conceived an evolution of presumed transmigrated souls, or *thetans*. Thetans are the spiritual essences of immortal celestial beings who existed eons ago, experimented for the purpose of pure diversion in corporeal human form, forgot their higher origins, and became trapped over time as Homo sapiens. In other words, the thetans' illusion (which Scientology overcomes) is that they are human, afflicted as they are by an amnesia about their celestial origins.

As Dianetics had its clear, Scientology has its "operating thetan" goal. An operating thetan is one who is aware of his or her archaic origins and who is "cleared," not only of the engrams of this present life but also of past lives.

Organization.   In transforming Dianetics into Scientology, Hubbard added not only a wealth of new doctrines to the movement but also a number of levels beyond clear toward which members should strive. Such a change was important in giving Hubbard more control over his new organization. Unlike Dianetics, whose main ideas were published in a book that anyone could buy, Scientology now sells its doctrines bit by bit in packaged copyrighted lessons that only certified auditors can teach. By adding titles, prestige, and promises of greater benefits to the various levels moving beyond clear to operating thetan,

Scientology can more easily monitor the knowledge of members. Likewise, Hubbard drew up strict certification requirements for auditors and other persons who might be promoting Scientology so that he could maintain the "orthodoxy" Dianetics had so quickly lost. Only Hubbard is free to change Scientology's beliefs.

In 1952 Hubbard established his headquarters in Phoenix and later in the decade spent a good deal of time in England setting up Scientology operations. He later moved his American headquarters to Philadelphia, then back to Phoenix, and finally to Washington, D.C. Each move was an opportunity to purge inefficient or disloyal members from the Church's leadership. New local Churches of Scientology were formed in other states during the 1950s by a franchise method that gave them a certain amount of freedom from the central organization. Not all Scientology affiliates could be immediately recognized as such by their titles, and the large number of organizations ultimately under Hubbard's control could be bewildering. Roy Wallis suggests that this pattern was deliberate:

> Hubbard was well aware of the value of corporate structures as weapons in the control of both his movement and its environment. A complex corporate structure maximizes the difficulty of surveillance, or investigation of the number of public images through which the movement can be promoted.[30]

Scientology's organization became more centralized in the 1960s, resembling that of a large corporation. It can now be thought of as a pyramid, with Hubbard at the top. Below him are his wife and a board of seven executive directors, each of whom supervises a separate division of Scientology (such as financial matters or certification procedures). Below these divisions are 27 separate departments, whose operations are strictly laid out according to *The Organization Executive Course*, drawn up, of course, by Hubbard and published in 1970.

In 1966 Hubbard formally resigned from his position as chief of Scientology, turning over all legal control to the board of directors. The change was purely nominal, however, and Hubbard relinquished very little power. High administrative officials are intensely loyal to him. Hubbard continually turns out new extensions to Scientology doctrine, a fact that continues to give him immense leverage over the movement's future.

The People's Temple

Origins. Most people who have only a sketchy knowledge of the cult controversy instantly recognize "Jonestown," a word that conjures up the worst images of stark horror and religious fanaticism gone amuck. For many persons Jonestown also has become a symbol of all that is potentially sinister and "wrong" with new religious groups, an unparalleled nightmare in American religion.

Jonestown did not begin as a nightmare, however. The People's Temple founder, evangelist Jim Jones, first came to public attention in 1953, when he founded the nondenominational Christian Assembly of God Church. Jones offered an urban ministry to the poor: soup kitchens, day-care facilities, drug counseling. As he was later to do in his Indianapolis People's Temple Full Gospel Church, Jones stressed racial equality, a message unpopular with many whites in the conservative Midwest of the 1950s and early 1960s. Still, while many might not have liked his radical stand against racism, Jones's operation was regarded as a legitimate church. His Indianapolis church was affiliated with the Disciples of Christ denomination, and in 1964 he was ordained as a Disciples of Christ minister.

Those early years are important for understanding Jones and what the People's Temple became. Jones and his church were persecuted, a fact that some observers say gave him a strong sense of paranoia and insecurity that, like a hair trigger, eventually went off when Congressman Leo J. Ryan and a mixed party of staff and news reporters visited Jonestown, Guyana, in November 1978. For example, one early result of Jones's Midwest experiences was, as sociologist James T. Richardson notes, a disillusionment with the American economic and social system. Jones subsequently became a passionate advocate of socialism. Richardson speculates:

> Why Jones adopted socialism is unclear, but it probably had something to do with his rejecting American society because of racism.[31]

Jones moved to Ukiah, California, in 1965, taking with him 100 members of his Indianapolis People's Temple. He claimed he had received a vision of a nuclear holocaust soon to decimate the United States, and he thought that Ukiah, with its protected Redwood Valley, would somehow survive the disaster. Later he settled the group in the predominantly poor black Fillmore district of San Francisco, then established another church in Los Angeles while he continued to manage his original People's Temple in Indianapolis. In all these locations he pursued the charitable operations that attracted poor inner-city blacks and a small contingent of liberal whites. Whole families joined, swelling his organization with children and persons of all ages.

At the same time, Jones hoped to do more than simply minister to the casualties of America's economic system. He intended to change it along the lines of socialism. He encouraged members to vote and become active in politics. In 1976, for example, hundreds of members traveled by bus to a Washington, D.C., rally led by Rosalynn Carter. Jones himself became involved in San Francisco politics as a member and later chairman of the city's Housing Authority in 1976–1977. Jones was riding high by the mid-to-late 1970s, and one interfaith group named him one of the 100 "most outstanding" American clergymen in 1975. In 1977 he won the Martin Luther King, Jr. Humanitarian Award, an irony in light of future events.

Beliefs. Originally Jones preached a fairly standard, fundamentalist Christian message stressing a literal brotherhood of all persons regardless of race. Whether as time went on he became emotionally unbalanced or turned into a shrewdly manipulative hypocrite is open to debate, but in the late 1960s his message began to change radically. J. Gordon Melton, Director of the Institute for the Study of American Religion, reports visiting a People's Temple meeting in San Francisco in 1971 and witnessing Jones performing "miracle" cures before the congregation:

> On the platform, Jones wore dark glasses. He told the audience that he had such powerful eyes, that the glasses were necessary to prevent the power radiating from his eyes and hurting us.
> In 1972, Jones was criticized for claiming to have resurrected over 40 members from the dead. He answered his critics that such was, in fact, the case and noted the length of time without a death at the People's Temple.[32]

Jones continued to make dramatic claims for himself that had the effect of increasing his power over members. At various times he stated that he was a reincarnation of Jesus Christ, Buddha, Karl Marx, and Vladimir Lenin. He had always used biblical scriptures to suit his purposes, but in San Francisco the Bible began to mean steadily less to his congregation, and was replaced by his own charismatic prophecies. For years Jones had encouraged his members to think of him paternally, to call him "Dad." Though some later defectors from the People's Temple undoubtedly distorted or embellished their experiences to make good stories, one ex-member's statement is no doubt reliable:

> In 1973 he [Jones] actually came out and said he wanted to be called *Father*, and he wanted us to pray to him. He wanted us to carry around his picture in our wallets.[33]

Jones introduced various new elements into the "theology" of the People's Temple besides his own visions. His conviction that the "Fascists" who would ultimately take over the United States had singled out the Temple for persecution was an idea that had been germinating ever since vandals and racists had harassed his church in Indianapolis. Growing criticism of him in the media, some outspoken reports by disgruntled defectors, and a very negative *New West* magazine exposé article that featured interviews with those same unhappy ex-members and the relatives of members added to his defensiveness. It has since emerged that Jones became a heavy user of various drugs during his last years, and they undoubtedly increased his loss of touch with reality if not his sense of persecution. This feeling, plus his growing belief in his own Godlike destiny, must have been mental torture for him.

Jones also became attracted to the idea of "revolutionary suicide," particularly after he moved most of his organization to remote Jonestown in 1977. Revolutionary suicide was the gruesomely romantic idea of Black Panther activist Huey Newton, who believed that a collective suicide, as a dramatic act of defiance, was a logical symbolic weapon to use in furthering socialism. Jones transformed this idea into a sacrament, staging ritualist "communions" at which followers were told they were about to drink, or had just drunk, poison. Sociologist Richardson notes:

> Jones seemed to understand the basic fact that ritual is often more important than belief; behavior usually predates belief. At the very least, the drills were analogous to fire drills for school children practicing what to do in a time of danger.[34]

Organization. The People's Temple was not typical of other so-called cults that largely recruited young adult (predominantly white) children of middle-class families in the early 1970s. Of the more than 900 persons who died at Jonestown, 137 were 11 years old or younger and 199 were collecting social security. More important, between 70 and 80 percent were black and from the lower economic end of American society.[35] A telling statement about Jones's practice of his preachings on racial equality was that few nonwhites made it very far into the upper ranks of his church.

Jones ran the People's Temple with an extraordinarily firm grasp. He was the final, charismatic authority who, in the end, literally exploited his life-and-death control over members. On a daily basis he supervised various aspects of the group's activities, but he did have the church organized into several layers of responsibility beneath him. Immediately answerable to Jones were his "angels," 15 to 20 physically attractive Caucasian women who acted as his assistants (and who on occasion also administered to his sexual needs). Below the "angels" was the "planning commission," a cadre of about 100 middle-echelon members (approximately one-third of whom were black) who actually ran the mundane operations of the People's Temple by coordinating orders from above with rank and file members, who were often organized into specific "teams" or "details" to cover specific tasks.

The entire organization was exceptionally authoritarian, particularly once Jones and the majority of his followers arrived in Jonestown. The planning commission, as a sort of members' review board, had been responsible for discipline in the United States. In Jonestown armed guards discouraged members' contact with the outside world and vice versa without Jones's permission. They ultimately kept many members at gunpoint during the macabre communion death when Jones urged his followers to drink cyanide-laced Kool-Aid and offer up one final, collective, sacrificial gesture of defiance to his "enemies."

EVALUATING THE CULT STEREOTYPE

How well does the prevailing stereotype of cults—that they all have essentially the same features and thus can be treated alike—stand up under critical scrutiny? When we demand facts and not merely pat generalizations to support claims about who and what the cults represent, how far does the current popular "conventional wisdom" take us? As we have seen in this chapter, the answer is: *not very far.*

None of the six major groups considered here closely resembles the formal definition of a cult as the starting point of a religion. Indeed, one of this chapter's major points has been that the label cult as currently applied is a buzz word that has been indiscriminately used until it has lost its usefulness. As to their *beliefs*, the "big six" new religions are worlds apart, even in the case of the two Hindu-based groups, the Hare Krishnas and the Divine Light Mission. One is monotheistic, theologically rigid, and monastic. The other is monistic, theologically open, and only partially communal. The Christian-based groups show no more uniformity than the Hindu groups. David Berg's fundamentalist, millennial scheme in the Children of God, with its expectations of violent upheaval and Jesus' imminent return, bears little resemblance to either Sun Myung Moon's plan for a benevolent Kingdom of God on earth or Jim Jones's concept of an ideal community. The Scientologists' doctrines have nothing in common with any of the other groups.

Structurally as well, the six groups are extremely diverse. Jim Jones, like L. Ron Hubbard, ran the People's Temple authoritatively, focusing the group's attention on his personality. Yet Scientology makes nowhere the demands on time and resources of members that the People's Temple did. The Children of God's far-flung "colonies" have left the movement decentralized rather than under Berg's close control; indeed, he is currently in the precarious position of becoming merely a nominal leader. Likewise, the Reverend Moon has a general inspirational leadership role in the Unification Church, occasionally stooping to involve himself in the mundane affairs of church leadership but often unconcerned about daily operations. Certainly he has, at best, only a loose control (on a daily basis) over the many scattered operations of the Unification Church. The Divine Light Mission is even more decentralized, and the Hare Krishnas (since their founder's death) now conduct their affairs in the classic style of a federation.

The *origins* of the six groups are quite dissimilar. Hare Krishna's Bhaktivedanta, who retired from business life as an elderly man, received the authority of a holy man passed on to him by teachers in a centuries-old Hindu tradition. Guru Maharaj Ji was born into more modern guruship in an ongoing Hindu movement and retained his title even after being disowned by his mother (herself a Hindu saint). The Reverend Moon and David

Berg each claim direct revelation from God as the source of their respective authorities. Not so Scientology, which is grounded (it claims) in the superior insight of its founder and in reliable scientific explanation.

Lifestyles of the six groups are not identical. Few Scientologists, except the highest leaders and staffs, live in anything resembling a communal lifestyle. Yet a communal lifestyle is precisely what the Unification Church and the Hare Krishnas have extolled to members as an important ideal arrangement. A core of the Divine Light Mission's members also live communally, but, unlike the Moonies and the Krishnas, many do not work communally. At the end the People's Temple did live communally in Jonestown, but for most of the group's existence members lived in conventional nuclear family households and worked at conventional jobs.

Finally, the claim that the new religions all have enormous memberships can only be accepted as the grossest exaggeration, and the further claim that they are spreading rapidly can be dismissed as virtual myth. With the exception of Scientology (whose members number in the several tens of thousands but who have few operational demands placed on their individual lifestyles), none of the new religions discussed here has numbered more than a few thousand members at its peak. Most groups, as we have shown, are now past that peak. Both the Children of God and the Divine Light Mission now number their *American* members in the *hundreds*. The Krishnas' size has stabilized at several thousand members, at most. That the public and the press still repeat estimates of total Unification Church membership as around 30,000 or more testifies to the vigorous "hype" job the Church's public relations office has engineered. Such commonly accepted estimates say more about the need for large Moonie membership figures that angry parents can point to in their lobbying efforts before public officials, and perhaps about the gullibility of news reporters, than about Moon's group itself.

In sum, any decision by reasonable people as to how to react to the new religions must take into account the facts that these groups are not the same in how they live, *or* in what they believe, *or* in what they have set out to accomplish. Decisions should be based on facts, not stereotypes and prejudice. Such new religions have received publicity—in some cases have sought it aggressively—far out of proportion to their real numbers. Ultimately what has earned all of them the label cult is the same pair of factors: first the unconventional attitudes and practices that do not conform to other mainstream religious groups, and second, the intellectual laziness of many people who do not wish to complicate the issue by recognizing the important differences among new religions. Many sincere people who practice this laziness, stereotyping all new religions as cults and treating them as one homogeneous category, would be horrified if it were suggested that they apply the same careless generalizations to all members of a given race or nationality.

We argue that neither the members of the general public nor law enforcement and government officials should be stampeded into legislating new laws or taking extreme actions on the basis of hysteria, fear, anger, or misleading statistics. Any meaningful response by larger society to unconventional religions must be made in terms of an informed, rather than a partisan or one-sided, viewpoint. Otherwise the long-run implications for American religion may be grave indeed.

3

The Cults' Challenge to America

Since the mid-1970s it has become commonplace for American newspapers and magazines to feature stories warning of the dangers of cults. Indeed, it seems as if our whole way of life is in imminent danger. Typical headlines in newspapers read "Cult Compared to Nazi Youth Organization," "Escapee Says Cult Wants 1984 World," "Cult Called U.S. Greatest Threat," "He Was A Walking Zombie," and "We Lost Our Child." The stories that follow such headlines depict nightmarish situations: innocent children being snatched off the streets and turned into virtual robots, pseudoreligions masquerading as legitimate Christian churches to conceal politically subversive activities, cynical gurus exploiting naive followers both physically and emotionally to accumulate power and money, and families being destroyed as cults turn sons and daughters against their own parents. While headline writers and journalists certainly search for the most sensational aspects of stories in order to capture readers' attention, this controversy is not merely the result of media hype. These articles usually reflect the inflammatory language used by opponents of the new religions, many of whom genuinely feel that they are dangerous for us all. But we need to ask: who are the opponents of the new religions and just what is it they find so alarming about these groups they call cults?

Our research has pointed to three institutions that have come into direct conflict with the new religions—government, church, and family. Only at the most general level can we find a common threat to all three institutions, and that threat comes in a challenge to their authority and legitimacy. Because the interests of the three institutions vary considerably, however, the type of challenge posed to each also differs. To make it more complicated, the new religions share few characteristics in common, which means that individually they do not present the same kind of threat to each institution. As we shall see, it is families of individuals who join certain of the new religions who are most vocal and hostile toward these groups. In fact, family members, primarily parents, form the core of what has come to be called the anticult movement. In order to understand this movement, let us take a look at the sources of conflict between government, churches, and families and the new religions.

GOVERNMENT

Conflicts between new religions and various governmental agencies have centered on the very legitimacy of the government, control over the means and use of violence, political activity by organizations claiming to be churches, and the rights and exemptions to which new religions are entitled as churches. Yet in this controversy various government agencies have proved more than capable of meeting the challenges posed by the new religions. In fact, none of the new religions has mounted what could be termed a serious or imminent threat to either governmental authority or legitimacy.

Legitimacy

Potentially the gravest threat to governmental legitimacy never fully materialized, as a result of the suicide/murders at Jonestown. Although the details are cloudy because there were so few surviving members of People's Temple, it appears that Jim Jones could have presented the American government with major political and diplomatic embarrassments. Jim Jones became increasingly disenchanted with America and paranoid about persecution in the years prior to the Jonestown tragedy. During the 1950s, Jones's interracial church in Indianapolis earned the enmity of residents of that conservative, segregated community. His move from Indianapolis to California in 1964 was motivated at least in part by a conviction that nuclear holocaust and mass extermination of blacks were imminent. Although People's Temple engaged in a variety of civic projects in California that assisted the poor and developed working relationships with many prominent political figures, Jones never escaped controversy because of questionable financial practices and shady tent-service healings. Somewhere along the way he also moved toward atheism and communism. It was the combination of his vision of imminent disaster in America and his growing commitment to communism that led him to establish the Jonestown community.

Guyana's socialist government was willing to offer sanctuary to Jones and his followers because of his political leanings. For the first three years, Jonestown was populated by only a few dozen young members of People's Temple. It was only after conflicts with ex-members were publicized and an exposé article in *New West* magazine prompted an official investigation of People's Temple that Jones began the mass exodus to Guyana. Yet even here he did not feel secure. People's Temple had come to the attention of federal officials. Representative Leo J. Ryan gave opponents a sympathetic hearing, which culminated in Ryan's ill-fated trip to Jonestown. By this time, Jones was conducting suicide drills based on the concept of revolutionary suicide and planning another migration from Guyana, probably to a Soviet-bloc nation.

It is difficult to calculate the magnitude of the propaganda victory communist nations would have gained by such a mass defection. Since World War II Americans have reveled in defections by communist intellectuals, dancers, soldiers, and athletes, taking them as evidence that communism is equivalent to tyranny and that no one voluntarily lives in a communist nation. America has experienced a few embarrassing moments when a handful of Korean War POW's refused repatriation to the United States and a few black militants fled this country for socialist nations during the 1960s. All of this pales, however, in comparison to the specter of nearly a thousand black and white Americans as a group openly rejecting America and migrating to a socialist country. Such an event would have played into the hands of the Soviet Union, which has made a concerted effort in recent years to portray the United States in the Third World as an oppressor of the disadvantaged in general and racial minorities in particular. As it turned out, the deaths at Jonestown were blamed on Jim Jones's deteriorating mental state and his fading ability to exert absolute control over his followers through a combination of force, deception, and mind control. Revolutionary suicide was never given serious consideration as an explanation for the deaths at Jonestown, even though it appears that a substantial number of individuals took their own lives without being forced to at gunpoint. As a result, the U.S. government did not suffer any major loss of face or feel great embarrassment. Jones was simply dismissed as a nut, a paranoid, and a fanatic.

Violence

Violence has been a red-flag issue in the volatile controversy surrounding new religious movements. With a few carefully defined exceptions, such as parents' rights to punish children, government maintains a total monopoly over the legitimate use of force, and hence acts of violence immediately trigger some type of governmental intervention. Both apparently senseless random violence and terrorist conspiratorial violence create public fear and insecurity. Thus, for government and the public alike the prospect of religious fanatics, who have already condemned conventional society, arming themselves for unknown purposes is frightening. There have been reports that various new religions have been stockpiling weapons. During 1980, for example, law enforcement officers raided a ranch run by a leader of the Hare Krishnas ostensibly in search of stolen property. What they uncovered instead was a large supply of semiauto-

matic rifles and shotguns. National spokesmen for the Hare
Krishnas disavowed the stockpiling of weapons and reportedly
censured the leader in question. A similar incident occurred
when students in a mid-Kansas college operated by The Way
began enrolling in a state-sponsored hunter safety course dealing
with firearms use. Spokespersons for The Way have defended
the large enrollments as a method of helping students overcome
a fear of firearms and allowing them to qualify for hunting
licenses. According to other reports, few students actually apply
for hunting licenses and large groups of members have been
observed firing rifles and and shotguns in remote rural locations.

Arms and ammunition also were discovered at Jonestown
following the suicide/murders, and Jones was known to
maintain a contingent of armed guards who patrolled the settle-
ment boundaries. But neither the quantity of arms nor the
patrols seemed particularly sinister in Jonestown's remote
jungle location. Nor is the practice of stockpiling weapons
characteristic of most new religions. Furthermore, it does not
appear that the groups anticultists most vigorously oppose are
more likely than others to possess arms. Recent reports indicate, for example, that a variety of religious groups such as the
Christian Patriots Defense League (founded by the Conservative
Churches of America) and Posse Comitatus have stockpiled
weapons and formed paramilitary operations. While such activities always raise concern among members of the public and law
enforcement agencies, they are quite common among groups
that feel themselves to be threatened and embattled. Organizations ranging from the Ku Klux Klan to the Black Panthers have
engaged in similar practices, and violent confrontations have
sometimes resulted. The new religions therefore do not appear
to have created a unique threat. Liberal firearms laws in the
United States promise to make gun control a continuing
problem involving radical groups of right-wing, left-wing, and
extremist religious persuasions.

Ultimately, it is the use of force, violence, or intimidation
with which the public and law officers are concerned rather than
the mere possession of weapons. There have been some cases of

force and intimidation both by and against members of new religions. All other incidents were, of course, dwarfed by the tragedy at Jonestown, where over nine hundred people lost their lives. Although it will never be known how many of those at Jonestown died willingly, it is clear that many did not. The five members of Representative Leo J. Ryan's party who died were killed in an ambush at the Port Kaituma airfield. Approximately two hundred children were murdered—either forced to drink the cyanide-laced Kool-Aid or unaware of its deadly contents. It was the tragic events at Jonestown more than anything else that raised fears of violence by new religions. Following Jonestown, opponents of the new religions began to play on the violence theme by labeling as cults various groups with no resemblance or connection to the new religions. The Manson family was dubbed a cult, and Patty Hearst became an example of the kind of mindless violence that could be expected from brainwashed cult members. Synanon, the group once heralded for its treatment of heroin addicts, was labeled a cult after the organization moved toward a communal type of organization. Addicts became permanent members of the community and intermarried and the group developed a paramilitary structure. Synanon captured national attention in 1978 when Paul Morantz, an attorney who had won a $300,000 settlement against Synanon, was bitten by a rattlesnake placed in his mailbox by group members. A series of instances in which opponents or investigators of Synanon were threatened and intimidated were later discovered, including one in which Patricia Lynch, a television producer for NBC, received repeated death threats following the televising of a negative report on the group in June 1978. These and other such stories were spread by opponents of the new religions in the hope that they could convince political leaders at all levels of government to begin a general crackdown on cults.

The most direct attempt to link the new religions to violence in general and Jonestown in particular involved the Unification Church. The anticultists began producing ex-Moonies (admittedly only a handful) who asserted that they too had participated in suicide drills. There were a series of stories in which comparisons were made between the People's Temple and the Unification Church and the latter was referred to as the "Suicide Cult." As it turned out, there appears to have been discussion by members of a few branches of the Unification Church about actions that might be taken in the event members were physically abducted and held by deprogrammers. In such cases, members discussed various forms of self-inflicted wounds (including the slashing of their wrists) that would force deprogrammers to obtain medical treatment for them. Once in a hospital, members planned to ask for legal protection and to contact Unification Church leaders. Since the suicide cult stories had little substance, they quickly ceased to draw media coverage. But coming on the heels of the unprecedented tragedy at Jonestown, these stories only served to deepen public suspicions toward all the new religions.[1]

The tragedy at Jonestown aside, there have been a number of instances of violence, force, and intimidation involving new religions. In some of these incidents both sides apparently have employed violence. For example, there have been reports of exchanges of gunfire and/or conflicts between fishing boats belonging to the Unification Church and local residents in places such as Gloucester, Massachusetts, and Bayou La Batre, Louisiana. Conflict has arisen over such issues as access to fishing grounds, which, according to informal tradition, are passed from generation to generation within fishing families, and unfair competition from the unpaid labor provided to Unification Church–owned boats and processing plants by Church members.[2] The recent hostility and violence directed at Vietnamese refugee families who have tried to fish the waters off the coast of Louisiana has demonstrated that this is largely an economic, not a religious, conflict.

Another series of violent confrontations took place between local residents in Moundsville, West Virginia, and members of Hare Krishna who had chosen this area as the site for their spiritual headquarters, Transcendental Village. In 1979, it was reported that there were huge caches of weapons at Transcendental Village, including military surplus, semiautomatic rifles, and thousands of rounds of ammunition, but the stockpile appears to have been a response to continuing local harassment. In 1973 two men armed with shotguns had wounded four Krishna members. In 1976 two local residents were convicted for shooting up the Village. In 1979 two trailers located at the edge of the Krishna property were burned. Immediately following this incident, a gasoline trail to two automobiles and a house belonging to a local resident was set and ignited, probably by Krishna members retaliating for the trailer burnings.[3]

Actually, there have been relatively few documented cases of new religions systematically employing force and intimidation. One of the most celebrated involved Scientologist harassment of Paulette Cooper, a free-lance journalist who wrote a scathing indictment of Scientology in her book, *The Scandal of Scientology*. In response to her criticism, Scientology launched a calculated campaign against her that spanned nearly a decade. According to documents later recovered from Scientology files at their New York headquarters, "Operation Freak-Out" was designed to "get P.C. [Paulette Cooper] incarcerated in a mental institution or jail or at least hit her so hard that she drops her attacks." Among other plans for this campaign were bomb-threat calls to an Arab consulate in New York City by a member of Scientology who had a voice like Cooper's and written bomb threats written on personal stationery stolen from her with her fingerprints on it. The campaign was so successful that Cooper was indicted by a federal grand jury in connection with the bomb threats. It was not until 1975 that those charges were finally dropped after Cooper volunteered to take sodium pentathol tests to establish her innocence.

There is no question that instances of cult-initiated violence and armed intimidation have occurred. In a number of undisputed, documented instances, many controversial groups such as Synanon and the Hare Krishnas have responded defensively to violence with violence. Yet the new religions have more often been the victims than the perpetrators of violence. The use of force has most frequently been associated with the forcible abduction and deprogramming of members of the new religions, a subject we discuss at length in chapter seven. There have been hundreds of coercive deprogrammings over the last decade, and a substantial number have involved the Hollywood-style abductions and chase scenes followed by a process akin to a classic exorcism ritual that attract sensationalistic media coverage. Because the idea that the new religions brainwash their members has gained such widespread acceptance and because the conflict usually pits sons and daughters against their parents, police, judges, and juries have been extremely ambivalent in their handling of these cases. Under any other circumstances, if an adult individual were abducted against his or her will, transported across state lines and physically con-fined, both police and FBI would immediately launch a major investigation. In fact, there has been little consistency to the handling of incidents when new religions are involved. In some cases, police, judges, and juries have sided with deprogrammers by refusing to press charges or issue convictions. In other cases, deprogrammers have been fined and imprisoned, and civil suits have been filed successfully against both deprogrammers and parents for actions taken during deprogrammings. However, since parents often are acting out of desperation and depro-grammers frequently receive large fees for their services, de-programmings continue in the face of obvious illegality and controversy.

Financial and Political Incursion

Local governments have come into conflict with the new reli-gions over public fund-raising activities, mostly involving the Hare Krishna group and the Unification Church. Municipal offi-cials have come under pressure from three sources: (1) local anticult groups, which see denying the new religions' financial base as an effective angle of attack, (2) leaders of charitable organizations, who resent these groups' skimming of local charitable dollars and fear that the public may become unduly suspicious of all fund-raisers, and (3) community residents who tire of being constantly besieged by Moonie and Krishna fund-raisers. There is no doubt that fund-raisers have little concern for the effects of their activities on local organizations and citizens, and municipal officials have responded by enforcing ordinances aimed at public solicitation. Attempts to control fund-raising through the use of local ordinances have not been very successful since the courts have found most restrictive statutes unconstitutional. For most communities, however, fund-raising teams are only a periodic nuisance, and in most areas where such fund-raising occurs frequently (such as airports) some mutual accommodation between new religions and officials has been reached. As long as fund-raisers obtain local permits, properly identify themselves, and do not harass pedestrians beyond an initial request for funds there is little local officials can do to contain their activities.

There have been several instances in which new religions have been charged with engaging in illicit political activities. During the Koreagate scandal, South Korean agents and diplomats were charged with paying bribes to U.S. officials in return for pledges of their continued support of economic and military aid to the South Korean government. Attempts were made to implicate the Unification Church in this affair because of the close ties between Moon and South Korean leaders. Ex-members of the Unification Church testified that they had been involved in lobbying for aid to South Korea. Their efforts apparently involved letter writing to congressional leaders, attempts to ingratiate themselves with congressmen and their aides, and efforts to persuade congressmen to visit a hotel suite in order to convey their pro-Korean message. Since there was little evidence that any of these efforts were particularly successful and since these offenses paled in comparison to congressmen accepting envelopes bulging with cash from South Korean agents, the matter was never seriously pursued after an initial investigation.[4]

Scientology was implicated in a more sensational case. The federal government had been suspicious of Scientology's claims for its "therapy" as well as its claims to be a church for some time and had been gathering information on the group. Scientology felt itself to be the target of unwarranted harassment and covert infiltration and responded in kind, seeking to compile evidence of federal harassment from documents contained in the files of federal agencies. On July 8, 1977, 134 FBI agents armed with battering rams, chain saws, and sledgehammers conducted a raid on Scientology headquarters in Los Angeles and Washington. Among the materials seized were stolen government documents, a lock-picking kit, and eavesdropping equipment. Eleven members of Scientology were brought to trial in Washington, D.C., and nine, including Scientology founder L. Ron Hubbard's wife, Mary Sue, were convicted of charges stemming from the infiltration of federal offices and the pilfering of government documents.[5]

In Sum: Government vs. Cults

As we have now shown, there have been numerous instances of conflict between new religions and various government agencies, but there has not been any particular pattern to this conflict. The challenge posed by the potential mass exodus of the People's Temple to the Soviet Union, for example, bears no relationship to the problems local communities face in controlling Krishna and Moonie fund-raisers. Furthermore, almost all of the issues that we have discussed involve relatively isolated incidents or limited intrusions into the political arena. Without evidence of any clear pattern of threat, no coalition of government agencies has had an interest in mounting a concerted campaign against cults. So, although there has been sporadic conflict between agencies of government and new religions, we must look elsewhere to find the roots of the anticult movement. Government at all levels — federal, state, and local — simply has not seen widespread threats to its interests.

CHURCH

The established Christian churches were well prepared to meet the cult challenge in the 1960s and 1970s, and, unlike the government, they have not held back from condemning and criticizing (sometimes in a *most* un-Christian way). At least from one perspective, American religious history has been an unbroken sequence of schism and conflict, and so the new religions represented yet another wrinkle on the familiar American religious face of radical challenge and establishment resistance. Virtually no church exists that has not been faced with factionalism, for example. Over the years the mainline denominations have been constantly confronted by new religions from both inside and outside the Christian tradition. The latest series of new religions differs only in that a number of them draw on Eastern philosophy and religion for their inspiration and appeal, which is predominantly to young adults. The contemporary new religions have presented the established churches with three basic challenges: (1) competition for youth, (2) violation of traditional church-state boundaries, and (3) "heretical" theology.

Competition for Youth

The 1960s and 1970s proved to be difficult times for such mainline churches as Episcopalians, Methodists, American Baptists, Presbyterians, Lutherans, and Congregationalists. Virtually all of these churches continued to lose members, and their largest losses occurred among young adults. Public opinion polls show that the percentage of American adults who report having attended church in the preceding week declined from a high point of 51 percent in 1957 to 40 percent by 1971. Simultaneously, public confidence in churches seemed to be eroding. In 1970, only 14 percent of the adults polled saw churches gaining influence in America. Both these measures of church vitality rebounded significantly by the end of the decade, but mainline denominations continued to struggle. At the same time, the fundamentalist and evangelical churches were booming and gaining influence as literally tens of millions of Americans declared themselves to be "born again."

It was during the early 1970s, precisely at the point that traditional churches were reaching their low point for church attendance, that the new religions grew most rapidly. The issue never really was that the new religions were luring significant numbers of members away from established churches. As we pointed out in chapter two, most of the new religions never achieved an active membership of more than a few thousand, and their high growth rates had peaked well before the midpoint of the decade. Instead, the issue for the mainstream churches, which viewed themselves as *the* representatives of Christianity, was that young adults were drifting away from them in disinterest and many were flocking to the "false" new religions. For the fundamentalist and evangelical churches, who were committed to winning souls to Christ, the issue was the strong attraction of youth to non-Christian or heretical churches. So the new religions posed a threat to the established churches — their very success in attracting visibly idealistic youth only served to highlight the mainstream denominations' inability to do so and *their* ability to attract youth to strange gods revealed the inability of the evangelicals to witness the ultimate truths of Christianity. Christian leaders were sometimes quite candid in discussing this embarrassment:

> . . . much of what we call the Church has failed — often miserably — in carrying out its role before God, itself, and the world. Though it is loved and even protected by the Lord, it has moved an embarrassingly great distance away from its original foundations . . . No doubt this apostasy has been a contributing factor to the spiraling sizes of these modern cults with their faulty saviors and practices.[6]

Violation of Church-State Separation

Although separation of church and state is a fundamental tenet of the American creed, in practice each institution has supported the other while avoiding interference in the other's legitimate domain. Thus, the state makes no attempt to tax much church property and defines "church" extremely broadly. Major political ceremonies such as inaugurations always include nondenominational prayers. For their part, churches avoid partisan political activity, although they often display the American flag and provide military chaplains for the armed forces. Even the fundamentalist churches, which have recently been moving toward greater political involvement, perceive much of their activity to be defensive in nature. From their perspective it is the state's intrusion into the moral and religious domains, through such actions as banning prayer in school and funding abortions, that is precipitating the confrontation. Some new religions, by contrast, have openly advocated elevating the church above the state, a position that all established churches oppose since it invites state regulation. (Likewise, the mainstream churches avoid overt, embarrassing competition with one another. There is an unwritten rule that they may seek converts among Asians, Africans, unclaimed individuals, native Americans, or convicts in prisons, but not from each other. There is an implicit gentleman's agreement, or Mexican standoff, that intense competition for converts is unacceptable in building church rolls.)

The best illustration of this violation of church-state boundaries is the Unification Church. According to the theology of Sun Myung Moon, the fall of man was due to Lucifer's physical seduction of Eve in the Garden of Eden. This first fall, which is referred to as the "vertical" fall, was followed by a second fall, when Cain slew Abel. This is referred to as the "horizontal" fall. All of mankind's problems can be traced to this dual fall, but it was the second horizontal fall that divided mankind into warring camps. In the modern world the cosmic struggle between the forces of Satan and God is supposedly represented by Godless communist nations and God-fearing democracies. America, Moon preaches, has been divinely designated as the archangel nation, the defender of democracy. In those areas of the world where the forces of communism and democracy are arrayed against each other, America has a divinely mandated obligation to combat the forces of Satan. It is on this basis that members of the Unification Church have lobbied for economic and military assistance to South Korea. In the final analysis, then, they see political problems, even international power politics, as spiritual problems. And the solutions must therefore be spiritual as well. By this logic political leaders must be subservient to spiritual leaders, and to Moon in particular, since only spiritual revelations can unlock the mystery of mankind's problems. It is precisely this kind of elevation of the church to a position of superiority over the state that established church leaders would feel compelled to disavow.

Heresy

Religion serves as a source of meaning and integration in the lives of individual believers, even if they do not belong to and attend a church. Religion provides a link to ultimate truth and supreme values and allows people to transcend the mundane, physical world in which they live. The degree to which these people incorporate religious beliefs and practices into their lives varies considerably. Many Christians pray for guidance in their daily affairs, attend church, send their children to Sunday School, are married by a member of the clergy, baptize their children, and express a preference for religious rites upon their death. Christianity thus continues to play a significant role in the family and in the major transitions in people's lives. In fundamentalist churches religious beliefs are likely to be even more specifically connected to individuals' daily experiences. Regulations of alcohol and drug use, sexual behavior, and husband-wife role expectations, for example, are based upon religious norms. A challenge to Christian religious beliefs is not just the clash of ideas; it undermines the legitimacy of activities central to believers' lives.

The new religions of non-Christian origin, such as Hare Krishna, Scientology, and the Divine Light Mission, pose a different kind of threat from the new religions that draw directly on the Christian tradition, such as the Children of God, the People's Temple, and the Unification Church. Fundamentalists in particular refuse to accept the notion that true spiritual fulfillment can be attained through any other route than biblical scripture and Jesus Christ. They openly attack the claim that mystical experiences or meditation constitutes an authentic spiritual experience:

A man can get hooked on certain experiences and thereby miss out on true human fulfillment. A Christian may ask if mysticism cannot be just this kind of egocentric exploration of man's spiritual capacity rather than a proper fulfillment of it, a type of spiritual masturbation in which desires and feelings that ought to be turned outward to the distinct, Person Creator God and Father of Jesus Christ have been introverted and debased.[7]

The new religions that identify themselves as Christian draw even more abusive criticism because they directly attack the Christian churches as well as the central tenets of Christian theology. "Moses" David Berg, for example, is contemptuous of established denominations, labeling them hypocritical, complacent, and lacking in spirituality. Fundamentalists respond in kind:

> The blunt truth of the matter is that the Children of God is a bastard orphan heresy. It is a bastard because it admits its mother to be a whore; an orphan because it pronounces its whore-mother dead; and a heresy because it has departed from the true teachings of scripture as those teachings have been passed down through the historic Church.[8]

Among the specific "innovations" on Christian theology that anger Christians most are the questioning of Jesus as the messiah, new revelations that supplant biblical truths, and the assertion that spiritual salvation requires good works by Christians rather than being an act of God's grace. The doctrines of the Unification Church illustrate these disputes nicely. Since Sun Myung Moon attributes the fall of man to Eve's sexual indiscretions, thereby illustrating his failure to live up to his divinely mandated responsibility, mankind must pay indemnity as a condition for restoration to God. Once sufficient indemnity has been paid, God offers a new opportunity for restoration and a divinely ordained messianic figure is appointed to lead the restoration attempt. Several such restoration attempts and messianic figures have appeared throughout human history. Jesus was the last. Each such attempt has failed, however. Now a new opportunity for restoration has been offered by God and a new messianic figure is on earth. Should mankind fail to recognize this opportunity and the messiah, additional thousands of years of suffering and indemnity will be required before the chance for restoration can again be earned.

The implications of such doctrines are abundantly clear to Christians. First, biblical scriptures are alleged to be incomplete. It is the new spiritual revelations that unlock the mysteries of the Bible and make the responsibilities of mankind clear. All established Christian churches, therefore, would have to defer to Moon and the Unification Church, the repository of ultimate truth. Second, Jesus failed in his attempt to save mankind, and, as a result, a new messiah is necessary. The savior Jesus in whose name many Christians pray is reduced in spiritual stature and will not be he who returns. Rather, a new messiah described by Moon (who, incidentally, closely fits his own description), is now due the spiritual loyalty of all mankind. Finally, salvation is no longer assured by belief. It must be earned, and, since the only course for restoration is that revealed to Moon and contained in the Divine Principle, traditional Christianity can no longer offer assurances of spiritual salvation. It is little wonder that Christians in general and fundamentalists in particular have reacted bitterly and angrily toward Unification Church theology. Fundamentalists have concluded that the Unification Church is yet another satanically inspired effort to prevent mankind from uniting under the banner of Christianity:

> Moon may have a strong hold on his followers, but the strings do not begin with him. Moon himself is more deceived than those whom he deceives. Moon is not the puppet master. Moon is the master puppet. Satan is the puppet master.[9]

In Sum: Churches vs. Cults

Of the three conflicts between established churches and the new religions, the battle over theological heresy is the most important. The attraction of youth to new religions rather than to many existing churches is an embarrassment, but not enough converts have been made to cause the churches a serious problem. The violation of church-state boundaries is a potentially explosive issue, but the new religions have never mounted a serious challenge to the state. Their doctrinal heresies, by contrast, are disturbing because they could influence the loyalty of church members and the authority of clergy. Here the churches are vulnerable since they really cannot prevent such heresies. Christian churches also face the problem of trying to preserve a common body of doctrine, even if at a very general level. After all, there must be *something* that is uniquely Christian and that all Christians share if Christianity is really a set of truths. In fact, generally shared doctrines form a thin veneer, glossing over pervasive doctrinal disputes, and every new doctrine or interpretation only reminds us of the differences. So in the face of visibility, vigor, and doctrinal innovation of the new religions, the established churches have pulled together to form a united front. Religiously affiliated presses have spewed out a torrent of tracts, books, and sermons warning against the danger of cults. Their real purposes are to rally the faithful and to crush heresy once again.

FAMILY

The conflict between the new religions and the family differs from the conflicts with church and government in that families suffer the "loss" of a son or daughter. Because the impact of the new religions on individual families is more immediate and devastating, relatives possess a greater interest in combating cults and a willingness to take more extreme actions than the other two institutions. It has been more difficult for families to establish means of communication with one another and to organize than it has for churches or government agencies because there have been no networks linking individual families already in place. However, shortly after the new religions began to appear and quickly gain new members early in the 1970s, opposition groups began springing up where the new religions were heavily recruiting. These anticult associations today are composed almost exclusively of ex-members of new religions and parents of current members, and they have clearly been the dominant organizing force in the campaign against the new religions. Their twin goals are to help individual families extricate their children from the new religions and to combat them directly by "educating" the public and lobbying for governmental support.

The anticultists have compiled long lists of groups they consider to be cults, but it is the three groups that recruit young adults and are organized communally—the Hare Krishna, the Unification Church, the Children of God—against which they have leveled their heaviest attacks. These three come closest to fitting the cult stereotype, although they differ from each other on a number of important dimensions. Attacks on the other three groups have been less intense. Scientology has been accused of being a financial ripoff and of engaging in mind control techniques, and is a significant target because it has by far the largest membership of the six groups. People's Temple came much closer to fitting the cult stereotype after its transportation to Jonestown than during its California days, but the suicide/murders effectively destroyed the church. Few anticultists had even heard of People's Temple prior to the tragic events at Jonestown, and were caught as much by surprise as other Americans. While the anticultists attempted to exploit the tragedy for their own purposes, the obliteration of the group eliminated it as a target. Only the limited usefulness of raising the specter of future Jonestowns remained. Divine Light Mission is only partially communal and therefore has not drawn as much fire from anticultists, although it is always prominently mentioned in their literature.

Context of the Conflict

The Children of God, Hare Krishna, and Unification Church have all consciously recruited young adults. "Moses" David Berg explained this policy by using the image of "new wine." There are "old bottles" (the older generation), "new bottles," and, in particular, dropouts from the System, who would be the containers for new wine. However they choose to put it, what all three groups correctly recognize is that the combination of idealism and freedom from marital and occupational constraints makes young adults the most likely age group to be responsive to their appeals. American youth has always been drawn to idealistic causes, springing to the nation's defense during wartime and manning the ranks of such causes as the civil rights movement, the Peace Corps, and Vista. These groups have in common a struggle against some problem, which, if it can be alleviated, will make the world a better place, *and* the possibility of an important, immediate contribution for each participant. Youth is in an excellent position to respond to idealistic crusades, because it has fewer domestic and career responsibilities and can rearrange its schedules to incorporate participation in a variety of social movements and political activities. Like many other movements before them, the new religions openly appeal to youthful idealism and capitalize on the availability of youthful converts.

The Hare Krishna, Unification Church, and Children of God are organized communally. Groups that see the world around them as deeply flawed and on the verge of catastrophe tend toward communal organization. They withdraw from the outside world and await the impending destruction (as the Children of God did by abandoning the United States for Europe), seek to change and save the world (as the Moonies do by announcing the advent of the messiah), or attempt to change and perfect individuals who have been corrupted (as the Hare Krishna do through the teaching of their meditative practices) as a means of resolving social ills. It is the combination of a belief that the present world is hopelessly corrupted and a utopian vision of the future that justifies their withdrawal from conventional society and total commitment to creating a utopia.

These communal groups strive to build total commitment and dedication to their respective causes.[10] As a result, they usually possess a number of characteristics in common:

1. *Personal sacrifice.* Members are required to abandon their previous lives and invest themselves totally in the communal group, sacrificing outside careers, possessions, and activities. It is common practice in each of the three groups for members to drop out of school and donate all their money and personal possessions to the church or temple. Members also engage in individual and collective acts of suffering and austerity. New converts to Hare Krishna go through a period of withdrawal and contemplation and Moonies conduct periodic fasts lasting a week or longer.

2. *Total loyalty.* Members are required to suspend former outside relationships that might compete with their total commitment to the communal group. Strong fraternal ties are developed within the group, and virtually all property, activity, and intimacy is shared. Converts to the new religions routinely break off romantic relationships (unless the lover or spouse also converts) and put considerable distance between themselves and family members. There are special negative terms to refer to outsiders—"Systemites" among the Children of God, "satanic" among the Moonies, and "demons" among the Hare Krishna—that serve to increase ties within the group by identifying a common enemy against which the group is engaged in constant struggle. Members refer to one another as members of a single family. In the Unification Church, there is a well-developed "fictive" kinship system. Moon and his wife are referred to as True Spiritual Parents (and distinguished from physical parents) and other members are one's brothers and sisters. In all three groups there are strong taboos against romantic or sexual attachments to other members, and celibacy is maintained until marriage. Hare Krishna members continue to live in communal quarters following marriage, and sexual intercourse is permitted only for the purpose of bearing children (and *then* rarely). Members of the Unification Church remain celibate for three years, are separated for 40 days following marriage, and sometimes continue to live somewhat separate lives even after marriage to continue church work. Such practices are designed to insure total loyalty to the group and prevent the formation of relationships that might interfere with commitments.

3. *Personal transformation.* Strong commitment to the group is developed by encouraging new members to think of

themselves as born again. The Children of God take on biblical names and the Hare Krishnas assign members a Sanskrit name from temple scriptures. Unification Church members refer to their "spiritual birthdays" (the date on which they joined the Church) as the point at which their lives really began. Some also adopt biblical names. The new identity is reinforced by constant negative references to former lives, public confession, self or public criticism, and penances or punishments when members do not live up to the ideals or standards of the communal group. All three groups vary their techniques, the objective being the denial of ego or selfishness. Any reappearance of the old self is strongly resisted. Moonies take long, cold showers if sexual thoughts or desires enter the consciousness and refer to such unwanted intrusions as their "fallen natures."[11] These techniques are effective because they are coupled with strong reinforcement for the member's new identity. Each person is part of a larger whole to which he has consciously subjected his self, and the group is powerful because of the cosmic events in which it is the prime mover. Individual strength flows out of group strength, and individual members feel a strong sense of purpose in even mundane daily affairs.

These characteristics are not unique to the new religions, of course. Organizations as diverse as religious monasteries and convents, military academies and basic training camps use similar tactics with the same ends in mind. The means for building intense commitment are well known, and have been employed by groups that have wanted total commitment from their members throughout history.

The conflict between families and the new religions must be understood in the context of their attraction for idealistic young adults and their communal organization. Although it may be hard for parents to comprehend, it is precisely the self-sacrifice and hardship that have attracted youth to the new religions. And it is the communally organized new religions that are most strict and demanding. As one writer observed:

The comfortable affluence of the life of the American dream seemed, for many youths, to lack a sense of ordeal, of challenge or hardship. Designated life plans (such as college, graduate schools, and professional employment) were merely carefully prescribed expressions of parental ideals. The alternative life is based on one's free choice, its constraints the result of personal decision, as opposed to the external forces of school, family or employment.[12]

At the heart of the anticult controversy is this understandable if tragic fact: young adults have left the paths that would lead them eventually to conventional careers and families, choosing instead bizarre groups that their families see as pure waste. The resulting conflict and misunderstanding between generations is a classic illustration of a clash of interests in which there probably is no right or wrong. There is, however, passionate disagreement and at times even hatred—but of a kind that can only occur between people who have loved, and in most cases still love, one another very deeply. Let us attempt to adopt the perspective of both youthful converts and distraught parents in order to understand the causes of this conflict.

Converts to the New Religions

Because they recognize the importance of attracting young adults, the new religions have concentrated their recruitment efforts on youthful subcultures or countercultures. The Children of God began when "Moses" David Berg took over management of the Huntington Beach (California) Teen Challenge Coffee House, part of the flourishing Jesus Movement of the 1960s. The Hare Krishna opened a center in San Francisco's Haight-Ashbury district and was extremely successful in recruiting members of the drug subculture. The Unification Church's single most successful recruiting unit is the Oakland Family, which recruited in the San Francisco–Berkeley area. In place of the heavy biblical/anticommunist doctrines taught elsewhere in the Unification Church, the Oakland Family preaches a much more humanistic message: Human beings have become alienated from one another and a new model community based on reciprocal love is needed to show humanity the only real solution to its deep dissatisfactions and alienation. Each of these groups has also organized mobile recruiting teams that travel the country in search of converts. By the end of the 1970s the Krishnas and Moonies had become familiar sights on city streets, college campuses, and airport terminals and bus stations.

From all accounts, recruitment campaigns by the new religions have yielded meager returns. The vast majority of youth is simply uninterested in their pitches, and the defection rate among members remains very high. To those youth who are drawn to the new religions the attractions are many and varied. They may be the devotion and commitment of the individual who recruits them, the quality of life in a communal group, the content of the theology, or the idealistic nature of the cause. We found exactly this kind of diversity among the many Moonies we interviewed in 1978. One stated his discontent with his former life this way:

> I was looking for a way to serve mankind. I wasn't happy or unhappy. I had no goal in mind, but I was seeking something substantial. I didn't feel really fulfilled. I felt there was something missing. I wanted to be more than I was.

Another member observed that he had been attracted to the Church because he "was impressed with their determination." A third recalled, "The people cared more than other places I had been. These people were going places."[13]

Once an individual has moved into the communal group, the single most important step in conversion, he or she is likely to experience a tremendous sense of euphoria and freedom, since all these groups are organized so that one fits in and belongs instantly. It is as if one had always been there, but the feelings of belongingness can be intense:

> I was always afraid of people with hate in their hearts...It's so wonderful to be in a place where you don't have to feel that fear. It's so hard to explain! (She blushes and is on the verge of tears.) When I first came here, I didn't know what

> Karen meant when she ran up and hugged me, and said, "At last you're home, welcome!" But now I know what she means. I am home.[14]

A Krishna devotee asserted:

> . . . the best aspect of life in the temple is the other devotees. Without them I would not stay here. They are so great. . . . We see Krishna together every day.[15]

No specific skills are necessary to join, and everyone is needed because the communal group relies upon each member working constantly for it. The work gives individuals a sense of importance as does the group's total acceptance of them. And there is the excitement of meeting and getting to know other members, learning the theology, traveling on recruiting or fundraising teams, and striving to build a utopian community.

A convert to one of the new religions is likely to feel a sense of freedom from many of the pressures of conventional society. Because all three of these groups strictly control sexual relations, the competitiveness among members of the same sex and the need to continually prove one's attractiveness to the opposite sex disappears. It is often startling for members to learn they can live on a day-to-day basis without needing much in the way of either money or possessions. The group openly rejects luxuries, and it takes care of all life's necessities. Possessions may come to be regarded as a burden. As a Krishna member put it:

> It makes no difference whether it is a new car, a pretty girl, a fine restaurant or the best acid that you can find — they are all the same. They create anxiety because as soon as you have one you want more. The only way out is to give it all up. Not just one or two, but all of them. Then you will realize that you don't need objects to feel important.[16]

Perhaps most intriguing of all may be a convert's discovery that within the communal group it is possible to live together, share, cooperate, and strive for high ideals without competitiveness. Members find there is another way of living that does not involve building one's ego and personal achievement; the alternative is finding your strength in the group and letting go of self. In a highly individualistic society like ours, this may constitute a revolutionary discovery. A member of Hare Krishna observed:

> One must serve Krishna constantly without ever thinking of yourself. We are filled up with pleasure by our service to Krishna. All the old pleasures are meaningless because they are selfish.[17]

While all these feelings and experiences are intense, they may not last. Members find that the struggle against ego and selfishness is continuous, a battle that is never won, and some wonder whether they are capable of making or willing to make that sacrifice. The group that seems so utopian, they gradually learn, is in reality not free of competition; only the stakes have changed and competition is less public. The warmth that new members feel is to some extent illusionary. As an observer of the Hare Krishna reported:

> Although the devotees were in close day-to-day proximity, the quality of their relationships lacked a specific personal intensity. Smiles, warm personal greetings, physical touching and hugging were virtually absent.[18]

Feelings have to be diffused to avoid intimacies that might divide the group, but many members come to wish for personal closeness.

None of these groups has made a significant impact on American society, and, after a time, members come to realize that their visions of a perfect world, both inside and outside the communal group, are much more remote than they had dreamed. Many members of the new religions finally decide to leave, but during the early stages of their membership, when they are discovering a new world, they find it hard to see why their families cannot understand and share their joy.

Parents

The consequences of joining a new religion are different for converts than they are for their families. What the new member regards as an exciting adventure and a fulfilling experience parents usually see as total disaster. A son's or daughter's conversion to a new religion poses two threats to families, parents in particular: (1) undermining parents' efforts to prepare their children for future careers and marriages and (2) undermining parental authority and family loyalty. A major goal and responsibility for parents is preparing their offspring for happy and successful careers and marriages. Parents take real pride in their children's success and happiness and toward this end encourage and sacrifice for their education, support personal achievement and development, reward independence and motivation, and try to breed a capacity for social grace in the variety of social settings their offspring will encounter. The communally organized new religions set out to systematically erase the self-interest and achievement orientation of members, who are encouraged to develop a capacity for love not reason, cooperation not competition, and selflessness not achievement. To parents who have worked and sacrificed for years to insure their children's success, a son's or daughter's renunciation of former goals can be a painful blow. The following two statements by parents of Unification Church members illustrate these feelings:

> Our twenty-two-year-old daughter, Anne...dreamed for years of being a public health nurse in Appalachia. Her dreams and ours were shattered suddenly last January 1974 when Anne came home unexpectedly and announced she was quitting nursing college and joining the Unification Church.

> Richard was three days into his senior semester as a pre-med student, University of Texas, Austin. He had a 3.989 grade-point average. The cult got him almost on the spot.[19]

Conversion to a new religion also threatens parental

authority. While parents want and expect their children to grow into independent adults, they often plan to continue as head of the family. Parents may lose the capacity to give their children orders at some point, but most hope their advice will be heeded and expect at the very least to be accorded respect. But as we have pointed out, communal groups try to put distance between converts and outsiders who have any emotional pull on them. By organizing themselves almost as families, communal groups seek to fulfill all their members' emotional needs inside the group. It is galling for parents to see their sons and daughters show respect and deference to group leaders instead of themselves. Even more threatening is decision-making by Church elders, not the family. Members might or might not be allowed to visit home for holidays or in the event of illness, marriage partners are discussed with Church elders and not parents, parents face the possibility of never getting to know or see their grandchildren, and members might even be moved abroad permanently (some Hare Krishnas were sent to India) without any parental consultation. Parents of a member of Hare Krishna state:

> He has abandoned his entire past life; has no interest in his former friends, nor in any of his family. His calls and letters are very few and far between, despite our numerous attempts to communicate with him. When we do speak with him it can never be on a personal level; it is strictly a sermonizing type of conversation. There have been serious illnesses within our family, but his responses have been negative, completely devoid of emotion.[20]

Parents of a convert to Children of God sum up their feelings as follows:

> It has certainly been a terrifying and sad experience for her family, to have her estranged from us...We love her so dearly—and it tears our hearts out to think of not being near her.[21]

Two families of Moonies lament:

> She has given up her freedom and is willing to go wherever

Moon sends her, to marry whomever he chooses, to do whatever he asks.[22]

She didn't even send her father a birthday card...She said she didn't even consider us her real parents, only physical parents. Moon and his wife were her real parents.[23]

How parents experience these two threats to family stability only serves to increase their fear and anxiety. Individuals are likely to be recruited by a new religion while they are away from home—traveling or on a college campus. The time between first contact and conversion to a new religion varies from a few weeks to a few months, but the conversion process may be well along before parents first hear of their child's developing interests. By then it may be too late to dissuade their son or daughter. Parents are caught totally by surprise since their offspring often had expressed no particular interest in religion, and, only a short time ago, finishing college, launching a career, and starting a family seemed assured. Parents feel they are caught in the middle of a living nightmare, a desperate struggle to save their child's life. They cannot believe it is happening to them. This is what they read about in the newspapers—the kind of thing that only happens to someone else's children.

If parents do manage to establish communication and spend time with their son or daughter, they may be shocked and frightened by what they find. In place of the normal college student they saw a short time ago is a person whom they literally might fail to recognize. A physical change of appearance is most dramatic in the case of the Hare Krishna. What parents see is someone dressed in flowing saffron robes, a son's head shaven except for a knotted pony tail, clutching a cloth sack containing prayer beads. Members of the Children of God and the Unification Church have at least cut their hair, given up distinctive personal clothing and jewelry, and abandoned cosmetics. They may exchange clothing with other group members. Because the clothing and grooming styles that lend individuals a distinctive appearance are absent, parents often have an eerie sense that everyone looks alike.

The time that parents spend with their son or daughter is

hardly more reassuring. Their offspring seem difficult to reach. Even if they are glad to see their parents, new converts may be mistrustful and ambivalent as parents try to talk them out of their new commitments, frustrated at their inability to share this new life with their parents, and reluctant to be separated from their group for very long. There doesn't seem to be much to talk about because only one topic really matters, and there is a total lack of agreement on it. Converts try to explain the sense of fulfillment they feel, the discoveries they have made about themselves, the sense of purpose and direction they experience. Parents hear that the messiah is returning and restoration of the world is at hand or about the joy and peace that can be found in chanting "Hare Krishna." They are hardly encouraged.

It is impossible for parents to put the pieces of the puzzle together. They press for answers. What does the return of the messiah, even if the Reverend Moon is the messiah, have to do with selling flowers on the street twelve hours a day? Where does the money go? Why isn't there more food to eat? How can "Moses" David Berg as the leader of a religious community approve, let alone encourage, female converts to sexually seduce men as a recruitment tactic? How can cheaply printed tracts containing obscenities and slurs on America be spiritual revelation? What does peace and happiness have to do with shaving one's head and endless, mindless chanting?

The situation is likely to polarize as converts' involvement in the communal group continues to deepen and parental criticism and negativity persist. Communication becomes less frequent and more strained. Parents become more desperate. What could possibly account for this sudden transformation of their son or daughter? Something must have been done to them. Parents begin to take the brainwashing explanation more seriously and some consider deprogramming.

In Sum: Families vs. Cults

Of the conflicts between the new religions and government, church, and family institutions it is the family-cult conflict that is the most intense. Individual families have suffered the loss of a son or daughter under circumstances that are threatening and frightening. Parents cannot completely understand what has happened or been done to their children. They feel they are locked in a desperate struggle with unscrupulous cults and their children's lives hang in the balance. It is for this reason that parents have banded together into anticult associations and opposed the new religions any way they can. It is for this reason, too, that when lobbying and appeals for help do not resolve their grievances they turn to vigilante-style actions to protect their interests. So it is the families of converts to the new religions that are the impetus for the anticult movement. Only a clash of interests of the magnitude we have described here is sufficient to generate a conflict with such rancor. There are no neutrals, only allies and enemies.

THE CULT CHALLENGE: TO WHOM?

As we have seen, the new religions have not posed a serious threat to either government or churches, although they have been a source of embarrassment and irritation to both. Government has been forced to arbitrate between the interests of new religions and their opponents, but the inconsistency of government policy indicates the real ambivalence of public officials to becoming involved in conflicts concerning religion. Churches also have acted in an ambivalent manner. On the one hand, they have felt obliged to support families, who after all are the backbone of church memberships and finances, and to defend themselves against heretical doctrines. On the other hand, churches have been reluctant to support legal action against cults because, once taken, any form of political regulation opens a Pandora's box of government control over churches. For this reason churches have sympathized with parents whose children have joined new religions but in general have stopped short of giving approval to forcible deprogramming or calling for government investigations.

The families of converts to the new religions, however, have shown no such ambivalence. Many parents uncompromisingly view themselves and their adult offspring as victims of unscrupulous cults, and many families have taken drastic actions to redress these grievances. There is a real clash of interests between converts to the new religions and their families. Thus in many cases parents and their children interpret the same experiences in different terms. Viewed from the parents' perspective, converts to the new religions have adopted courses that abandon years of work and sacrifices and jeopardize promising futures. It is because all this seems so sudden, so unexpected, so unexplainable, and so unacceptable that parents lean toward a brainwashing interpretation. But to youthful converts in search of a meaningful integration of their lives, an idealistic promise to make the world a better place, and an alternative to American competitiveness and individualism the new religions are an exciting discovery. To them joining a new religion is an act of self-affirmation, what psychologists term "self-actualization." Such youthful idealism is no stranger to researchers of social movements; however, to individual families it is downright disconcerting, even terrifying.

There is no easy resolution of this clash of interests. Parents are correct in their assessment that converts to the new religions are turning their backs on their pasts as well as on previous plans for the future. These youth may indeed come to regret their naiveté and exuberance in later years. Meanwhile, it is no small sacrifice for either the converts or their families. But the converts are quite correct in *their* contention that they are adults, however inexperienced in long-range decision-making, and therefore possess the right to chart their own courses in life. The real irony is that in most instances the conflict does not persist. Left to their quests, most converts to the new religions ultimately drop out and resume their former lives. Of those who remain as members, most ultimately settle down into stable, if unconventional (by outside standards), lifestyles and pursue alternative, sometimes prestigious careers within the movement. The possibility for family reconciliation increases with the passage of time, however much parents feel estranged and separated from their offspring initially. But in the meantime the battle is heated and passionate, and it is to a consideration of the specific charges and countercharges in the cult controversy that we now turn.

4

Joining the New Religions: Brainwashing or Conversion?

There is a certain horror all of us experience when we imagine an individual stripped of his autonomy and free will, not just physically but *mentally*, so that he becomes merely a soulless, humanoid shell under the control of others. The essential human aspect of the person—his ability to reason, to decide between good and evil—is removed, transforming him into a dangerous (even repulsive) creature subject to any destructive whim of his controllers. This theme runs through our popular culture and folklore, from Hollywood's fright-film zombies and the innocent little girl victimized by the Devil in *The Exorcist* to beliefs in demonic possession, which can be found in virtually every major religious tradition since antiquity. In modern times we have seen it played out in frighteningly real terms: in the stories of American servicemen taken prisoner and "brainwashed" by communists, in the gruesome Tate-LeBianca murders by the Charles Manson cult, and in the kidnapping and apparently brutal transformation of millionaire heiress Patricia Hearst into "Tanya," the machine-gun-toting Symbionese

Liberation Army guerrilla. Whether one calls it "brainwashing," "mind control," or "spirit possession," the notion of one personality subverting another's power to act and think independently has remained a powerful, resilient explanation of otherwise seemingly unexplainable behavior.

Since the early 1970s a number of parents have been claiming that just such a possession phenomenon is occurring at alarming rates in the United States. The alleged victims are their adult, college-age children. The alleged perpetrators are the gurus, prophets, and messiahs of the new religions: charismatic leaders such as the Unification Church's Sun Myung Moon, the People's Temple's Jim Jones, the Children of God's "Moses" David Berg, Hare Krishna's Bhaktivedanta Prabhupada, and the Divine Light Mission's Maharaj Ji. Their mind-control methods, claim parents and other anticult spokespersons, start with high-pressure indoctrination conducted in isolated rural workshops where arousal of fear and guilt are alternated with warm approval and "love-bombing." These techniques are combined with a frenetic round of activities (including silly or childish games to break down inhibitions), minimal sleep and inadequate diet to heighten suggestibility, and endless repetitions of doctrines (sometimes mixed with singing or chanting) to numb normally critical reasoning abilities. The results are persons reduced to childlike dependency, unable to think for themselves, unquestioning toward leaders' demands, and capable of obedience that might even prove self-destructive to physical health and safety.

And how do sensible young adults ever get mixed up with such groups in the first place? The anticult answers vary. Ted Patrick, co-author of *Let Our Children Go!* and originator of the practice known as deprogramming, has claimed the Unification Church leaders use "spot hypnosis" to snare recruits and pass the secrets of the technique down through their lieutenants to street witnessing teams.[1] (In a deposition made under oath during one civil suit Patrick even claimed that they emanate invisible energy rays through their fingertips!)[2] Most anticultists take a less occult route and maintain that these groups employ garden-variety deception (such as concealing their true identities by trying to pass themselves off as conventional Christians or representatives of drug-rehabilitation programs) as well as such ploys as flattery, flirtation, or just the promise of a free meal and warm fellowship. In any event, idealistic youth are allegedly beguiled, seduced, and hoodwinked into attending dinners, lectures, or weekend workshops where they are subjected to the mind-control techniques described above. Moreover, anticultists add to the sense of imminent danger by claiming that these irresistible techniques have an almost foolproof success rate that is swelling the ranks of cults nationwide. Patrick, for instance, claims there are as many as 20 million persons involved in cults at the present time.[3]

Ex-members of cults offer shocking testimonies that seem to confirm these claims. Consider the following sample testimonies of former cult members taken from newspaper articles:

> I think I was hypnotized at first. Basically by the girl that met me because she kept staring into my eyes and I kept being attracted to her eyes. Then, during the meal, it's very possible for some sort of drug to make me more susceptible to the lecture. Then after that it was brainwashing because I was hooked. I wanted to stay there. I wanted to learn what they had to say. There was repetition all the time. Very appealing. The more I heard the more I rejected my family, the outside world.

> I became involved by going to a dinner and a few of their lectures, but, by attracting you and using spot hypnosis, placing suggestions in your mind on a person-to-person basis, using their hands a lot and telling you anything you are wanting to hear, they draw you deeper into the church and into the cult.

> There were 14 hours of lectures interspersed with singing and games. The whole time I was never left alone. I went off to the bathroom and was reprimanded for being inconsiderate and breaking group unity.

> I learned to hypnotize people and went out to witness, bring in new people. In Berkeley we were bringing 30 new people every day. And they were hooked by that first supper and

lecture...[I would] walk up to them, stare at their eyes, get their attention and hold their attention...We were trained to do as our leaders did.[4]

Because of the nature of such cult testimonies, parents and anticultists staunchly deny that "real" conversion to these groups is occurring (whatever else the young adults involved may think). Rather, they claim it is *pseudoconversion*, and as such it should not be protected by the First Amendment. Neither should concerns for violating religious freedoms prevent government investigation of the exploitive charlatans and megalomaniac demagogues operating these con games under the guise of real religions.

This brainwashing claim is both the essence of anticult theology *and* the subject of this chapter. Undoubtedly the question of whether the new religions routinely brainwash their followers is the single most sensational issue in the entire cult controversy. Associated with it are other assumptions, such as the exploitive character of the leaders of these groups and their ultimate motives. Before we examine current claims of brainwashing, however, we need to consider briefly just what brainwashing is and is not.

BRAINWASHING AND THOUGHT REFORM

Much has been written since World War II about a greatly misunderstood process called *brainwashing*. Books on the subject from the late 1950s and early 1960s have recently been taken down from the shelf, dusted off, and used to legitimate anticultists' claims that mind control is a real large-scale menace. To most Americans there is something sinister and immoral about brainwashing. Thanks to such films as *The Manchurian Candidate*, they have a vague awareness that the Chinese communists invented it and used it on American prisoners of war. Actually the term brainwashing is a misnomer, for in the process referred to the mind is not "washed," nor is it erased or drained of all conscious thought. "To wash a brain" is only a metaphor (and a poor translation of the Chinese). What really occurs is the replacing of old attitudes and beliefs with new ones,[5] which can be accomplished in either of two contexts, one emphasizing spontaneous voluntary participation, the other utilizing terror and coercion.

An example of the voluntary type can be seen in the late 1940s and early 1950s, when the Chinese communists developed workshops called "revolutionary colleges" to accomplish attitude change on a mammoth scale. Their goal was simultaneously to rid the population of medieval Confucian perspectives and to disseminate Maoist communist ideology as efficiently as possible. Robert J. Lifton, a psychiatrist who conducted extensive interviews with Western and Chinese refugees who had been put through *szu hsiang kai tsao* ("ideological reform," or *though reform* as he preferred to call it), found a standard procedure followed in these colleges:

1. *Group Identification.* Camaraderie was emphasized, the atmosphere was cordial, and the group leaders acted more like older, wiser camp counselors than grand inquisitors. Members were encouraged to be frank in revealing their feelings and questions about propaganda lectures that emphasized the corrupt exploitive regimes of the past and the responsibilities of citizenship under Maoist communism.

2. *The Period of Emotional Conflict.* Here self-criticism in front of the group, along with introspective essays, confessions, and testimonies of past "sins" against the people were encouraged. The group leader informally singled out the more "progressive" members and used them to foster peer pressure on others both to demand unflinching self-criticism and to reward ideological conformity with approval and acceptance. The atmosphere began to resemble a religious revival with all the elements of sin, guilt, shame, and repentance. Individual members literally experienced what psychologists term a *catharsis*—an emotional purging.

3. *Submission and Rebirth.* Group members prepared autobiographies reflecting their new "enlightened" Marxist perspectives of themselves, their families, and their society. These were submitted not only to the group for further criticism but also to communist party members until every-

one was satisfied that each individual was ideologically "correct" in perspective.[6]

To social psychologists and sociologists familiar with group dynamics and interpersonal behavior there is nothing at all mysterious about attitude changes in such situations. Social psychologist Kurt Lewin, who performed the same feats regularly in laboratory experiments during the 1940s, observed:

> Many social habits are anchored in the relation between the individuals and certain group standards...Perhaps one might expect single individuals to be more pliable than groups of likeminded individuals. However, experience in leadership training, in changing of food habits, work production, criminality, alcoholism, prejudices, all indicate that it is usually easier to change individuals formed into a group than to change any one of them separately. As long as group standards are unchanged, the individual will resist changes more strongly the farther he is to depart from group standards. If the group standard itself is changed, the relation between individual and group standards is eliminated.[7]

In one classic study of a factory by sociologist Seymour Lieberman, workers with distinctly prounion, antimanagement attitudes immediately switched to antiunion, promanagement attitudes when they were promoted to foremen. During a later recession, when many of these same foremen were reduced to worker rank, they did an about-face and reassumed their former attitudes, as if merely changing hats.[8]

In another classic study, sociologist Sanford N. Dornbusch examined the indoctrination techniques of the United States Coast Guard Academy. Cadets there are initially stripped of their former civilian identities: their heads are shaved, uniforms are issued, and previous jobs, achievements, and family ties are not only devalued but often cadets are not allowed to even refer to them. A new system of rewards and punishments gradually shifts their values and elevates the new goals of the military academy over any other loyalties or interests. Contact with the outside world is strictly controlled. Letters and visitors are not allowed initially. Even personal reflection on the whole experience by cadets is discouraged—diaries are forbidden. By conventional civilian standards the lifestyle of the Coast Guard cadets is restrictive and even repressive. It remolds values and alters personalities. It disciplines individuals and shapes their perspectives, but it does not render them robots. Similar techniques are routinely employed in all armed forces' boot-camps, as well as in a number of current Roman Catholic convents and monasteries.[9]

Whether one considers such indoctrination settings and processes moral or immoral is of course a matter of personal value judgment. (A good many fundamentalist Christian ministers have benefited during religious revivals from at least an intuitive sense of how to create conditions similar to those of the Chinese communists.) It is a well-established fact, however, that human beings have a psychological need to perceive continuity between their actions and their attitudes. Also well understood is the tendency for people to take their cues as to what is appropriate behavior from others around them and from their reference groups or peers, to continue to act out rewarding roles and to drop or extinguish the nonrewarding ones. The Chinese in the revolutionary colleges were *not* transformed into zombies, deprived of conscious thought and rendered mentally incapable of initiative. They *were* exposed to constant and sometimes subtle pressure to start talking "the party line" and abandon traditional precommunist ideas. They experienced rewards, and saw others rewarded, for doing this. Their emotions were systematically played upon by group leaders who established personal bonds with them and then used these to help arouse feelings of guilt and shame. Thus, by creating a situation where individuals could be pressured into saying things they might not otherwise say, then rewarding them for making such statements and providing a rationale to justify further ones, workshop leaders led participants to come to *want* to say what they began gradually to say and believe. Manipulated and indoctrinated? Certainly. Rendered unthinking automatons and mindless robots? Hardly.

The coercive type of attitude change occurs less frequently

than the more voluntary type for several good reasons. One is that it is more costly and time-consuming. The "target" person has to be abducted (or captured), imprisoned, and then "waited out" until physical and/or psychological endurances begin to weaken. Meanwhile, the energies of numerous individuals have to be tied up in guarding, arguing with, and caring for the target. Since the goal is actual attitude change, the person has to be put into a psychological state of suggestibility. To achieve this end, the captors may use drugs, food and sleep deprivation, repeated terrorizing (perhaps beatings or threats of execution), interrogations, and ideological argument. It is not very efficient, nor—at least as far as the Chinese communists' reported brainwashing of U.S. servicemen during the Korean War—is it effective for very long. For example, Alan Scheflin and Edward Opton, in their book *The Mind Manipulators*, point out that of over 3500 American POWs captured during the Korean War only about 50 ever made procommunist statements and only about 25 refused to be repatriated when the war ended. The authors compare those figures (50 out of 3500, or about 1 percent) with the enlistment in the Confederate army of Union soldiers captured during the Civil War: 2 percent, or roughly a two-to-one ratio.[10] Psychologist Edgar Schein, who studied repatriated prisoners of war and Chinese indoctrination methods in the early 1950s, distinguished between mere collaboration (cooperation done to avoid punishment or obtain amenities such as food and cigarettes) and true ideological *conversion*. While acknowledging high rates of often trivial collaboration, he nevertheless stated about the communists' conversion efforts: "...one can only conclude that, considering the effort devoted to it, the Chinese program was a failure."[11]

Thus, the psychiatric literature on brainwashing, which anticultists frequently cite but which they apparently have never read carefully, makes no sweeping claims about terrifyingly effective methods of subverting human reason. The diabolical Fu Manchu, who can rob men of their free will, and the psychological tricks worked on Americans in *The Manchurian Candidate* are more Hollywood than reality. Indeed, many psychologists' qualified statements about brainwashing actually undermine its more highly publicized stereotypes as promoted by anticult spokespersons.

In sum, a process resembling brainwashing, which requires imprisonment and a high degree of coercion, is relatively rare and has questionable effectiveness. Thought reform is a more common phenomenon but requires voluntary participation by the target of attitude change. While much has been made of so-called brainwashing or thought-reform techniques as some little-known set of powerful procedures that devious communists discovered, these techniques actually represent fairly straightforward extensions of basic principles in psychological conditioning and group dynamics. These same principles are routinely applied in psychiatric therapy, in learning situations by weight control groups, in alcohol and drug abuse correction, by industrial psychologists, and even in mass media advertising. Under certain conditions they can be relatively effective, but they are far from foolproof. What really struck postwar observers of abused POWs as shocking, therefore, was not the existence of such attitude-change techniques per se but their use in psychological warfare. This is an important point to remember when anticultists claim that cults employ sinister, as yet poorly understood mind-control techniques: *Such techniques, even where it can be shown they are used, are neither mysterious nor new, nor have they nearly the effectiveness attributed to them by popular writers.*

THE CASE FOR BRAINWASHING IN NEW RELIGIONS

In chapter two we provided evidence to challenge claims that the new religions all share specific cultic communal organizational features or that they can be lumped together under some simplistic label such as cults. Here we want to analyze critically the brainwashing allegation by considering the actual evidence that mind-numbing techniques, combined with deception, are standard recruitment tactics used by these groups. Assuming that accusations of brainwashing can be shown to be at best distortions, we will examine the source of such well-publicized accusations later in this book. We will see that as with most distortions some limited occurrence of manipulation has been exaggerated well out of proportion to its prevalence and that in a conflict of interests some persons have a direct stake in perpetuating stereotypes.

EVIDENCE FOR THE USE OF DECEPTION

First let us take up the matter of deception being used in recruitment by cults. Anticultists maintain that these groups routinely employ deception to woo perfectly reasonable, intelligent young adults into settings they otherwise would not enter, and there subject them to mind-control techniques. In reality, however, how widespread is deceptive recruitment? If we consider individual groups instead of simply stereotyping them, we find that the amount of fraudulent misrepresentation and outright lying in recruitment has been grossly exaggerated. For example, Scientology often tries to recruit prospective adherents by mailing out a long personality-inventory questionnaire to persons, which they are encouraged to return to a local office for a "free analysis." There is no misrepresentation as to Scientology's identity. Clearly printed at the top of the form is the group's affiliation. (Once it is returned to the office, a representative of the Church will indeed provide the analysis, and since all nonmembers are presumably in need of help, not surprisingly the prospective member will be told he either requires assistance or can achieve his potential even more fully by signing up for Scientology courses. However, Scientology does not attempt to hide its identity in the process.)

Or consider the enthusiastic and rather visible witnesses for Krishna. Uncounted college campuses and city parks have witnessed the chanting, dancing performances of shaven-headed members in saffron robes. Typically a person approached in the street by a Krishna is invited to a vegetarian banquet followed by "a little philosophy." However, as sociologist Thomas Robbins and psychologist Dick Anthony have noted,

> it is difficult to envision anyone joining the Hare Krishna movement without being aware at the outset of involve-

ment that this sect, whose members are visible on streets
dancing and singing and wearing long robes and shaved
heads, constitutes a highly unusual group possessing a
distinctly eccentric and ritualized lifestyle.[12]

The Krishnas' exotic appearance and ascetic, monastic lifestyle
are in fact their main appeals in recruitment. Logically, therefore, it would be counterproductive for them to hide these
features and pretend that they were middle-of-the-road Presbyterians. (It *is* true they abandon their robes for conventional
clothing and don wigs when they disperse into airports to fund-
raise, for obvious reasons of minimizing public resistance, but
that is to solicit money, not members.)

Or, if you were handed any of the pamphlets of the Children
of God that shrilly predict the imminent end of the world, often
laced with the pornographic drawings and sexually explicit
poetry that characterize prophet David Berg's later visions,
would you think you had just encountered another group of
Pentecostals? Undoubtedly not. The Children of God do employ
a form of deception in recruiting at times, but we have yet to see
it used in this country. In England the group has become notorious for its practice of "flirty fishing," in which the more attractive female members, single *and* married, hang out in singles'
bars and discotheques in order to meet unattached males and, if
necessary, sleep with them in order to "bring them to Jesus."
Flirty fishing was designed to attract professionals and older,
better-educated persons who would be turned off by fundamentalist Bible-thumping. It was the brain child of Berg, who in
his later years has switched wives, lived polygynously, and
encouraged his staff to do likewise. Obviously Berg puts
survival and growth of the movement above the sexual integrity
of individual COG families. Flirty fishing is not prostitution in
the legal sense since no money is exchanged. But it is unquestionably the most controversial method of missionizing yet on
record. Its results have not been officially tallied, but they
appear to be slim. Only a handful of men have become full-time
members of COG colonies. Though flirty fishing is indeed a
deceptive recruitment device, from the standpoint of lonely

males looking to pick up attractive women in bars for an evening of casual sex, it is questionable as to just who is using whom. At any rate, most American youth recruited into the movement meet up with it on beaches and city street corners through pamphlet-passing missionaries who do not hide their sectarian affiliation.[13]

Nor do missionaries for the Divine Light Mission, or for other Eastern groups such as Bahaiism or the Happy-Healthy-Holy organization, all new religious groups that have sought members on large university campuses, try to pass themselves off as anything other than what they are. That is no doubt the reason their memberships are so tiny. The Guru Maharaj Ji attracts so few members because he still claims a unique spiritual status in an era when many young Americans are skeptical of omnipotent gurus and are less eager to escape into exotic Eastern religions than they are to find well-paying jobs.

Jim Jones's People's Temple attracted persons just like any inner-city church: through the soup kitchens and other charitable services Jones provided the community, his sermons that emphasized charismatic healing and interracial cooperation, and his active involvement as concerned clergyman in local politics. By the time he began to portray himself to members as something other than simply an ordinary minister, the group had ceased vigorous recruitment in the community and begun to draw inward, seeing itself separated from a larger hostile society.

The Moonies, or followers of the Reverend Sun Myung Moon's Unification Church, have usually been singled out as *the* representatives of the deceptive cult. Ex-members have recounted how they engaged in systematic misrepresentation to lure college-age adults into supposed educational discussion groups such as the Collegiate Association for the Research of Principles (C.A.R.P.) or placed misleading classified advertisements in newspapers that portrayed the group as the Peace Corps. There is no question that the Church has used such ploys in the past. We have experienced deception ourselves on certain occasions. To say, however, that the group as a whole relies on systematic fraud in its recruiting is simply untrue. At most dinners, lectures, or workshops across the nation to which street witnesses bring potential recruits, there are beaming pictures of Sun Myung Moon hanging on the walls. "Guests" view slide shows and films about Moon and the Unification Church and sit through tedious theological lectures that would leave anyone of even modest intelligence with the unmistakable impression that this is not merely a group of enthusiastic Protestants or Up With People.

In actuality, most of the deception-in-recruitment claims about the Unification Church, which have been generalized indiscriminately to the entire movement, can be traced back to the Church's unique West Coast wing in Berkeley, California. This wing has traditionally been atypical of the larger Unification Church in many respects, not the least of which is its more humanistic, less theological orientation and its willingness to cut ethical corners in recruiting new members. The "Oakland Family," as its members call themselves (or the New Education Development Systems, Inc., as it is registered with the state of California), has since the mid-1960s systematically recruited young adults from the San Francisco Bay area for the Unification Church while publicly denying any formal affiliation with Moon's organization.[14] Initially persons are invited to an evening of free food, singing and entertainment, and a lecture on human values and problems of alienation in which little of religion (much less of Moon or his messianic hopes) is mentioned. Only during its extended weekend and weeklong workshops does Moon's place in the movement gradually emerge *after* the participants have established emotional bonds with group members and come to develop some commitment to its activities. This strategy of placing less emphasis on biblical doctrine and millennial religious hopes has consistently proven successful in attracting West Coast college-age adults who are open to eclectic philosophical alternatives but who would be immediately turned off by something smacking of traditional Judeo-Christianity. It is *not* the approach followed by most Unificationist missionary teams, which no doubt accounts for their relatively meager results compared to the conversion successes of the Oakland Family.

Are we claiming then that most anticult claims of deceptive

recruitment in cults taken as a whole actually are only over-generalizations from the Oakland Family's pattern of misrepresentation? In a word, *yes*. How such a stereotype ever developed and became accepted can be easily explained. The Oakland Family, operating in the cosmopolitan San Francisco Bay area with the Berkeley campus and city of San Francisco acting as two immense magnets drawing free-floating searching youth from all over the country, has been the most successful recruiting arm of the Unification Church. It is also one of this country's largest and oldest permanent Church centers. The Unification Church has also, since the mid-1970s, been the officially designated number-one target of the anticult movement as well as one of the most highly publicized new religions.[15] That the Church, and correspondingly its most notorious wing in California, should typify the fears, concerns, and grievances of parents is quite natural.

Moreover, a process of "self-fulfilling focus" has insured that once attention was called to its existence by angry parents, the Oakland Family would come under increasing scrutiny by the media. Self-fulfilling focus basically means that publicity begets further publicity. Because some journalists wrote sensationalistic articles on the group, others (not to be outdone) followed suit until, by the late 1970s, reporters were routinely "going underground" to wander the Berkeley campus or San Francisco's Fisherman's Wharf in hopes of being invited to the evening lectures by unknowing Oakland Family street missionaries. Afterward, such journalists, mistaking the Oakland Family as typical of the larger Unification Church, published lurid "exposés" of deceptive recruitment in various popular magazines and newspapers. In doing so they established a folklore of deception as a common tactic in all Unificationist mission work. Anticult spokespersons have fanned the fire by generalizing beyond the Oakland Family and the Unification Church to *all* nonconventional religions, such as the Hare Krishna movement, the Divine Light Mission, and Scientology. The fact that reality does not resemble the stereotype seems not to disturb them. Many journalists have publicized these accusations uncritically. The mechanics of news reporting virtually guarantees that once an allegation with or without some truth to it has been published somewhere, somewhere else another journalist researching previous articles as background for his own piece will, because of deadlines and editorial pressures, uncritically include it as fact. Thereafter the allegation takes on a well-nigh independent life of its own.[16]

Anticultists would reply to this argument that even if a cult does openly identify itself, deception nevertheless occurs because the eventual costs, sacrifices, and later life entanglements are not clearly spelled out during conversion. The young person ordinarily does not think ahead to such details as the possibility that someday, after years of service, he may have second thoughts and leave the cult, possessing no marketable skills or worthwhile education, that he will have built up no savings or pension, or that eventual marriage to a cult member will pose numerous complications and tragedies. Naive youth, in other words, do not fully appreciate what they are getting into, and the cult certainly does not help them consider the long-term implications of joining. In the case of Scientology, anticultists argue, the person who innocently goes to receive his free analysis and ends up signing for courses is never told that he will be continually pressured to keep signing up for an endless series of lessons. Likewise, young Moonies and Krishnas can in no way know the possible regret they will one day feel for having squandered precious years on fund-raising for gurus and messiahs rather than spending the time preparing for "useful" careers and forming conventional families.

This seemingly reasonable complaint of indirect deception is nevertheless specious. Religious conversion cannot be handled like purchasing a washer and dryer, complete with limited warranties for parts and labor and money-back guarantee. To require a new religion to lay out for a potential convert a contract stating precisely where and what he will be doing in twenty years' time or to provide a laundry list of future subjective and material sacrifices balanced against benefits and rewards is to ask the impossible. We would consider it absurd if we demanded the same of conventional churches when they take in converts. One might as well ask partners entering into marriage to know all aspects of living together before the ceremony. At some point there is simply risk and future uncertainty.

Furthermore, it is not generally admitted (or perhaps even known) by anticult critics that various new religions do attempt to "screen out" the serious seekers from merely curious faddists and immature or unstable persons by maintaining probationary periods before conferring full membership. Of course new religions capitalize on the naiveté of many young adults. But the same could be said of armed services recruiters who seek enlistments among high school seniors. Naiveté is, after all, one reason behind a young person's attraction to idealistic religious crusades and groups determined to change the world. Their naiveté, however, does not automatically prove they are deceived.

EVIDENCE FOR THE USE OF MIND-CONTROL TECHNIQUES

As scientific research shows, true coercive persuasion, or brainwashing, is rare and not nearly as effective in changing attitudes as is commonly believed precisely because it relies on imprisonment and force. Coercion tends to produce overt compliance, not changes of mind. From time to time stories in the press surface in which a person attending a high-pressure weekend workshop at the Oakland Family's remote rural farm in Boonville, California, suddenly finds the scene gone sour, demands to be driven back to San Francisco immediately, and has to wait for some time, but this is clearly not the same thing as the brutal containment of POWs. To maintain any parallel with POW experiences, anticultists have to claim that there exists *psychological* coercion or subtle group pressure equivalent to physical restraint as the force prohibiting young adults from simply walking away from religious indoctrination sessions. This claim moves the whole anticult explanation closer to the phenomenon we discussed earlier as *thought reform*, i.e., Lifton's definition, into which participants enter voluntarily and find a low-key but deliberate system of rewards, peer pressure, and orchestrated involvement. The claim of psychological coercion is misleading because it relies as much on subjective impression as on objective fact. Clearly there is manipulated attitude adjustment in such situations, but it hardly constitutes destruction of an individual's capacity to think or reason.

In sifting through research on various indoctrination techniques of the new religions gathered by trained anthropologists, sociologists, and scholars of religion (as opposed to the testimonies of angry ex-members of cults and unsympathetic reporters), what reliable evidence exists for the contention that mind-numbing mind-control techniques that obliterate conscious control of one's daily activities are routinely employed? If we are talking in terms of indoctrination and deliberate attempts to replace old values and attitudes with new ones, then such reshaping processes exist. The fact that new religions do not provide equal time for opposing viewpoints or that they slant arguments in their favor is certainly nothing remarkable in religious education. But if we want documentation of more ruthless manipulation, such as keeping people awake for days at a time, starving them, or exercising them to the point of exhaustion, all in order to break them down to states of suggestibility, we find little evidence produced by trained observers to support the brainwashing stereotype.

Scholars have observed and experienced indoctrination techniques, both with their presence as researchers known to their hosts and covertly, in such controversial groups as the Moonies, the Hare Krishnas, the Divine Light Mission, and Scientology. In some cases, particularly in the more monastic communal groups such as the Unification Church and the Hare Krishnas, researchers *have* found processes similar to what Lifton termed thought reform. After all, many of these groups are seriously bent on changing the world, including the beliefs of the people in it, and it is not surprising that they discovered the relative efficiency and effectiveness of group dynamics principles in reforming attitudes that have been long known to psychologists. Many groups have deliberate disciplines or exercises to help "train" the mind to block out extraneous or frivolous thoughts and competing desires. These include chanting, meditating, and praying. But new religions do not want to produce robots or zombies. Rather, they want members with newly committed viewpoints, values, and preferences. One cannot enter a Hare Krishna or Moonie communal center, for example, and continue to carry along the outside world's middle-class intellectual baggage of notions of privacy and individuality. A new style of life, complete with new orientations to make it work, must be learned.

Contrary to what many anticultists claim, most young adults are not terribly impressed by or attracted to such confining lifestyles. Of those persons who give it a try, many cannot or do not learn how to make such a demanding lifestyle work. Carroll Stoner and Jo Anne Parke, journalist authors of *All Gods Children*, create a false picture of the situation when they claim: "Barely a soul is immune to the pleas and promises of the 'new religions.' "[17] The facts suggest otherwise. In chapter one we discussed the relatively small *real* membership figures for even the better known cults—evidence clearly against claims that they are able to appeal to or seduce alarmingly large numbers of youth.

Our own research on the Oakland Family's recruitment and indoctrination practices, which included interviews with staff personnel and personal observation, revealed that about one person in a hundred approached in bus terminals, city parks, on the streets made it as far as the weekend retreat where intensive indoctrination efforts resembling thought reform were made. Of those who went through the high-paced, high-pressure weekend activities, only about half stayed for the following weeklong seminar that generally led to membership[18]—poor results indeed for a group supposedly possessing the secrets of "spot hypnosis." The fact that the Oakland Family could recruit between 30 and 50 new "Moonies" each month (though many soon dropped out after "graduation") is testimony more to persistence and hard work than to effectiveness. (Perhaps more damning to the stereotype of Moon's followers as mindless automatons is the fact that the first graduating class from Moon's Unification

Theological Seminary in Barrytown, New York, whose students represent the elite of Unification Church members, witnessed a 17 percent defection rate soon after graduation.)[19]

Our intensive interviews with an initial sample of approximately 50 Moonies in Texas (and later with others) on their conversion experiences shocked us after all we had read in the media and been told by anticultists. Persons who had been in the movement for six months or longer were relatively ignorant of (and uninterested in) the Reverend Moon's doctrine. Moreover, they acknowledged this fact openly, and it did not seem to bother them. One young woman said: "The Unification Church offers me a communal way of life, and good communes are hard to find nowadays." As we probed further we discovered that persons not only stayed in the group for various reasons (excitement, travel, idealism, lifestyle) but joined under different circumstances for a multitude of motives. One fellow frankly acknowledged his previous sexual maladjustment ("I always had the feeling that women enslaved me"), which became irrelevant in the celibate fund-raising/witnessing teams and restored his peace with God. Another, a Vietnam veteran who had seen his share of wartime atrocities and carnage, had joined to help put an end to future wars. Some males joined because they were romantically attracted to the young women who recruited them; some members had felt alienated and aimless before they joined; others found Moon's theological explanation of human history and contemporary events compelling enough to enlist. Many were not terribly unhappy before they joined the Unification Church, but after hearing its message they saw an opportunity for self-actualization. They could simultaneously make the world a better place and improve their own spirituality.

Nor were many members the product of "overnight conversion." A number had rejected the movement after their first contact with it and took weeks or even months to study its doctrines before deciding to join. Their high degree of introspective sensitivity and reflective candor in discussing their reservations about the Unification Church contrasted strikingly with anticult claims that we are supposed to be dealing with mindless robots and unthinking slaves. New members were supposed to be kept lethargic and subservient because of inadequate protein-poor diets, but we ate their food, often dropping in unannounced for dinner in cities such as Arlington, Houston, New York, and San Francisco, and found it nutritious. Instead of minimal sleep designed to dull members into suggestibility, we found the same five- or six-hours-a-night regimen familiar to millions of college students, interspersed with occasional naps. Moonies were supposed to be kept in states of mental confusion by continually poring over Moon's scripture *Divine Principle*, but in moments of relaxation we found them reading Tolkien's *The Lord of the Rings* and the potboiler biography *Jackie O!* Every working moment was supposed to be consecrated and devoted to the sole purpose of ushering in the Kingdom of God on earth, but they spent Sunday afternoons at the movies seeing *Star Wars* and *Oh, God!*

Most important, we found conversion had been misinterpreted by outsiders, including parents, as an event rather than a process. Many persons participated on an experimental basis, weighing the benefits (such as self-fulfillment and spiritual growth or lifestyle satisfactions) against all the previous comforts they had surrendered and the acute grief they knew they were causing their families. Continuance in the movement, as was their joining, represented the result of continually examining the cost-benefit ratio of membership. Just as falling in love realistically involves a process of initial attraction, progressing into a deepening, more complex relationship of commitment, many members' conversions to the Unification Church are best understood as processes that might be interrupted or terminated at any time, not as discrete one-time events. True, there are cases of "love at first sight" and there are persons who make on-the-spot decisions to enlist in the Church. But these instances are nowhere near as prevalent as the brainwashing stereotype has made them out to be.[20] Our discovery is similar to what sociologist James V. Downton, Jr., concluded about conversion to Guru Maharaj Ji's Divine Light Mission: "While thoughts of conversion normally bring to mind images of sweeping change, the fact is that both conversion and commitment are gradual in their development. Small steps, not giant strides, are the normal course."[21]

Downton found that many young, college-age Americans who had become disillusioned with the hedonistic shallowness of the late 1960s drug culture but who felt unable to return to conventional middle-class lifestyles gradually drifted into the exotic subculture of an Eastern religion. As if at a lush smorgasbord of religious options and possibilities, some sampled the Divine Light Mission and rejected it, others tried it out for a while before moving on to something else, and a few plunged into it as committed devotees. The guru's message was so general, however, that it could not hold the interest of most who were initially attracted to it. In 1974, when the guru placed more restrictions on who could live in Divine Light Mission ashrams, defections increased. If his followers were indeed brainwashed zombies, or simply unquestioning, gullible youths unable to think for themselves, why is it that so many made the decision to leave after the guru disillusioned them by marrying his secretary that same year?

Anthropologist Francine Daner noted a high turnover among Krishna devotees and described a six-month preconversion probationary period now mandatory for those interested in joining. This waiting period was instituted in the mid-1970s to reduce the growing problem of "blooping," i.e., dropping out, which occurred as long as prospective members were not first tested for sincerity and gradually acculturated to the group's strict monastic lifestyle. The Krishnas realize their spartan life of religious devotion is not for everyone. Far from plucking youth off college campuses and city streets indiscriminately, they, like the modern Roman Catholic church in its recruitment for the priesthood, take some pains to make certain (on the part of both parties) that the decision to join has been given serious consideration.[22]

In their study of the UFO cult of Bo and Peep (two former Texas academics who preached that true believers would soon be assembled in an alien spacecraft to experience accelerated spiritual advancement into higher forms elsewhere in the universe), sociologists Robert Balch and David Taylor (who joined the group covertly) encountered a low-key process of indoctrination based primarily on discouraging members from discussion of their doubts, questions, or reservations with one another and acting out certain designated roles within the group. Even the marks of thought reform were absent. The typical member was what they termed a "seeker," a person who had already dabbled in or tried out various occult and unconventional philosophies. Seekers were likely to move on after sampling what was to be gained from the UFO group as were initiates to the cult life. Members even developed a deliberate style for dealing with outsiders, mumbling monotonically and staring blankly and glassy-eyed to cultivate the impression of having been profoundly transformed (thus confirming anticult expectations of brainwashed individuals). But having seen cult life from the inside, when members were not under public scrutiny and could be themselves on occasion, Balch concluded:

> The private reality of life in a religious cult usually remains hidden beneath a public facade of religious fanaticism. . . The first step in conversion to cults is learning to *act* like a convert by outwardly conforming to a narrowly prescribed set of role expectations. Genuine conviction develops later beneath a facade of total commitment, and it fluctuates widely during the course of a typical member's career. Many cult believers never become true believers, but their questioning may be effectively hidden from everyone but their closest associates.[23]

The grisly events in Jonestown in 1978 might seem to offer some evidence for the existence of brainwashing since a large number of persons did drink poisoned Kool-Aid at Jones's command. But not all participated voluntarily. Over a hundred were children and had to be forced to swallow the deadly mixture. The few survivors tell of armed guards herding many people together and making them drink at gunpoint. A tape recording of those last few minutes of the People's Temple colony, played repeatedly on national television news broadcasts, reveals a din of weeping, crying, and the repeated demanding of order by Jones. Jones and a nucleus of his temple's leaders may have been fanatics, but there is no evidence that the majority of members were brainwashed. They were full of fear and confusion, but they did not calmly drink poison and lay down robotlike to die.

Even in psychiatry, there is accumulating evidence based on sophisticated testing that shows no pathological or ill effects of cult membership on individuals. For whatever reasons and dissatisfactions in their lives that prompted them to join, young adults entering into these controversial groups have often not been found to show any incapacity to act or think rationally and independently. For example, researchers concluded after one study of cult members that "it would be fallacious to label all of these religious followers as more emotionally disturbed than their peers."[24] Elsewhere, in an article appearing in the prestigious *American Journal of Psychiatry*, psychiatrist J. Thomas Ungerleider and clinical psychologist David K. Wellisch, who together studied 50 members and ex-members of cults, stated similar findings:

> No data emerged from intellectual, personality, or mental status testing to suggest that any of these subjects are unable or even limited in their ability to make sound judgments and legal decisions as related to their persons and property.[25]

In another article Ungerleider and Wellisch discussed their in-depth analysis of two cult members who had been forcibly abducted by deprogrammers but who successfully resisted deprogramming. The authors confirm: "The two abducted group members were able to make informed decisions and were in no way legally mentally incompetent."[26]

There are, of course, psychiatrists and other specialists who disagree with such findings. Prominent among these are Harvard psychiatrist John G. Clark, Jr., and psychologist Margaret Singer.[27] We do not want to paint a picture of unanimity on the cult issue among mental health specialists. However, the anticult stereotype of all such experts' agreeing on the psychic dangers of new religions, which a few outspoken professionals have led the public to believe, is false.

THOUGHT REFORM IN THE OAKLAND FAMILY

As there are claims of deception being employed in recruitment, there are also allegations of high-pressure manipulation and tactics akin to thought reform used by new religions. These assertions do have some *limited* basis in fact. We stress the word "limited" because just as various new religions differ from each other in the many ways we have noted, they also differ in indoctrination. In our discussion of the deception allegations, we noted that only the Moonies seem to have engaged in systematic deception and then only in one West Coast faction of the organization. The other five major groups we consider cannot reasonably be accused of hiding their identities to attract members. If one wishes to stretch the definition of deception to include not explaining to potential members the full range of possible future costs and benefits or not providing equal time for options, then virtually *no* existing religious organization—from Episcopalians to Christian Scientists to Zen Buddhists—is strictly honest.

In our investigations of the brainwashing/thought reform charges we have found that once again a reliable set of observations by various independent researchers invariably leads back to the Unification Church's Oakland Family. The first Moonie missionary outpost in the United States was established in the San Francisco Bay area in 1959, and though that branch did not immediately show impressive growth (in part because it *did* explicitly identify its millennial goals) the Church continued to maintain operation there during the late 1960s. The leaders who ran the Oakland, Berkeley, and San Francisco missions, beginning in 1965, changed the thrust of their initial proselytization message from religious to secular-humanist. Instead of emphasizing Satan and sin, they stressed alienation and love. Throughout the 1970s the Oakland Family was supervised by Dr. Martin Irwin "Mose" Durst, a professor of humanities at Laney College in Oakland with professional training in social psychology and sensitivity group therapy (he is now president of the Unification Church of America), and his assistant, Kristina Morrison, who had completed all course work (but not her dissertation) for a Ph.D. in psychology. Durst is an entertaining, ingratiating, articulate speaker with a flair for capturing the interests and imaginations of idealistic young adults. He continued the humanistic approach initially to attracting youth and only gradually introduced the religious themes so integral to the Unification Church's existence. Together Durst and Morrison put their training in techniques of attitude change to effective use in the weekend workshops and extended training sessions of the Oakland Family.

An examination of how this well-publicized Unification Church unit has been able to produce as many members as it has should clear up much of the mystery and misunderstanding surrounding the brainwashing stereotypes. Readers should keep in mind two additional considerations: first, most unconventional religious groups in contemporary America do not employ such complex, systematic recruitment tactics (nor, indeed, does the Unification Church as a whole), and second, the Oakland Family's results are not nearly as impressive as the brainwashing stereotype suggests.[28]

The Oakland Family relies on three elements in its recruiting practices: vigorous but selective witnessing, "hooking" potential members with a message that does not at first sound very religious, and building emotional bonds that generate fast commitment.

Casting a Narrow Net

Since the early 1970s the Oakland Family has been the most effective recruiting arm of the Unification Church. Part of its function is to supply the Church with the type of person most able to serve its mission. This person must be idealistic, energetic, and healthy as well as mobile, with few commitments such as a career, a mortgage, a spouse or children. He or she must be able to drop other involvements and devote all time to the Church's projects. Such a person is college-age, or in the 18 to 24 age group, legally adult (or almost so), unmarried, and essentially on his or her own with few responsibilities to anyone else.

This is a description of the potential Oakland Family recruit, and Family missionaries concentrate their efforts in areas where such people can be found in great numbers. Missionaries watch for young adults carrying backpacks in city parks, at bus and train stations, and on beaches. They set up display tables near Fisherman's Wharf and on the Berkeley campus of the University of California, advertising a beautiful rural retreat where personal development can take place. In short, they canvass areas around the San Francisco Bay high in turnover of mobile, sometimes transient, youth. In our interviews with members of the Oakland Family and with Oakland Family "alumni" scattered throughout the country working for the Unification Church, we encountered numerous similar accounts of what members were doing when they first became acquainted with the Family:

> I was attending a Unitarian convention as a youth delegate after graduating from high school. I decided to backpack through the country and gradually work my way home.
>
> I had just graduated from high school but hadn't found a job yet.
>
> It was after graduation [from high school] before I was going to start college in the fall.
>
> I married right after high school... I had gotten a divorce, was taking LSD. I was sitting on a beach when this missionary came up to me.

The Reverend Moon, like the Hare Krishnas' Bhaktivedanta, is reported to have recognized explicitly the idealism and open-mindedness of young adults for recruiting purposes. At one point he even stated that persons over forty (that is, immobile, mortgaged, career-concerned parents) were "sacrifices on the altar of god," essentially beyond hope for mobilizing in his movement. He was no doubt correct, for the sorts of sacrifices and round-the-clock activities that fill an Oakland Family member's daily routine (or the routine of other Moonies) would be out of the question for adults who have such responsibilities as earning a living and raising children. Thus the net cast by Oakland Family recruiters is a narrow one, a point dramatically shown to us when we (both in our thirties) first visited the Oakland Family's center in the heart of San Francisco during an evening recruitment program. Aside from Durst and Morrison, we were the oldest people there, standing out conspicuously like faculty members at a fraternity open house.

"Hooks" and "Plants"

Used car salesmen, psychotherapists, and politicians all understand the value of "hooks." Hooks are the "angles" or "openings" that attract customers, convince patients to discuss their problems frankly, or interest voters in a political platform. Not all individuals are influenced by, or are susceptible to, the same hooks. Thus discovering which ones work best in any given case is an art requiring practice.

"Plants" or "stooges" have always been used by speakers wishing to influence a crowd. Plants appear to be ordinary members of an audience but in reality are working for a speaker. When a snake-oil salesman at a frontier outpost in the Old West asked, after making exorbitant claims for his medicine, "Now, folks, who wants to be the first to buy a bottle?" it was the plant in the crowd who barged forward crying "I do! I do!" In an audience he laughs loudest at the speaker's jokes, applauds most vigorously, and generally gives other members of the audience the impression that for him the speaker's points are incredibly insightful. In the final analysis a plant's job involves deception: he must appear to have no connection with the speaker or sponsor, his actions instead seeming to be spontaneous. Therein lies his effect.

The Oakland Family has used both hooks and plants with success. In fact, they are indispensable elements in its recruiting routine. The most general hook is the nonreligious pitch, which Durst and his assistants present when a street missionary first brings a prospective recruit to a dinner and lecture at the San Francisco center. West Coast Moonies learned during the early

1960s that talk of the Second Coming, particularly when Christ was supposed to arrive from South Korea, quickly turned off all but a handful of persons. As a result, Durst's fast-paced introductory lectures propose no messiahs, suggest no neobiblical analyses of world problems, never mention South Korea, and neither Adam nor Eve (much less the Reverend Moon) is ever brought up for discussion. The dominant theme is the alienation of human beings from one another, couched in existential philosophical terms and richly punctuated with humor and lively pantomime. It is a powerful hook for some idealistic youth who are concerned about the world they live in yet are confused as to how they might best contribute to making it better.

More specific hooks are sought and created. Though to outsiders the precise ratio of Moonies to non-Moonies during a lecture is unclear, in reality there is always one Moonie for every guest, if not more. The task of each Family member is to engage the guest in conversation, probing all the while for hooks—interests, hobbies, talents, hometown—and then flatter the guest by dwelling on them. Rather than attempt to weed out likely from unlikely members at this point, everyone is graciously encouraged to learn more about the Oakland Family. Everything from clothing worn at the dinner to piano-playing talents is praised. Neil Salonen, former president of the Unification Church of America, even instructed members on how to observe openings so as to create the impression that members had much in common with guests. These hooks are discovered and cultivated deliberately to build rapport and break down suspicions. Often female members are paired with male guests, and vice versa, which sometimes makes a powerful impression on visitors. Some church members frankly confessed to us that it was sexual attraction that first led them to consider becoming more involved in the movement. While such motives may not be pursued for very long if one decides to continue associating with the Oakland Family, they undoubtedly represent one important, effective hook.

The average guest at an Oakland Family dinner and lecture has little reason to suspect that this group is really a recruiting arm for the Unification Church. Oakland Family missionaries frequently deny their mission in public. The guest also has no idea how many of the other young adults milling around the center before and after dinner are members. An experienced observer of the movement could tell, however. The Moonies wear conservatively cut hair. The men wear no mustaches, beards, or even long sideburns. The women wear dresses rather than slacks. Both sexes tend to take the initiative in conversations, probing for and exploiting hooks. But to a naive guest there are no obvious cues. Thus, when the lecture by Durst or an assistant begins, the guest has no way of knowing how many of the clapping, cheering persons in the audience are plants dispersed to amplify applause and create the impression that the lecture is well received, that the jokes are indeed hilarious. In such group situations laughter and excitement are contagious. But what to the guest appears to be genuine appreciation of the speaker's message or Family members' skits may be only rehearsed affectation and forced enthusiasm. Yet without knowing this fact, a guest believes such behavior carries the ring of authenticity. It can create subtle pressure to cheer, clap, and roar with laughter along with the group. After all, the guest thinks, everyone else is having a great time and sees something profound in the lecture. And so the guest laughs and applauds along with the others.

Such participation in a group, as social psychologists have shown with abundant evidence, can produce subtle but demonstrable attitude change.[29] If the participation is viewed by the guest as voluntary and neither coerced nor bribed, then attitudes about it come to match the behavior. Concretely this means that after an evening of applauding speeches and laughing at corny jokes, despite the fact that the group pressure to join in basically prompted the applause and laughter, a person comes to remember the speeches and jokes as important and as irresistibly funny. What sociologists call "pluralistic ignorance," i.e., the fact that the guest cannot easily identify other guests and therefore cannot easily gauge the true (as opposed to the manufactured) audience response to what is presented, works to the advantage of the Oakland Family when it recruits.

"Love-Bombing"

After cajoling a young person into visiting the San Francisco center of the Oakland Family with promises of a free dinner and fun entertainment, the Family invites him or her to their farm at Boonville, California, for a weekend of seminar workshops. The Boonville farm is the indoctrination site of the horror stories told frequently by ex-Moonies. At Boonville the guest encounters an atmosphere and series of activities for which he or she is usually unprepared. The individual is suddenly involved with the group on a twenty-four-hour basis, privacy disappears, and even acts normally considered private become group-supervised. One sociology graduate student who went "underground" to observe the weekend experience reported that he was followed by his Moonie host into the toilet!

Aside from the lack of privacy, however, there is a continual use of hooks and plants. Guests are discouraged from talking to anyone else unsupervised (ostensibly to prevent any "negativity" from developing) to keep down the awareness of who is a Family member and who is a guest. This lack of awareness is important to the Family's routine since at times during the weekend, when everyone is encouraged to open up and discuss intimate thoughts, doubts, and fears, the plants provide moving testimonies that include tears and expressions of gratitude to all the wonderful people in the Family for their concern. If you were to visit the Boonville farm regularly over a year's time, you would see that the apparent spontaneity is actually a rehearsed sequence and that the same persons break down and sob on cue, weekend after weekend. However, to the naive guest who is unprepared for such emotionalism and for whom plants are not easily distinguished from other guests, the situation seems much less contrived.

The daily schedule is fast-paced and filled not only with lectures, testimonies, and discussions but also with exercises designed to break down inhibitions. These are familiar to social psychologists but appear at first glance silly to outsiders. They introduce "group hugs," where participants link arms over each other's shoulders, contests to see how many people one can introduce oneself to in thirty seconds, and skits pantomiming children and animals. These are interspersed with lusty cheering contests and spirited games of dodgeball and volleyball. The pace is deliberate: as observers (both scholars and former members) have pointed out, there is little time for reflection, to ask questions or critically follow up points made in the lectures. Real intellectual analysis is discouraged and even cut off by group leaders. The emphasis is on developing in a "positive" way. Any attempts to dwell on inconsistencies in the lectures or to pursue alternative answers to the questions raised are gently rebuked as "negative."

Toward the end of the weekend, aspects of the group's religious nature are gradually revealed. By then, however, for many guests the situation has changed and the revelation that this group possesses an important religious dimension has much less impact than it would have had two days earlier. It is not that many guests have been moved by the plants' testimonies, nor is it that hooks have been found and exploited. An additional element, which the Family members refer to as "love-bombing," comes into play.

Love-bombing means showering a person with flattery, attention, kindness, and expression of concern and love. It involves hand-holding, plenty of eye contact, and professions of empathy. Guests are lavishly rewarded with appreciation for opening up and giving personal testimonies. They are encouraged to tell more and cheered for their courage when they do. The emotionalism of the plants' testimonies is mixed in with love-bombing as are the frenetic games and childish skits. Sometimes love-bombing can be carried to ridiculous extremes, as one sociologist who visited Boonville for a weekend related. During dinner his assigned "buddy" kept offering him the food off his [the buddy's] own plate. When the sociologist turned away momentarily and then looked back, he found the Moonie had even peeled his banana for him.

It is this feeling of being smothered with affection and kindness that produces in some guests a feeling that what the group has to offer is unique and valuable, that makes them want to stay and learn more in the ensuing weeklong workshop. Such expressions of naked emotion and unrestrained spirituality from peers are rare for many young adults. The nurturant atmosphere, coupled with the security of a communal group, undoubtedly makes further participation attractive to the minority of young people who stay. The religious dimension revealed at the end of the workshop is no more disturbing to them than eventually seeing through the rehearsed "spontaneity" of workshop testimonies and love-bombing. By then they believe that it was all done for their own good, and they will learn how to do it themselves from watching more experienced members.

Such techniques of manipulation—particularly the creation of an impression of popular acceptance of ideas in a group—are certainly not limited to the Moonies, whatever we may think of their deceptiveness. Evangelist Billy Graham, for example, regularly employs similar ones. In a study of one evangelistic crusade in 1974, two sociologists found that the Billy Graham Evangelical Association employs local volunteer "counselors" whom it trains to help members of the audience "make their decisions for Christ." These counselors attend an intensive training program over several weeks that includes the learning of hand signals for counselors to communicate during Graham's sermons and final "altar call" and even directions on using breath mints before encountering potential converts. The behavior of these counselors is remarkably similar to what plants in the Moonies' workshops do:

> Counselors begin their work after the singing, testimonials, collection, and Billy Graham's sermon, which culminates in the altar call. At the moment of Graham's invitation to "come forward to Christ," counselors and choir members begin moving forward to an area usually in front of the speaker's platform or rostrum. To a naive member of the audience or a television viewer, this movement creates an illusion of a spontaneous and mass response to the invita-

tion. Having been assigned seating in strategic areas of the auditorium or arena and given instructions on the staggered time-sequencing for coming forward, the counselors move forward in such a fashion so as to create the illusion of individuals "flowing" into the center of the arena from all quarters, in a steady outpouring of individual decision. Unless an outsider or observer of these events has been instructed to look for the name tags and ribbons worn by those moving forward, it is all too easy to infer from these appearances the "charismatic" impact of Graham and his invitation. These strategies promote the respectability of making a public commitment and represent methods calculated to manipulate the consent of the passive, the uncertain, the wary, and the indecisive.[30]

EVALUATING CLAIMS OF BRAINWASHING

The entire concept of brainwashing, as we have seen, is a misnomer. It is repudiated by many sociologists, psychologists, and psychiatrists as a crude euphemism. Worse, it is a distortion of a real, understandable process of attitude change that is neither mysterious nor unusual in American society.

The stereotype of cult recruitment includes key elements of deception and mind control. The deception allegation is clearly exaggerated. Only the Moonies—and then only one component of the Unification Church—practice deception as to their origins and goals with any regularity. Most of these new religions are too radical and demand too much of new members for deception to keep potential recruits interested very long. In such cases as the Hare Krishnas or the Divine Light Mission, the accusation that all such groups deceive in recruiting is absurd.

Attempts to shape attitudes are a part of every church, school system, military establishment, and government. Ultimately there is nothing inherently wrong, in the moral sense, with the practice of shaping attitudes, even if it brings about radical change. The "wrongness" depends only on whether we approve of *who* is shaping the attitudes and for *what* purpose. This is the fundamental issue with which we as citizens must come to grips. Over a century ago Roman Catholics supposedly practiced mind control but Protestants did not. Today nobody seriously claims that the Roman Catholic church brainwashes its members more than any mainstream Protestant church. Has the Catholic hierarchy radically altered its method of indoctrinating clergy and lay members? It would be hard to see how. Rather, public toleration for Catholics has increased, and with toleration has come an acceptance of them as legitimate and noncontroversial. Mind control is more in the mind of the perceiver than some individual, identifiable practice.

Unquestionably, nearly all (if not all) the new religions seek to shift personal values and goals in a dramatic fashion. But the important legal and moral question is: do such efforts leave members uncritical, semiconscious, virtually compliant, quasi-comatose zombies who are blindly obedient to the whims and orders of new religious leaders? The evidence suggests otherwise. How would supporters of the brainwashing/mind control stereotype explain high turnover rates in memberships of the Unification Church, the Hare Krishnas, and the Divine Light Mission? (To answer that their memberships have not declined runs counter to the facts.) Why did so many of Jim Jones's followers have to be forced at gunpoint to drink cyanide-laced Kool-Aid? Moreover, why have a number of psychiatrists and psychologists found no reasonable evidence of stunted mental functioning? Surely something so obvious in human behavior as the inability to make a rational, independent decision would be apparent to any trained mental health professional.

The brainwashing stereotype is clearly inadequate to explain the otherwise normal daily behavior of thousands of Scientologists who pay their taxes on time, raise families, competently work at their ordinary jobs, and vote for public officials in elections. Neither does it help us understand the *real* behavior of Hare Krishnas and Children of God members who must make complex organizational decisions in their growing bureaucracies.

In this chapter we have argued that self-fulfilling focus by the media is a prime reason for generalizing the Oakland Family's deceptive high-pressure style to all branches of the Church and beyond that to all cults. In the Oakland Family situation, with its large mobile San Francisco Bay population and intensive media coverage, this exaggeration is understandable. The Oakland Family instituted a fast-paced agenda that includes plenty of group-centered activities, sensitivity games to break down participants' inhibitions to open up fully, Oakland Family plants who spontaneously offer teary emotional confessions and testimonials, and minimal (though certainly not dangerously low) amounts of sleep. All the familial elements of thought reform, from guilt arousal to flattery and praise for "saying the right things," are present in this indoctrination setting. The weaknesses and fears of a recruit are unearthed, played upon, and the result is a person prepared, after just one week or even one weekend, to go off on an idealistic crusade and act as if he or she will reshape the world.

Occasionally newspaper articles appear in which a journalist attends a Moonie indoctrination workshop elsewhere in the country, but they are tepid compared to the exposés of the Oakland Family. Careful examination of the articles that attempt to describe in detail the brainwashing process allegedly used by Moonies will reveal that nine times out of ten references are made almost exclusively to the Oakland Family. The press's emphasis on the Oakland Family, the Family's ability to recruit heavily, and the Unification Church's many defections and departures through deprogrammings have insured that much attention has been devoted to the Oakland Family's methods.

But if cult brainwashing is largely a stereotype or myth, are the ex-cult members who tell horror stories about their involvement self-serving liars or simply deluded? If mostly myth, why do some outspoken psychiatrists and psychologists defend the anticultists' claims? The media may have played an important role in giving such accusations broad exposure through self-fulfilling focus, but reporters and journalists did not fabricate their stories. And the hard-sell deceptive recruitment efforts of a small utopian sect on the West Coast cannot reasonably account for how other unrelated groups have been drawn into the controversy and labeled brainwashers. Neither the media nor the Oakland Family are the primary myth-makers.

To understand in concrete terms the origins of the brainwashing stereotype we must look to the very heart of the anticult movement: the families of the persons who have joined new religions, the angry ex-members themselves, and what actually goes on during a deprogramming. We will do this in chapter seven. Only then, after seeing who stands to gain or lose by promoting the brainwashing stereotype, can we understand the social and psychological processes that produce it.

5

The Leaders: Gurus and Prophets, or Madmen and Charlatans?

Stories about cults frequently include pictures and descriptions of the gurus who lead them. These are the pied pipers who lure followers to give up their possessions, forsake their former lives and friends, and parrot their leaders' words as gospel truth, slavishly attend to their every wish, and profess total obedience to them even to the point of sacrificing their own lives. One searches for the source of their magnetism in newspaper photographs, but what is seen is a motley assortment of unprepossessing features. Sun Myung Moon is old and balding. In flattering photographs he appears to be benevolent, even fatherly. In photographs of his public speeches, however, his grimaces and wild, karatelike gestures suggest a man in a fanatical rage. Hare Krishna founder Prabhupada, by contrast, is always shown in his monk's robes with the expression of a benign, tranquil holy man from the East. Guru Maharaj Ji has been at various times portrayed as a precocious adolescent lecturing his elders, as young Jesus is often pictured lecturing the priests at the temple, or as an older teenager dressed in modish Western clothes, looking more like a rock celebrity than a guru. "Moses" David Berg strikingly resembles his namesake: a gray-bearded Old Testament patriarch. L. Ron Hubbard, whose picture has rarely been seen in recent years outside Scientology centers, looks as if he would be completely at home among a group of corporate executives. Finally, there is the infamous Jim Jones, who—shorn of his impenetrable black sunglasses—is indistinguishable from any Midwestern small-town minister.

These modest, unassuming appearances belie both the leaders' own claims for themselves and their followers' adulation. L. Ron Hubbard, who his followers affectionately call "Ron," is regarded as a guide and friend in the process of self-discovery rather than as a spiritual master. Nevertheless, his doctrines are treated as absolute truth. Jim Jones claimed that he was the reincarnation of a number of famous people, including Karl Marx and Jesus Christ, and boasted a number of extraordinary powers. His followers called him "Dad" and, with his encouragement, always carried his picture in their wallets. David Berg regards himself as a prophet who receives messages concerning the imminent Second Coming. Guru Maharaj Ji, particularly during the early 1970s, had no reservations about accepting the rather exalted title of Perfect Master and Lord of the Universe. Prabhupada was referred to by his followers as His Divine Grace and now, after his death, is regarded by many of these same followers as a reincarnation of Krishna. The Reverend Sun Myung Moon has left little doubt in the minds of many of his disciples that he is the Messiah. Even in public interviews he has not avoided a comparison to Jesus Christ. In one he responded:

Q: You are obviously saying that you are a prophet, but do you also consider yourself the New Messiah?
A: We are in a new Messianic age. But 2,000 years ago Jesus Christ never spoke of himself as a Messiah, knowing that would not serve his purpose. I am not saying, "I am the Messiah." I am faithfully fulfilling God's instructions.
Q: But you don't rule out the possibility that you are the Messiah?
A: Let God answer you, let God answer the world.[1]

How can we explain the awe and reverence with which disciples treat these men and the Godlike images they have of themselves? Do these leaders really possess ultimate authority over their followers, and, if so, is it the result of unscrupulous domination or willing subservience?

LEADERSHIP

All groups have leaders, individuals who maintain power over other group members. The power leaders are able to exercise varies for different groups and, at least to some extent, with the personal qualities of an individual leader. It is not surprising that a military officer has more power over his troops than a social club director has over club members or that one military officer is able to gain greater loyalty and respect than another officer with the same position and title. In the cult controversy the real dispute is whether leaders maintain their positions through deception, manipulation, and coercion or through personifying the values and ideals of the group in such a way that followers willingly become disciples. The anticultists contend that mind control, physical deprivation, and intimidation are used to keep members docile and compliant. Members of the new religions contest this charge, asserting that they are deeply committed to their cause and willingly make personal sacrifices.

This dispute is difficult to resolve because human behavior is more complex than the arguments of either side. While we often think of relationships as either voluntary or coercive, many are both. After individuals join a group, they may permit themselves to be subjected to deprivation or coercion. For example, alcoholics or drug addicts who voluntarily enter treatment centers do so with the expectation that they will be deprived of these substances and that they will be physically confined or forcibly restrained if their behavior becomes unmanageable. Students who join fraternities or enter military academies anticipate a period of hazing during which they will suffer indignities. Volunteers in elite military units know they will be subjected to a schedule that may involve spartan living conditions, subsistence level rations, a few hours of sleep each night, absolute obedience to superiors, and long days filled with strenuous exercise. The reverse situation is also possible: individuals may be coerced into joining a group and later continue participation on a voluntary basis. For example, a mentally ill person might have to be forcibly taken into custody and physically restrained. Later, that patient, after recognizing his or her own illness, may consent to continue treatment on a voluntary basis. Whether the relationship begins voluntarily or coercively, some individuals are willing to experience the coercion because they see it as being in their own interest.

GURUS AS CHARLATANS AND MADMEN

Since human beings can join an organization voluntarily and as a result voluntarily experience extreme deprivation and coercion, rejecting brainwashing allegations does not necessarily imply that coercion does not take place. However, if members of new religious groups are systematically deceived, manipulated, and exploited by gurus who are charlatans, then sacrifice and deprivation, even if voluntary, are seen in a different light. Even if one rejects brainwashing allegations, important questions remain: To what extent do leaders of the new religions use members for their own private ends? What are these leaders' true motives? Is there coercion and, if so, are the gurus responsible for it? Are followers who make major personal sacrifices disciples, as they believe, or dupes, as the anticultists believe?

Attacks against the leaders of the new religions are an important component of the anticult campaign. The gurus provide a who and why for the process of exploitation the anticultists contend is taking place. It is these men who ultimately are responsible for cults; they are the brains behind the conspiracy; it is their warped needs and desires that give cults life and form. Four themes run through anticultist attacks on the new religions' spiritual leaders. First, the men are charged with simple greed as their real motivation — the new religions are just a new variety of get-rich-quick schemes. Second, they are seen as having political ambitions, with political programs, not spirituality, as their real agendas. Third, anticultists believe that leaders of the new religions have a lust for power, and this is the explanation for the ever-present need to subjugate followers. Finally, these men are not sincere, the anticultists allege, and do not believe their own claims. Spirituality is only a superficial cover for darker, hidden motives. In a word, they are charlatans. Such charges are extremely difficult to evaluate, for in order to get full and final answers, one would have to gain access to the gurus' innermost thoughts and feelings. Since such evidence is not obtainable, the leaders' behavior patterns must be compared to anticultist portrayals.

Wealth and Greed as Motives

Some of the new religions have amassed large amounts of money and property, although their wealth hardly compares with that of the mainline denominations. The Unification Church, for example, probably grosses between $25 and $50 million per year in the United States from street solicitation alone. Its South Korean headquarters operates a variety of profit-making enterprises, including an anticommunist training school, which government bureaucrats attend, and a small arms and munitions factory supported by government contracts. The Church also seems to have strong links with conservative industrial leaders in Japan who fund various projects. Finally, both the Korean and Japanese branches of the Unification Church have several hundred thousand members who make donations. Although the total wealth of the Unification Church is known only to its leaders, there is no doubt that it is substantial.

This money does not all go directly into Moon's pocket, however. The Unification Church spends vast sums on projects to further its goals.[2] During the early 1970s, for example, Moon conducted several nationwide speaking tours, appearing in virtually every major American city. Independent estimates of the cost of these tours run as high as $8 million. The Church also has poured millions into its New York City daily newspaper, *The News World*, in an effort to present its philosophy to the public. Additional millions have gone to sponsor Unity of

Science and New Ecumenical Research conferences with the aim of bringing scholars together to study and discuss matters of concern to the Church. The Church also supports the Unification Theological Seminary, where future Church leaders are provided theological training. In addition, it has purchased a lot of real estate around the country for use as Church centers. Finally, the Church has helped finance a variety of businesses to provide employment for its members and has established new branches in many foreign countries. All this is costly. Why does Moon expend all this money on Church projects? Surely he could siphon off more money for himself if he wished. There are probably two reasons why he does not. First, he has seen the Unification Church grow from a small band of loyal disciples to a large, worldwide organization. If he is to preside over a vital, dynamic organization, he must pour resources into it. If he is to continue to play the role of messiah, aspiring to unify all other churches, the momentum must appear to be in his direction. Since the Unification Church no longer seems to be growing rapidly either in Korea or in the United States, Moon may well be locked into a strategy of pouring resources into the Church in order to prevent stagnation. Second, he personally does not need money. As sociologist John Lofland, who has studied the Unification Church since its arrival in the United States, put it:

> If his aims were mere wealth and movement power, he need not have gone to all that trouble and expense to get them. He already had a large amount of both.[3]

Nonetheless, the Church provides for many of Moon's major expenses. There are Church-owned estates and limousines reserved for his personal use. He travels the world at will and has a staff to cater to his every need. He spends much of his time aboard his yachts engaged in tuna fishing, his favorite pastime. Even though he has no formal, legal control over many Church assets, he has no financial worries. Since Moon already possesses great personal wealth from his many Church-run businesses in South Korea and has high expectations for his movement, it seems logical that he would invest resources heavily in the Church. Moon may be accused of empire building, but personal greed does not seem a likely motive for his actions.

The other two new religions that have generated very large annual revenues are Hare Krishna and Scientology. In addition to soliciting in the streets and hawking books in airports and on street corners, the Krishnas operate one of the largest incense companies in the world, producing products worth millions of dollars each year. Like the Unification Church, ISKCON appears to be reinvesting much of this money to spread its message and way of life. Large sums are spent on missionary work in India, particularly in Bombay, where the Krishnas are building a large temple and retreat center. The Krishnas also operate several business enterprises such as their incense, cosmetic, and publishing companies and have opened centers for worship and recruitment in many cities across the country. They own a 1000-acre farm in Moundsville, West Virginia, where they are constructing a model community and a large, lavish temple devoted to the worship of Krishna. However the money left over from such activities and projects is spent, it does not go to Prabhupada. Prabhupada's lifestyle remained virtually unchanged during the twelve years he spent in the United States prior to his death in 1977. Despite ISKCON's growing wealth, as Carroll Stoner and Jo Anne Parke, whose treatment of the new religions in *All Gods Children* could hardly be termed complimentary, conclude, "None of the reported wealth has gone to make Prabhupada a wealthy man. He continues to lead the life of an austere Hindu monk."[4]

Scientology relies almost exclusively on course fees to generate revenue. Becoming clear can be a very expensive proposition, often costing members thousands of dollars. Since the Church of Scientology is much larger than either ISKON or the Unification Church, a great deal of money is earned through these classes. Estimates of annual revenues from sales of classes to members and nonmembers run as high as $100 million. In contrast to the Moonies and Krishnas, members of Scientology are paid for the services they provide to the Church, although some members lead introductory classes in order to pay for advanced classes. In any event, Scientology incurs great expenses because members do not live communally or work full-time for the Church without pay. The margin of profit therefore is probably considerably lower for Scientology than for the Unification Church or ISKCON.

Whatever the size of Scientology's profits, it is clear that L. Ron Hubbard is not in need of money. During the 1950s, his self-help therapy, Dianetics, was extremely popular and *Dianetics: The Modern Science of Mental Health* became a popular best-seller. The profits from his extensive science fiction writings, lectures, and therapy made him independently wealthy. Yet he has taken a variety of actions that have aroused deep suspicions about his motives. Shortly after Hubbard unveiled Dianetics, a variety of individuals began to administer independently Dianetics therapy. Hubbard moved quickly to regain control by establishing formal credentials for those who could legitimately offer the therapy. Whether this was an attempt to maximize profits once he had discovered how popular Dianetics was becoming or an attempt to prevent others from modifying his ideas and exploiting the name Dianetics at will is impossible to know. Dianetics quickly evolved into Scientology and was reorganized as a Church. Critics have charged that this transformation was no more than a clever tax dodge. In recent years, Hubbard has continued to "discover" further stages of personal enlightenment toward which his followers work, often at considerable expense. Critics have charged these new "revelations" are merely a means of keeping followers hooked on Scientology and to keep the money flowing in. It is certainly possible to interpret Hubbard's actions as designed to maximize wealth. However, at least at the present time, it seems more likely that Hubbard, like Moon, is empire building because he wishes his vital organization to survive him.

Whether or not this movement deserves to be condemned is, of course, an arguable issue. There is a tendency on such issues to compare the realities (or even the excesses) of what new religions do with inflated conceptions of the motives and actions of conventional churches and their leaders. Realistic comparisons of empire building among L. Ron Hubbard, Sun Myung Moon, Pat Robertson, Jerry Falwell, and Billy Graham would probably reveal more similarities than differences in style. From one perspective there is little merit in arguing that Hubbard or Moon is no more or less money-oriented than many other religious leaders. Take, for comparison's sake, the case of the well-known (and respected) television evangelist Rex Humbard. In April 1980, Humbard pleaded with viewers to send contributions to his organization so that it could cope with a $2.5 million deficit in its operating budget. Some of his debts were at least four months behind in payment. Researchers Jeffrey Hadden and Charles Swann in their book *Prime Time Preachers* noted:

> Humbard's appeals brought in $4 million and wiped out the debt. About the same time, a Cleveland *Press* writer discovered that Rex and two of his sons, who work with him on the television ministry, had purchased a home and condominiums in Florida valued at $650,000 with down payments of $177,500 in cash. A lot of people have long believed that preachers, especially the evangelical variety, have their hands in the offering plate. In light of this belief, the timing of Humbard's corporate debt and personal investment certainly didn't make him look very good. And he didn't help his own cause any when he told the prying *Press* reporter, "My people don't give a hoot what I spend that money for."[5]

Yet the fact that Moon, Hubbard, and others lead new religions and are so frequently accused of greed raises some doubt that personal greed is the *real* issue.

In contrast to the Unification Church, Hare Krishna, and Scientology, the Divine Light Mission and the Children of God do not possess a great deal of wealth. Throughout its history, Divine Light Mission has been financed by contributions from members, ashram-run businesses, and festivals that members must pay to attend. While the festivals were reasonably profitable, Divine Light Mission never grew large enough to generate a great deal of money either from festivals or member donations. Since Church-run businesses were largely small, local enterprises, they also failed to earn a great deal of revenue. As a result of some overly ambitious projects designed to spread its message, Divine Light Mission has faced severe financial difficulties. Despite these problems the Guru Maharaj Ji has continued to maintain an extremely affluent lifestyle, complete with mansion, limousines, and expensive, fashionable clothing. According to some reports, during the mid-1970s the guru was receiving five hundred dollars per day for his personal expenses. Some premies, according to reports, decided their guru needed his own private Boeing 747 jet, and Maharaj Ji responded with delight at the idea. However, the guru's lavish lifestyle has been the source of considerable controversy and even defections among premies due to Divine Light Mission's precarious financial condition. It is fair to conclude that Maharaj Ji comes closest to fitting the anticultists' stereotype of a leader living in luxury at the expense of his followers.

The Children of God have raised funds in a variety of ways, ranging from donations of funds and property by members to publicly selling their literature. Member donation has not been as profitable as literature sales since the group has not experienced a great expansion of membership. As the religious tracts Children of God devotees sell are rather inexpensively printed, these "sales" in many respects amount to public donations. Nevertheless, the Church seems more interested in spreading its message than in making money. Children of God runs a number of youth-oriented nightclubs and music-related businesses, but these are more important to the Church for their recruitment value than for money. Despite its modest income, the Children of God pours substantial funding into international proselytizing. The Church claims to have founded colonies in over 80 countries, and the cost of establishing and sustaining these missions must be substantial. Members continue to live frugally, consistent with their theological beliefs, and there is no evidence that David Berg personally departs significantly from this lifestyle.

The People's Temple amassed a large amount of wealth through donations of money and property from members. Jim

Jones maintained tight control over Church funds, although it is not clear whether he intended to put any of this money to personal use. There were disturbing signs, however: Jones appropriated the social security checks of the many elderly members of People's Temple and transferred the ownership of Church-owned nursing homes into his own name. Still, it is difficult to conclude that Jones hoped to exploit his Church financially. Whatever else may be said about Jim Jones, he did not live an affluent lifestyle. Furthermore, the cost of moving his entire congregation to Guyana must have been extremely high, and Jones was contemplating another expensive migration to either Cuba or the Soviet Union. Given these massive projects, the funds at Jones's disposal do not seem excessive. And if wealth and luxury were his primary objectives, it hardly seems likely that he would have led his flock to the primitive jungles of Guyana.

The degree to which leaders of the new religions seek personal wealth clearly varies. At one extreme we find Prabhupada, living a totally ascetic life, and at the other the Guru Maharaj Ji, who regards unlimited luxury as his birthright. There is no doubt that those leaders who desire to live in affluence do so, and for the most part, their followers seem to accept and expect this. Most leaders seem more interested in building churches than in accumulating greater personal wealth. Since they have spent much of their lives building churches, their motives are hardly unselfish. The churches are extensions of themselves, and the churches' immortality seems their prime concern. Regardless of how we may feel about their empire building, however, it seems clear that simple greed is not the sole motivation. The same amount of energy, devoted more directly to amassing wealth, could have been much more lucrative.

Political Ambition

One of the anticultists' major allegations is that the leaders of new religions are using the movements to gain political power for themselves. This allegation does not apply to most of the leaders. David Berg has gone into seclusion in Europe. Prabhupada lived a life of ascetic retreat until his death. Neither

L. Ron Hubbard nor Guru Maharaj Ji has expressed political ambitions. Only Jim Jones and Sun Myung Moon could be used as evidence that these spiritual leaders secretly harbor political ambitions.

Jim Jones was a potential revolutionary. Although he was involved with a variety of civic projects in San Francisco and gained the trust of some of that city's political leaders, he became more radical with the passage of time. His fears that a massive repression of blacks was imminent, that a nuclear holocaust was inevitable, and that governmental persecution of the People's Temple would continue created more of a defensive than an offensive stance, however. He made his initial move to California to found a refuge from nuclear devastation. His move to Guyana was triggered by government investigations of the People's Temple, and his plans to migrate to a socialist country were based on fears of continuing government persecution. Despite his support of international socialism and his rejection of the United States, he does not seem to have been politically ambitious except as political alliances would protect his Church.

Of all the new religious leaders, the Reverend Sun Myung Moon has shown the greatest interest in politics. His concern stems directly from his vision of a worldwide theocracy. From Moon's perspective, the source of all mankind's problems has been a refusal by mankind to live up to God-given responsibilities. In Moon's vision of theocratic socialism, the church must be superior to the state and political solutions must flow out of spiritual revelation. Only if government is sensitive to God's will can mankind's problems be solved and true potential realized. Moon, therefore, quite openly advocates a close working relationship between church and state in which the church is the ultimate authority.

In addition to Moon's theological interest in politics, he has been made sensitive to political currents as a result of his Church's origins in South Korea. Prosperity and even survival in dictatorial South Korea would have been impossible had Moon not been a shrewd politician. There is no doubt that Moon is well connected to the South Korean political elite, although his political fortunes in his home country have fluctuated significantly over the last several decades. Since the assassination of dictator Park Chung Hee and Moon's failure to win great influence in Washington, D.C., his political future is indeed questionable. But the Korean government contracts with his arms and munitions factory and his leadership training school are convincing evidence of his continuing closeness with government leaders, at least in South Korea.

Moon has not shown the same political shrewdness and sensitivity in the United States, however, perhaps due to major cultural differences in political expertise. A number of Moon's provocative statements have received widespread publicity and elicited angry criticism. Moon, for example, has been quoted as saying:

> The time will come, without my seeking it, when my words will almost serve as law. If I ask for a certain thing, it will be done. If I don't want something, it will not be done.[6]

Another frequently publicized quote is, "I will conquer and subjugate the world. I am your brain." In addition to rhetoric, Moon has involved himself in a variety of political activities that have angered many Americans. Followers lobbied in Congress for a closer alliance with South Korea based on Moon's designation of that country as the New Israel. During the Koreagate scandal his remark briefly became an issue. There is no doubt that Moon's greatest political error was attempting to develop close personal ties with Richard Nixon during the Watergate period. The noisy demonstrations he organized in support of the Nixon presidency and his statements to the effect that God had chosen Nixon to rule and therefore only God could remove him from the presidency created strong public anger and hostility. Following these events, media coverage of the Unification Church became consistently negative. Assessing Moon's political ambitions is difficult at this point. Most of his political initiatives backfire and, in recent yeras, he has remained in seclusion. Whatever political aspirations Moon might have, widespread public hostility toward the Unification Church and the failure to continue to attract large numbers of American youth mean that such plans now are little more than fantasies.

If the new religions are just a cover for seeking political power, it is not apparent from the actions of most leaders of these groups. Most have shown little inclination to become involved in political affairs, although a number have condemned America as thoroughly corrupt. Only Jim Jones and Sun Myung Moon have been politically active. Jones's actions were largely defensive in nature, and he did little in the United States to further his socialist convictions. Moon has been much more politically active. There is little doubt that he courts government power, and Americans would have reason for concern if Moon had any real chance of achieving his goals. His willingness to support a repressive regime in Korea and his advocacy of a theocratic form of government are hardly reassuring. However, Moon stands little chance of ever gaining political influence because the Unification Church is no longer growing rapidly and has committed several fatal political blunders. Still, concern about his intentions is not sheer fantasy.

Power and Domination as Motives

The most consistent and emotional charge made against leaders of the new religions has been that they wield dictatorial power over church member activities. This is a key element of the brainwashing allegation. The guru's insatiable lust for power provides the explanation for manipulation and abuse of members of the new religions. Some statements by leaders of the new religions, frequently quoted by the anticultists, do little to allay the fears of those who believe them, for example, that of Guru Maharaj Ji:

> So whatever extra you have got, give it to me. And the extra thing you have got is your mind. Give it to me. I am ready to receive it. Because your mind troubles you, give it to me. It won't trouble me! Just give it. . . So just try to be holy and

> try to be a good devotee, a perfect devotee of that Guru who
> is Himself perfect, who is really perfect.[7]

Statements like Moon's classic "I am your brain" have
frightened new religions' opponents, who have taken them as
evidence of all gurus' evil intentions. We have already considered the allegations of brainwashing and find little supporting
evidence. Even if followers are not brainwashed, they may be
subjected to highly authoritarian rule. Let us consider the issue.

There is no doubt that the major decisions affecting the course
and development of each of the new religions have been made by
their founder/leader. For example, the People's Temple migra-
tions from Indiana to California and from California to Guyana
were dictated by Jim Jones, and the whole concept of the ideal
community, Jonestown, was his. It was L. Ron Hubbard's
inspiration that made a spiritual quest out of Dianetics. When
the Guru Maharaj Ji decided his premies had become too
laggard, he tightened control over followers by organizing
communal ashrams. Moon also moved rapidly toward tight
communal organization shortly after arriving in the United
States. In each case, some members left and those who
remained were forced to substantially restructure their lives.
Prophecies of impending doom or deliverance by the Children of
God, Unification Church, and People's Temple have produced
frantic activity and willingness to ignore rules of conventional
society in the name of a greater cause and a higher truth. From
this perspective, leaders of the new religions clearly have a tremendous capacity to instantly transform the lives and priorities
of members.

While the spiritual leaders of the new religions do control the
major economic and organizational decisions, their authority
has not gone unchallenged. For example, "Moses" David Berg
has had problems asserting control over his movement. As two
sociologists who have closely followed developments in the
Children of God put it:

> . . . while the case is often made that the Children of God is
> a community under the personal control of David Berg,

there is evidence that since 1971 his exhortations to the
effect that the organization develop in small groups...had
been ignored by the intermediate leadership.[8]

While Berg eventually won the fight, he was forced to threaten
to cut off communication with the rebellious groups in order to
do so. There has been ongoing conflict between the East and
West Coast branches of the Unification Church, although
efforts have been made not to let outsiders become aware of it.[9]
The West Coast's more deceptive recruitment practices have
been a continuing irritant to the East Coast because of the negative media coverage resulting from such practices. Friction has
continued despite Moon's attempt to resolve the factionalism
within his American movement by appointing the West Coast
branch's leader as president of the Unification Church in
America. When the Guru Maharaj Ji married his secretary, after
admonishing his followers to lead a life of abstinence, half or
more of the core members of Divine Light Mission defected,
hardly suggesting total control by the guru. There is evidence
that Jim Jones was beginning to lose control over the People's
Temple. In addition to the loyalty of his trusted lieutenants,
Jones had the total support of the senior citizens at Jonestown,
who felt they owed Jim Jones everything. Jones was able to bring
issues before the entire community for a democratic vote with
complete assurance of winning. By the time of the Jonestown
tragedy, however, a group of dissenters was beginning to find
means of circumventing Jones's control and the outside world
appeared increasingly hostile to Jones. The suicide/murders at
Jonestown may well have indicated a growing sense of desperation and loss of control rather than the iron-handed rule so
widely assumed. The degree to which leaders are able to control
and shape the churches they found vary considerably.

The extent to which leaders of the new religions manage the
day-to-day activities of members' lives also varies. The
Reverend Sun Myung Moon continues to direct the major
organizational and financial decisions within the Unification
Church, but most members, who are scattered across the
country and around the world, rarely see him. Many have never

even met the man they call their spiritual parent. L. Ron Hubbard remains in relative seclusion aboard his fleet of yachts, Sea Org, off the Atlantic coast. David Berg deliberately withdrew from active leadership of the Children of God several years ago through an open letter to all members, "I Gotta Split." Although Berg attends annual meetings, he does not appear to exercise much influence over ongoing Church affairs. Indeed, observers of the Children of God have noted substantial differences in the lifestyles and operation of the various colonies. There is a similar pattern in Hare Krishna. Temple lifestyles differ considerably, and members apparently have some choice in locating a temple where they feel personally comfortable. The pattern was evident even before the death of Prabhupada. In the case of the Divine Light Mission, many members apparently left because there was so little organization and discipline. Maharaj Ji simply shows little interest in such matters. Only Jim Jones closely controlled the daily round of his members' lives. He was able to do this both because the size of his congregation was small and, once the move to Guyana had been made, almost completely isolated. Certainly evidence exists that some of the new religions are organized in a highly authoritarian way and have been coercive, but with the exception of People's Temple, it is not the gurus themselves who dominate members. Yet all these men have some influence over their followers, and several have an enormous amount of influence. The more spectacular cases have received widespread publicity. Sun Myung Moon, for example, picks marriage partners for many converts to the Unification Church, sometimes without their having met one another prior to the matching ceremony. Moonies refer to Moon and his wife as "True Parents," as distinguished from their physical parents. Female members of the Children of God have been willing to have sexual relations with potential converts following Berg's assertion that this was an acceptable way of demonstrating the power of love. Jim Jones was able to convince a large number of his followers to join in a mass suicide. Even if we leave aside such sensational illustrations, it is clear that many members of the new religions significantly alter their lives. Krishnas and Moonies, for example, turn their backs on conventional lives and sometimes their entire past, including family and friends. Members of Scientology and Divine Light Mission may live more conventionally, but their entirely different vision of the world reorders values and priorities. Gurus do play a major role in such transformations. How can we reconcile apparently conflicting indications of leaders' power?

There are two answers. The first is that the most visible, dramatic changes in members' lives occur in communal groups, and, in this situation, the leader's influence is indirect. Moon and Prabhupada cannot monitor each of the many communal groups scattered across the country. Once communal groups are established, they tend to be self-sustaining. There is intense pressure for total loyalty and commitment, and leaders and followers both have a stake in maintaining the group. Because participation is voluntary, pressure is intense. Each member has made a substantial personal sacrifice and commitment for the group, and all members therefore look to others' sacrifice and commitment to sustain their own. Leaders usually play a major role in establishing a communal organization, but they may be quite remote from day-to-day operation without any noticeable consequence. Of course, there are cases where leaders do exert ongoing personal control, as Jim Jones did, but this is not usual.

Communal groups can create very intense peer pressure to conform on members, particularly when either doom or salvation is believed to be on the horizon. Under these conditions such groups typically separate themselves from conventional society, which is viewed as corrupt, in order to maintain their own "purity" or to save themselves from their inevitable holocaust. The Children of God, Hare Krishna, Unification Church, and People's Temple have all organized communally and to varying degrees have withdrawn from conventional society. The isolation of the People's Temple in Jonestown is the most dramatic case, but the other three groups also keep members quite isolated. Contact with outsiders is generally limited to occasions when members are recruiting or fund-raising, and ties with former friends and family members are strongly discouraged if in any way they threaten total commitment to the group.

An isolated communal group creates the potential for total social control. Members of such groups often are taught that leaving the group will result in their spiritual (and sometimes their physical) death. To the extent that members really believe that the group possesses ultimate truth and power (and this varies just as degree of belief in conventional churches does), they may be afraid to leave. Cutting off ties with outsiders may create feelings of vulnerability and dependence. Members who have openly denounced and rejected friends and family may feel compelled to stay. The longer individuals remain in a communally organized new religion, the more completely their lives are tied to the group. All of their friends, marriage partner, church, careers, and children are intimately tied to the communal group. The whole group as well as its leaders thus has tremendous leverage over each individual. To leave or to dissent may be to lose everything. Members may also feel a sense of obligation to the group. Not only has each individual made a major personal commitment to the group, but members usually have actively recruited others. Recognizing that one's own commitment is waning can engender guilt about leaving behind those whom one recruited. The fact that large numbers of individuals do, in fact, leave suggests that such obstacles are not insurmountable. Nevertheless, the feelings of fear, guilt, dependence and vulnerability indicate how intense the pressures on individuals can be.

It is important to recognize, however, that the gurus themselves may or may not play a central, personal role in generating such feeling. Jim Jones obviously dominated the lives of his followers in a very direct way because his congregation was limited in size, collected in a single location, and, in its last days, physically isolated in a remote jungle community. Other new religions simply do not have the capacity to exert such total control over their followers. The situation at Jonestown was exacerbated by Jones's strong feelings of paranoia and persecution, his heavy use of drugs toward the end of his life, and his personal manipulativeness. The suicide/murders at Jonestown were as unique as they were tragic, and little purpose is served in trying to generalize from that extraordinary incident.

Authoritarianism is not solely the result of communal organizations. There is a second factor. Leaders are able to exert so much control over their followers' lives and decisions because followers attribute extraordinary qualities to their leaders. Why does this happen? One reason is that individuals who join a new religion do so because they find something intensely rewarding about their new relationships. Whether it is the warm, sharing, idealistic environment of a communal group or the insights gained through therapy or the sense of inner peace that comes from meditation, the relationship works for these individuals at this time. The fact that other communal groups, therapies, or forms of meditation might be equally rewarding is irrelevant to them. This is similar to lovers attributing unique qualities to one another because of the rewards of a relationship, even though each might have found an equally worthwhile experience with someone else. The leader gains the credit for such rewards (or is blamed for failure) because he is believed to be the original source of the reward.

Followers also elevate leaders to heights in order to justify personal decisions and commitments. After all, if an individual is about to transform his or her entire life, one must be able to justify such a dramatic break with the past and to feel confident about taking such a large risk. To the extent that converts can believe that new beliefs and lives are ultimate truth, that others also believe, and are willing to risk, they have a much greater sense of confidence and security. The leader is the visible, personal symbol of the group. If all group members share a commitment to the leader, each can be confident of others' commitment to the group. Attributing and constantly acknowledging extraordinary qualities to the leader is, therefore, a means of demonstrating deep commitment. And this serves the interests of the followers fully as much as it does the leaders.

One indication of the role followers play in the elevation of their leaders is the creation of stories that endow leaders with superhuman qualities or deeds. L. Ron Hubbard, for example, is reputed to have engaged in both time travel and astral projection (i.e., leaving his physical body in his astral, or spirit form, to travel distances) and to have encountered spirits from other galaxies. Sun Myung Moon has been raised to heroic stature in a number of stories. After meditating on the tragic life of Jesus as a young man it is reported he wept all night long, and in the morning his tears had saturated the mat on which he slept and soaked through the ceiling to form a puddle on the floor below. Moon is believed to have special rapport with animals, who can sense his special qualities; for instance, animals have congregated around him when he visited a zoo and tuna have jumped onto baitless hooks he cast into the sea. Leaders are also described in superhuman terms. Sun Myung Moon is believed by many Moonies to be the Messiah; the Guru Maharaj Ji is believed to be the most extraordinary person ever to have lived by premies; followers of David Berg present him as a great prophet; and members of Hare Krishna treated Prabhupada as a reincarnation of Krishna. In each case followers attributing extraordinary qualities to leaders justify their own commitment to each other and to the leaders.

The leaders themselves claim extraordinary qualities and deeds, such as seeing visions, conversing with God, and combating Satan. In order to maintain their position, leaders constantly have to demonstrate extraordinary qualities, which creates considerable pressure for leaders even though followers are willing to accept heroic tales rather uncritically. Partly for this reason, leaders often issue such new prophecies as "Moses" David Berg's periodic forecast of the destruction of America or Sun Myung Moon's prediction of dates for the restoration of man to God. The lack of confirmation of such prophecies does not seem to be important to many believers, since the failures can be explained. What is important is that the leader continually confirm his position by having visions and making prophecies.

If follower and leader wish to confirm the leader's unique spiritual status, it is easy to see why leaders exercise such authority. The more a leader moves or is moved toward a Godlike position, the more complete must a follower's obedience be. While there are some restraints on the process, charismatic authority poses a danger. In the case of the People's Temple, for example, not only did Jones and his followers create heroic tales, but Jones engaged in deliberate deception and manipulation to preserve his position. He produced a bloody shirt with a bullet hole in it and claimed to have been shot but left unharmed. He arranged for confederates to shoot up his church and then as a demonstration of his telepathic powers described his attackers in great detail. Jones's activities show the potential for the abuse of charismatic authority. For this reason, most churches that were founded by a single charismatic leader gradually place controls on succeeding generations of leaders. Yet it is important to recognize that while leaders do, in fact, have a great deal of authority over individual members, much of this authority comes from the followers.

Sincerity

Even if it is true that new religious leaders are not motivated solely by political ambition, or a need for domination and control, the question of basic sincerity remains. Are they in reality what they appear to be? Are they genuine? Such questions are extremely difficult to answer, of course, because we seek to compare inner thoughts and feelings with outward actions when we can only observe the latter. It may be that new religious leaders are not motivated by any single need such as wealth or power but still may be charlatans.

One test of sincerity is whether a leader's founding of a church fits in with a pattern of a devout, religious life or represents a sharp departure from it. While far from a perfect test, this at least indicates continuity of purpose. By this standard most of these leaders would have to be judged as reasonably sincere. David Berg had been an ordained minister in the Christian and Missionary Alliance some years before starting his coffeehouse ministry, Teens for Christ, in 1968. For at least twelve years he has continued to invest his time and energy in building the Children of God despite the fact that there has never been a very large membership or financial profit. Sun Myung Moon had a vision of Jesus commissioning him to become the next messiah or "Lord of the Second Advent" at the age of sixteen and began preaching the revelations he had received at twenty-six. In 1954, he founded his church in Seoul at the age of thirty-four. During the years that followed Moon worked tirelessly, spreading his church and his message around the world. Moon has devoted virtually his entire life to building the Unification Church, developing an elaborate theology (the Divine Principle), and following the course which he believes God laid before him more than forty years ago. Prabhupada became a Krishna as an adult and, in 1944, at the age of forty-three founded the Church's magazine, *Back to Godhead*. His religious commitment continued to grow and at fifty-eight he became a Hindu monk. Six years later he brought his message to the United States, spending the remaining twelve years of his life developing ISKON in this country.

Jim Jones began a career as a preacher only a year after high school graduation. Four years later he founded the Christian Assembly of God church (which later became the People's Temple) and subsequently was ordained as a Disciples of Christ minister. Like Moon, he devoted virtually his entire adult life to the development of his church, although he never produced an elaborate, distinct theology as Moon did. The Guru Maharaj Ji is the son of a Perfect Master. He became the head of Divine Light Mission at the age of eight. Only thirteen when he established a branch of Divine Light Mission in the United States, he has continued to play the role of Perfect Master into which he was born. Precisely when L. Ron Hubbard developed Dianetics remains a mystery, but he had worked on his ideas some time before publicly unveiling them in 1950. For the last thirty years he has continued to develop the implications of his ideas and has steadily integrated his therapy into a religious framework. Of the six leaders, only L. Ron Hubbard "added on" a theological doctrine, within two years of the public introduction of Dianetics. Whether this represented an attempt to gain tax-exempt status and greater control over auditors or simply a natural evolution in his thinking is impossible to determine. Each of these men has thus been involved in a long-term effort to develop a church; most of them have come either from a well-established religious tradition or developed new theologies. New religions do not represent dubious operations that suddenly appeared in the early 1970s.

A second test of sincerity is the extent to which a leader has suffered persecution or made major personal sacrifices in the course of developing churches. It is not clear that either L. Ron Hubbard or David Berg has experienced much personal sacrifice aside from the recent condemnation of all new religions, but each of the other leaders has endured some type of persecution. Jim Jones left Indianapolis for California due, in part, to the persecution he faced for racially integrating his congregation. It is also true, of course, that he had been sexually promiscuous from the early days of his ministry and faced criticism for this. Prabhupada renounced his family and left his job in order to devote his life to the worship of Krishna. The Guru Maharaj Ji could have remained in India as head of the Divine Light Mission and lived a life of luxury as a revered spiritual leader. Instead he chose to come to the United States against his mother's wishes. His movement has never achieved great strength in this country, and his mother has revoked his title and claim to his former position in India. Sun Myung Moon was imprisoned twice by the communist regime in North Korea and subjected to extreme physical deprivation and punishment, apparently on the complaint of a group of Christian ministers. He was briefly imprisoned nearly two years later, in 1955, on charges of injuring public morals (i.e., sexual promiscuity) and draft evasion, but those charges were later dropped. Yet the fact that each of these leaders has made some major sacrifice for his beliefs suggests that they are not mere charlatans.

A third test of sincerity is the degree to which the leaders have exploited their respective churches for personal advantage. This is probably the most complex issue and one on which the record is mixed. More questions can be raised than can be resolved, but it is important since deep moral concerns are involved that the issues not be ignored. Greed and lust for power aside, certainly the most sensational charge is that of sexual perversion and manipulation. As discussed in chapter three, charges of sexual impropriety against leaders of new religions have been common throughout American history, and there is a similar pattern in the new religions. In 1955, Sun Myung Moon was charged with having sexual intercourse with female converts to purify them, an allegation vigorously denied by the Unification Church and for which no concrete evidence was ever produced. In any case, since the Unification Church arrived in the United States there has been no hint of sexual impropriety; indeed, the anticultists have complained of the sexual abstinence practiced by members following conversion.

David Berg's most controversial doctrine was that of flirty fishing, in which female members are encouraged to become "happy hookers for Christ," if necessary, to demonstrate God's love to potential converts. In addition, some married women in the Children of God also were shared with Berg and others as part of the philosophy of total love. Jim Jones regularly had sexual relationships with members of his congregation dating back to the initial founding of his Indianapolis church. The relationships were both heterosexual and homosexual, involving both married and single individuals. According to J. Gordon Melton, a scholar who has extensively studied the People's Temple, Jones led an unrestrained sexual life himself but tried to intrude in others' sexual relationships so as to orient their feelings to him. Melton reports that "among the actions taken by Jones were: (1) forcing members to strip in public, (2) forcing members to admit to homosexuality and lesbianism, (3) advising couples to abstain from sex altogether, (4) ordering public confessions of sexual acts and conduct, (5) rearranging marriages and commanding divorces."[10] Jones openly bragged both of his sexual prowess and of his sexual encounters.

Charges of sexual perversion or manipulation are difficult to assess, for three reasons. First, such charges are extremely damaging to religious leaders because they are viewed as a basic violation of trust and a true spiritual relationship. Since these charges have such an impact they may be made in times of conflict simply for the advantage provided. Second, reorganization of sexual relationships is common in communally organized groups. Leaders often attempt to control sexual expression because intimate relationships between members pose a potential threat to intense commitment to the group. The question becomes where the individual's first loyalties lie, and in communes the answer must be that they lie with the group. The usual pattern in a communal group is some degree of sexual abstinence with sex controlled by group leadership. However, some groups encourage "free love," which should prevent deep intimacies between individuals. Third, sexual attraction between charismatic leaders and their followers has always proven difficult to control. Relationships between ministers and parishioners, doctors and patients, teachers and students, and psychiatrists and clients have all shown a high potential for sexual abuse. Throughout American history, the lives of charismatic leaders ranging from George Washington to Martin Luther King, Jr., to John F. Kennedy have shown a similar pattern.

Given the likelihood of charges of sexual impropriety against charismatic leaders it is difficult to take the allegations against Sun Myung Moon seriously without any substantiating evidence. There is no doubt that sexual practices within the Children of God are bizarre by conventional standards. A number of the group's members left when Berg began pushing the idea of flirty fishing. Little evidence about the degree to which women volunteered for flirty fishing or wife sharing exists. To the extent that one's marriage and church membership are held hostage to participation in these activities, they obviously are open to condemnation. The case of the People's Temple seems the clearest by far. Jones apparently set a double standard for sexual practices, used sex to humiliate and punish members, forced false confessions of deviant sexual practices, and sought to break up relationships on personal whim. Still, of the six leaders, only Jones clearly used sex abusively for his own personal advantage. Given the frequency of sexual violations between admired, revered leaders and followers, the new religions hardly stand out as hotbeds of sexual perversion.

These simple tests of sincerity are not conclusive, and there is no available test or evidence that leads to definitive conclusions. In all probability these men, much like the rest of us, are neither totally sincere nor hypocritical. About all that is available to us is the patterning of these leaders' lives and actions, and, by this standard, they do not appear to be charlatans. How history will judge them remains to be seen.

GURUS AND RELIGIOUS CHANGE

We have assessed the anticultist allegations about leaders of the new religions and find the realities much more complex than the anticultists' stereotypes. There is little evidence that greed is the primary motivation of these gurus. Several of them were independently wealthy before starting their churches in the United States, and most reinvested massive amounts of money in their churches. It is much more likely that they are empire builders than quick-buck artists. There is limited evidence of political ambition. Only Sun Myung Moon projected a role for himself in government, but his political ineptness surely destroyed any real opportunity for him to exert political influence. The issue of personal power and domination is extremely complex because human beings are capable of voluntarily placing themselves in coercive relationships and sometimes have trouble extricating themselves. The power of cult leaders is not monolithic, for they face considerable difficulty in maintaining control over their churches. Still, some of them do exert enormous influence over their followers. There are both positive and negative aspects of this influence. On the negative side, members can be subject to intense social pressure, which ultimately is sanctioned by leaders, in communally organized new religions. These pressures can leave members feeling fearful, dependent, vulnerable, and guilty. Both leaders and group members may play on such feelings to maintain the loyalty that is so vital to communal groups. On the positive side, members are willing to serve as disciples and leave themselves open to far-reaching control by their leaders. Furthermore, followers have as strong an interest in the guru-disciple relationship as the leader does. There certainly is a danger of abuses by charismatic leaders who face considerable difficulty in living up to the superhuman qualities with which their followers endow them in maintaining their authority. As some of the tactics used by Jim Jones suggest, deliberate deception and manipulation can occur in situations where followers want to believe and leaders need to consolidate their own power. In general, however, there is very little hard evidence of extreme exploitation resembling slavery. Finally, it is difficult to conclude that leaders of the new religions are insincere. Most have been pursuing religious conviction throughout their lives and even have endured some persecution. However one may feel about their self-pretensions, goals, and beliefs, there is little evidence that they have taken advantage of their churches for personal gain.

Even if we can conclude that the leaders of the new religions are fundamentally not exploitative charlatans, a feeling of uneasiness may remain. These men do, after all, have enormous influence over others' lives. Followers may engage in extreme acts, whether or not these are particularly dangerous to anyone or violent in nature, which they might not do otherwise. There is a danger in charismatic authority, as it is a form of leadership usually emerging when great change is in the making because great change requires great energy and great commitment. To those who are not part of that effort, the whole affair may look extremely risky and absurd. Surely the parents of the men who left behind their jobs and families to follow Jesus of Nazareth must have been worried and fearful. From our current perspective it was worth the price. Millions of people over many centuries have found deep spiritual satisfaction in the teachings of Christianity. Many other large, stable churches—from Mormons to Christian Scientists to Jehovah's Witnesses—have followed a similar course. In all these cases, and most others as well, charismatic authority gradually is diminished once the founder/leader dies because it is too risky and unstable. Herein lies a real human dilemma. Religious freedom and religious diversity will certainly result in new groups with charismatic leaders at the helm challenging the established order. That is the history of religion in America. This kind of leadership always involves risk and sacrifice. We cannot have change without risk and we cannot foresee which of the challenges to the old order will become the pillars of a new and equally satisfying order. The essential question each of us must answer is to what extent we are willing to protect our short-term sense of security and order at the cost of stifling diversity, change, and freedom of expression. There are no easy answers.

6

Fund-raising and the New Religions: Charities or Rip-offs?

All of us have been approached in shopping centers, in airports, at our place of work, or even on our own doorsteps by individuals professing to be raising money for charitable causes. The pitch is a familiar one: "Hello, my name is Janet and I am collecting money for the United Way [or the Little League, or an interdenominational church group]." Whoever makes the pitch awaits our response, smiling, fully expectant that we will respond with some donation, however modest. Sometimes we instantly recognize the organization the solicitor claims to represent—the United Way, the Heart Fund, or an anticancer group —and sometimes the group is smaller, more local, or more obscure, one about which we have little or no information. But fund-raising organizations always present us with titles and sentimental appeals that are difficult to turn down. After all, when people are volunteering their free time on behalf of homeless mothers, civil liberties, disaster victims, wayward children, Christian brotherhood, the destitute, or those stricken with crippling diseases the least we feel we can do is acknowledge their effort with the gift of a few dollars.

Most of us are comfortable with such giving. We feel some pride and satisfaction in supporting a worthy cause and are not unhappy that we can express our principles and have a tax break as well. Yet the coin has two sides. Many of us feel some discomfort when we are approached for a donation. We usually do not know the solicitor. Is the solicitor who he or she claims to be? And for all but a handful of prominent national charitable organizations we know little or nothing about the groups requesting money. As a result, all of us at times have wondered which of the seemingly endless list of charities we should support and how much of our hard-earned money actually is used to solve the problem or help the group that asks us to give in the first place. Generally such doubts surface briefly, when the fund-raiser is standing in front of us with outstretched hand, when a co-worker has come to our office or shop to pick up our pledge card, or when we are in the process of writing an annual donation check. Yet these doubts disappear just as quickly because we do not have any easy way of checking the identity of fund-raisers or finding out where the money goes. In the end we usually give despite any reservations, and hope our gift is not wasted.

Doubts about the ultimate use of charitable solicitations have been intensified recently as some new religions have gone after a share of the charitable dollar. In many cases new religions have been able to capitalize handsomely on the knee-jerk tendency that Americans have to give away at least small amounts of money without pressing for much detail about the solicitor or the charity in question. In some cases fund-raisers for new religions are deliberately vague in identifying their affiliation, raising questions of deliberate deception, misrepresentation, or outright fraud.

The furor over religious fund-raising is not limited to the new religions' tactics and purposes, however. There is anxiety among many clergymen and conventional church groups that the electronic pastors of the media—the Pat Robertsons, the Jim Bakers, the Robert Schullers—are siphoning dollars away from local church congregations, using an oversimplified "Praise the Lord" theology and old-fashioned hustle to build network empires. At recent meetings of the National Council of Churches of Christ in the United States, concern has been raised that monies donated to these media "charities" are not really "helping" anyone through mission work or aid to the poor but instead are only going to pay for higher salaries and yet more air time. But whether new religions or television evangelism is being considered, one result is that many people are asking a fundamental but unresolved question: What is a charity? The best way to answer this question lies in taking an honest look at the way American charities operate. It will thereby become evident that many, if not most, charities fall somewhat short of the charitable ideals they profess. Critics of the new religions tend to cloud this issue by comparing what conventional charities *say* with what some new religions *do*.

THE CHARITY MAZE

Charitable giving is an American tradition whose roots can be traced back to ancient Judeo-Christian beliefs. In pre-twentieth-century America, private philanthropy, in the absence of a developed welfare state, became an essential for the ideal citizen. Giving was both a moral and a civic duty. Throughout our history the rich have been expected to contribute a portion of their wealth to provide some relief for the less fortunate and to benefit the community as a whole through such activities as patronizing the arts and supporting libraries and universities. Even the most ruthless nineteenth-century "robber barons"— the Stanfords, the Vanderbilts, the Rockefellers, and the Carnegies—returned some of their enormous wealth to the public. Gradually such attitudes pervaded the growing, affluent middle class. Since World War II there has been a rapid increase in the number of groups competing for charitable dollars. The combination of the high American standard of living and the charitable impulse has caused the number of dollars available to charities of all types to balloon. By the mid-1970s Americans were giving to charities at a rate of $20 billion each year.[1]

What Is a Charity?

A garden-variety dictionary definition of a charity is an organization that provides help to the needy. At first glance this definition seems clear-cut and straightforward. When we are confronted, however, with the broad range of groups actually seeking charity dollars from the public, one can see how ambiguous the whole concept of "charity" really is. Ideally, what most people have in mind when they think of charity is the Good Samaritan model: an individual who extends personal assistance to someone else in need who in turn immediately and visibly benefits from this gift. But the reality of charitable giving in the United States is far different.

In practice we tend to treat as charities all organizations that have managed to gain tax-exempt status from the Internal Revenue Service. Sometimes we add the stipulation that nonprofit organizations must have passed muster with one of the watchdog groups that evaluate charities for accountability and public disclosure, such as the National Information Bureau. Usually, however, approval from such independent groups merely involves some basic financial disclosure statements. But a number of well-known nonprofit organizations, such as the Muscular Dystrophy Association and the Billy Graham Evangelistic Association, have failed to comply with requirements for complete approval by such private agencies as the NIB, which means that even such watchdog agencies' available lists of approved groups do not separate legitimate from fraudulent charities very well. Furthermore, given the capacity for "creative accounting" within large bureaucracies, the financial disclosure information probably identifies only the most flagrant and inept of the fraudulent charities.

What we are left with, then, is a veritable maze of groups as diverse in the type and quality of services they offer us as are those of colleges, automobile service stations, and mutual fund operations. Some charitable groups simply sell a product on the open market and use the profits for charitable purposes. A church-run bookstore is a good example. Other groups provide us with a product that has limited market value or at an inflated price with the understanding that we regard the purchase as a contribution. Girl Scout cookies or an Audubon newsletter illustrate this arrangement. In still other cases, like the National Cancer Society, we receive nothing directly in return;

our entire contribution presumably goes to fight cancer.

Not only do charities differ in what they give us personally as an inducement to make a donation but also in their different goals. At one extreme are groups such as the United Way, which helps many different local causes, or the Heart Fund, which attacks a widespread health problem that might affect any of us. At the other extreme are groups that fight rare diseases or give aid to a cause in which few people feel they have a stake.

The Charity Game

Most Americans do not ask too many questions about the operation of major well-known charities, partly because they have few ways to check up on their actual operation, partly because they naively assume the charities will use the money as they say they will. At a time when many charities have become large, impersonal bureaucracies and when the donor rarely knows the person who solicits the donation, giving becomes literally an act of faith. In his book *Give! Who Gets Your Charity Dollars?*, journalist Harvey Katz underscores this point:

> We're vulnerable enough as consumers. But, in the market place we are at least dealing with something tangible most of the time. Not so in the charity world—we can't kick the tire of the Red Cross before sending in a donation. We are at the mercy of our own faith.[2]

Thus for the most part charities escape careful public scrutiny. Most people have only a vague idea of where the money goes.

The most common complaints about fund-raising by some of the new religions are that no one can really find out where all the money goes, that from what can be discovered the money does not appear to be used for any charitable purpose, and that heavy-handed, deceptive tactics are used to obtain "donations." There is a surprising overlap between these complaints and the actual scene among conventional charities. To demonstrate this, let's take a look at how the "legitimate" charities stack up on the counts by which new religions are criticized.

Most Americans seem genuinely shocked when they discover how much money goes to the fund-raisers and organizational overhead and how little money actually trickles down to meet directly the problem the donors believe they are helping eliminate. A good example is the respected March of Dimes campaign (formally the National Foundation for Infantile Paralysis), one of the most successful and best-known charities in recent American history. The March of Dimes grossly overestimated the prevalence of polio during its twenty-year crusade between 1938 and 1958. The fact is polio never reached the epidemic proportions claimed by the National Foundation and fully half of all known cases did not even involve paralysis. Furthermore, many of the victims were adults, a statistical fact belied by the now famous poster image of a young child in leg braces. Finally, most Americans still do not appreciate how little of the money they gave went to combat directly even the limited number of reported polio cases. Journalist Katz estimates that only about 6 *percent* of the *half billion* dollars raised through public solicitation (or a total of about $33 million) actually went for polio research. The rest was eaten up by overhead (i.e., public relations, office costs, miscellaneous expenses, and sheer waste).[3]

The idea of voluntarism that we associate with charities has been overplayed and exaggerated, often by the charities themselves, which prefer to portray our giving as "our" idea, not theirs. Yet actual surveys of the public's attitudes toward charitable solicitations reveal considerable resentment and annoyance at being aggressively set upon by friends or total strangers in public or more subtly by employers, ministers, and other leaders to whom we are beholden in some fashion. One researcher[4] reported typical reactions from individuals subjected to these kinds of appeal pressures:

> Too much pressure, too many campaigns . . . You are made to feel unpatriotic if you don't give.

> I don't like it. It makes you feel forced into it, shamed into contributing. You feel like hell if you refuse.

> When I get them Easter Seals I feel put upon—but I usually

send them the dollar. But I don't like it. You feel the obligation; if you keep them and don't pay, it's like stealing.

I find it irritating to be approached by women waving a can at you.

Employees in many organizations are required to make a monetary pledge to various charities, sometimes in percentage amounts. Often they are pressured, if not required, to sign and return pledge cards even if they decide not to make a donation. Many church members are familiar with dated weekly pledge envelopes, which they are strongly encouraged or instructed to return with a stated donation. Most people don't seem to vent these feelings openly, however, apparently because they think others will regard them as lacking in civic responsibility and personal generosity.

Then, too, there is the matter of deception. Even the most prestigious causes have not been immune to the temptation to employ deceptive fund-raising tactics. For example, sociologist David Sills reports how the March of Dimes in its crusade against polio used a potentially misleading hook to boost donations. One volunteer gleefully recounted the following incident to him:

I'll never forget one thing we did. We pulled into the Market Basket [supermarket] Friday night. We said [over a loudspeaker] — the parking lot was full of cars you see — "There's a *killer* loose in this vicinity!" People jumped out of cars — that got a lot of attention you see. Then we informed them that it was infantile paralysis that was loose. Next day downtown everybody was talking about it, and they gave "like mad."[5]

Imagine the furor that would have been raised if such a stunt had been concocted by the Hare Krishnas!

Similar reports have surfaced regarding fund-raising practices by the Congress for Racial Equality (CORE) and the Southern Christian Leadership Conference (SCLC), both major civil rights organizations. In an exposé on the popular CBS network's *60 Minutes* it was revealed that in the late 1970s both groups employed the same fund-raising organization, which became the target of numerous complaints as a result of its deceptive appeals. Donors were given the impression that they were contributing directly to the expenses of the civil rights campaigns when in fact their donations were being used to purchase advertising space in a limited-circulation magazine. Not only were donors misled but, to make matters worse, little of the money ever reached the civil rights cause. The fund-raising organization kept *90 percent* of all monies received, so literally only one dollar in ten ever reached the civil rights movement. (Of course, CORE and SCLC had overhead expenses that further diluted the possible impact of individual contributions.)

It is not our purpose to suggest that most charities in the United States are rip-offs, nor are we trying to justify wrongdoing by any group including the new religions. We do think that an honest look at conventional charities reveals that they are very much like other organizations and place a high value on survival and prosperity. For example, after polio was conquered the March of Dimes looked around for another disease. It shifted to birth defects; then it was fund-raising as usual.

Charities try to gain as much control over their "market" as other kinds of organizations do. As their interests dictate, they band together into the United Way or remain separate to maximize their charitable cash flows. Each uses whatever strategies it can to stimulate public feelings of obligation to support the "cause." Neither do they rush to reveal any more about their operations than forced to. For example, it was only recently, and under heavy pressure, that Billy Graham began making financial disclosures about his multimillion-dollar organization. The new religions proceed along much the same lines.

To evaluate the new religions' fund-raising practices, we need to understand what they do and why, specifically how they raise their money and its purposes. It is to these issues we now turn.

FUND-RAISING BY NEW RELIGIONS

As we have pointed out, the six major new religions possess very different beliefs, organizations, and goals. Not surprisingly, therefore, both their needs for money and the ways in which they have gone about fund-raising are also distinctive. The public stereotype that all the new religions engage in deceptive panhandling is simply not true, but it has led to an across-the-board campaign to prevent all new religions from fund-raising. (As we shall see, relatively few of the new religions resemble the prevailing stereotype.)

What are the reasons the new religions need money? Their needs vary. For example, like the Jehovah's Witnesses, the Shakers, and other well-known Christian sects, the Children of God expect an imminent end to this world as we know it. Their major objective is to warn everyone of Christ's Second Coming in this century and the terrible fate that will befall those who do not harken to the message of God's chosen prophet, David Berg. The end is coming, regardless of what humanity does, so there is no need to store up material goods or wealth beyond the movement's survival needs. For COG, therefore, money is raised largely to broadcast their message and provide living expenses for the faithful while they await the millennium. These funds come from the sale of pamphlets and newsletters, or what they call "litnessing."

The Divine Light Mission resembles the Hare Krishnas in that its members are interested primarily in individual change that will ultimately lead to a better world. But the premies are much less aggressive than the Krishnas in their world-transforming efforts. Nor do their beliefs, which stress self-enlightenment, lead them to establish lavish, expensive temples. In the main, Divine Light Mission activities are supported by cooperative enterprises, such as bakeries or craft shops, run by local communal ashrams. Premies do not panhandle or fund-raise in the streets. In this sense the Mission is much like such late-nineteenth-century utopian communal groups as the Oneida and Amana communities in this country.

The People's Temple and Scientology differ as much from one another as they do from the other four new religions under discussion. Scientology, like the Hindu-based Transcendental Meditation Movement, essentially sells a service on a contractual basis. One pays set fees for specific packages of lessons. There is neither street solicitation nor public sale of literature. Most of the money obtained from the lessons goes to pay for buildings, publications, and salaries of the full-time staff, as is the case with conventional churches. The People's Temple began as a conventional church in which members were encouraged to make regular service offerings and to volunteer their time and energy for various church projects. Gradually, members felt stronger pressure to turn over their pensions, social security checks, bank accounts, and other personal possessions to the community. Thus, by the time the group moved to Jonestown, its method of raising money changed most radically, toward a classic communal community. Little attempt was made to obtain funds from the general public, and the colony supported itself largely through a combination of subsistence agriculture, members' contributions, and donations from the church branch that remained in San Francisco. Beyond moving expenses there was little need for large amounts of money since the group had little expectation of using it to change the world in any radical way.

The two new religions that come closest to the fund-raising stereotype are the Unification Church and the Hare Krishnas. Both groups seek to raise large amounts of cash, although for somewhat different reasons. (The Hare Krishnas do not rely exclusively on street solicitation for incoming cash. Much of the movement's revenues are generated by the Spiritual Sky Incense Company, which sells incense and a variety of toiletries nationwide. The Unification Church has set up various fishing, restaurant, and crafts businesses, but none has produced as much profit — when they have produced profit — as the Krishnas' incense company.) The Moonies' goal of restoring the Kingdom of God on earth entails the transformation of whole societies and economies. This enormous undertaking involves great amounts of money as well as political influence and mass conversions. Change of this magnitude is an expensive proposition. The Krishnas also envision change on a grand scale, but they seek world improvement through meditation, asceticism, and devotion to Krishna. From their perspective, then, individual change must precede institutional change. The Krishnas' goal is to create the most favorable circumstances to promote this change. This goal, practically speaking, translates into building lavish temples dedicated to Krishna, which in their splendor and scale are reminiscent of the most ornate Western European cathedrals and churches. These temples serve not only to honor Krishna but also as islands of refuge from the corrupt world where devotees can focus their energies on spiritual improvement.

Thus, of six well-publicized groups known as cults, only two approach the fund-raising stereotype that many people associate with all unconventional religions. It is worth examining Moonie and Krishna fund-raising techniques in some detail and also worth understanding the rationales behind them. Although both groups need a lot of money, why do they turn to public fund-raising? After all, isn't it somewhat ironic that they turn for a handout to the very societies they condemn? Don't they see themselves as hypocritical when they lambaste American society as materialistic and then turn around and gladly take its money?

The answer is found in the fundamental dilemmas that face groups that simultaneously condemn the world and seek to change it. Having rejected the world as corrupt, they feel compelled to withdraw from it as completely as possible. Such changes can quickly be seen in their speech, their clothing, their food, how they spend their time, and where they live. Yet, curiously enough, they also need the outside world, for it is the outsiders and outside institutions they wish to save and reform. Their problem therefore becomes one of how to get the resources—money and converts—necessary to create the change they seek while avoiding the corruption of the outside world. It is a bit of a juggling trick and poses the major challenge for such groups. Historically most groups have solved this problem in one of two ways: They either sell some communally produced good or service (for example, the famous silver craftwork of the nineteenth-century Oneida community) or they rely on public begging. The latter alternative is most attractive in a situation where members have few skills to sell and where the change they seek is imminent. Modern-day, affluent American society has made this traditional choice more lucrative than it has ever been before.

For both the Moonies and the Krishnas, fund-raising has been elevated to a religious ritual. Money collected is not regarded as being for the movement, but as being "restored" or returned to God (or Krishna) through His stewards or servants on earth. As one former Hare Krishna member explained the fund-raising rationale in a television interview, "We're here to make a lot of money for God."[6] Likewise, the Reverend Moon has even claimed that the inscription "In God We Trust" on U.S. currency means that

> it is God's money. Every bill or coin says so. You are the stewards and God has deposited His wealth in your hands.[7]

Moonies regard the funds they labor so hard to gather in three ways. First, the money goes to further the Unification Church's diverse operations, which is to them a direct blow against Satan. Second, they believe that each time a person on the street makes a contribution (whether or not the donor realizes it) to a Moonie, both parties have jointly made an offering to God. Third, Moonies believe the ultimate reason anyone makes a contribution is that the donor, however unconsciously, senses the unconditional love the Moonie radiates. Because the ability to love all others on a spiritual plane is the basis upon which the Unification Church expects to transform the world, members strive continuously to increase this capacity. Unification Church members thus interpret successful fund-raising as a sign of their own personal spiritual growth.

Given the importance of fund-raising to the Unification Church and the Hare Krishnas, both spiritually and financially, it is not surprising that they have worked to find the most effective possible techniques. Yet their options have been limited, as they cannot solicit contributions from such donors as corporations, foundations, and civic clubs. In fact, they rarely are allowed on the premises of such organizations. Nor are wealthy philanthropists a likely source of funds. These limitations automatically rule out large donations and many prime fund-raising locations. The most lucrative remaining alternative is solicitation in public locations from which they cannot legally be barred. Therefore, Moonies and Krishnas abound at (some would say infest) street corners, shopping centers, and airports. It is the concentration of fund-raisers in such heavily traveled locations that leads to popular overestimates of membership in new religions.

Such public solicitation offers the Moonies and Krishnas a number of advantages. Areas of heavy human traffic present the opportunity to approach a large number of people during the course of a day, and most of those individuals possess at least some spare change. People passing through airports or walking along the street usually are in a hurry, and most do not appreciate being stopped by a stranger asking for a donation. The Moonies and Krishnas are able to take advantage of this. The individuals they stop are suddenly faced with a choice of rebuffing the solicitor or making a donation. Many people simply pull a quarter, half dollar, or more out of their pockets and give it to solicitors to avoid being assertive or rude. Many are too busy to inquire into the group's identity or purposes. Often a solicitor has only to state that he or she is representing a Christian youth group in order to win some change. Even when the Unification Church or the Hare Krishna groups are clearly identified, many persons buy their way out of a momentarily inconvenient situation, and the solicitors are only too happy to let them do so. So we are confronted with the ultimate irony—many individuals who detest the new religions are precisely the ones who end up being their financial backers. (We have interviewed numerous individuals who unwittingly made donations in such circumstances.)

Picking the right location, however, is not the whole story. Both groups have developed panhandling techniques and are willing under at least some circumstances to engage in deliberate deception. Observation of a number of fund-raisers for the Unification Church and the Hare Krishnas indicates that they develop the same streetwise sense possessed by successful panhandlers in any urban area. The tricks of the trade are numerous and, by all accounts, successful. One tactic to which many Americans have been subjected is having a small American flag, flower, or lapel pin suddenly stuck on one's shirt or coat before there is any chance to refuse. A donation is then requested. Many people feel it difficult or awkward to turn down the solicitor under such conditions. Another tactic is to stop passersby and engage them in conversation, creating a momentary inconvenience. A surprising number of Americans are completely immobilized by this maneuver, at least long enough to be pressured into giving a donation. One easy way to escape the solicitor is, of course, to make a small donation. A third tactic used by fund-raisers is flirtation or flattery with sexual overtones. "You'd be dangerous single," one Hare Krishna woman cooed to a young male during a covertly filmed NBC television documentary. "You must be intelligent to be in the Air Force," a serviceman was told. "How beautiful your hair is," a Hare Krishna fund-raiser told one elderly woman.

The most successful fund-raisers do not walk up to anyone with the same standard pitch. Instead, they gradually develop a sense of whom to approach and what kind of line to employ. One ex-Hare Krishna explained that she learned to "tune in to a person's interest" when she began her approach. A top fund-raiser in the Unification Church was more specific in her descriptions. She told us how to elderly couples she consciously played the role of dutiful granddaughter in order to evoke a sentimental response. Encountering a group of businessmen walking toward her on the street she studied the "body language" of the group, deliberately picking out the leader from his position in the group's center. She knew that if the leader gave the others would as well. Confronting a husband and wife strolling in a shopping mall she always approached the wife so as to avoid even the remotest appearance of flirtation. Once the wife was put at ease and perhaps sympathetic even an unenthusiastic husband would contribute. The fact that this woman set a record that day (one she later broke herself) by raising a thousand dollars is testimony to her savvy. On that day there was a driving rainstorm in New York City, soaking her as she solicited donations from cars at a stoplight. The sight of a freezing, drenched young woman evoked considerable sympathy from motorists.

In addition to lines and manipulation, however, Moonies and Krishnas have employed deliberate deception. They have issued pious denials that they have encouraged or allowed such tactics, but there remains little doubt that these continue to be employed. The reason deceptive techniques are more than occasional mistakes by overzealous members lies in the pressures under which fund-raisers operate. Moonies and Krishnas are taught that they hold the key to the salvation of mankind in their hands. The whole world could be transformed if their efforts are successful. Under such conditions it becomes easy to slide into a perspective where the end justifies the means. One Krishna stated this viewpoint clearly: "It's legitimate if God's doing it; we're representing God." The Reverend Moon also has encouraged this point of view:

> Telling a lie becomes a sin if you tell it to take advantage of a person, but if you tell a lie to do a good thing for Him that is not a sin. Even God tells a lie very often . . . [8]

Members measure the gains they have made in their capacity to love others largely in terms of their donations. In a situation where spiritual purity is believed to bring donations it is very easy to reverse the logic and assume that donations, however obtained, are evidence of spiritual purity.

Deception has been built into fund-raising practices to the extent that both groups have developed special languages to legitimate it. Hare Krishna members have been taught that all outsiders are "demons" and that "soliciting from demons helps to save them." The Unification Church regards outsiders as Satanic and even gifts given unwittingly or for inappropriate motives contribute to the donor's ultimate salvation. The Krishnas refer to their deceptive practices as "transcendental trickery" and the Moonies use a similar euphemism, "heavenly deception." Although members of the Children of God do not rely on public solicitation, they use similar terminology ("spoiling Egypt") that justifies deception of nonmembers, or even shoplifting. Given these rationalizations, members have no more difficulty engaging in deceptive fund-raising practices than a well-meaning mother has in feeding bad-tasting medicine disguised as candy to a sick child.

The bottom line in all this is that public solicitation is an extremely lucrative practice for the new religions, far more profitable than any other alternative open to them. There are high returns — all tax exempt — and low overhead costs. So they continue to rely on it despite the fact that it has created a great deal of hostility toward them. It is not hard to see why if we examine a few hypothetical but realistic figures. Let us begin with the assumption that a fund-raiser standing in the flow of pedestrians in an airport corridor or on a city sidewalk can stop two people each minute, or one hundred and twenty people each hour. Of course, many persons immediately reject an appeal, so more contacts per hour are possible. It would be easy for a fund-raiser working a ten-hour day (and most work more) to *contact* twelve hundred people. If five out of six individuals contacted refused to make a donation, solicitation would still yield two hundred donors each day. If donations averaged fifty cents each, a fund-raiser would take in $100 per day.

On the basis of a five-day week and a fifty-week year, each fund-raiser could collect $25,000 per year. One thousand such fund-raisers could therefore gross $25,000,000 per year. And remember: it is tax free. The reader should note that these are *conservative* estimates. Since members turn over all proceeds from their fund-raising and live most frugally, there is a considerable profit involved.

EVALUATING THE FUND-RAISING ISSUE

What anticultist stereotypes would have us believe in terms of the new religions' fund-raising activities is that all of them are some unscrupulous guru's get-rich-quick schemes. Anticultists try to create feelings of moral indignation in all of us by comparing the public relations claims of conventional charities with the worst excesses of fund-raising practices by the new religions. They also lump all new religions together as panhandlers, which as the evidence shows is not true. As we have seen, the reality of much charitable fund-raising is very different from the Good Samaritan ideal. If we compare the new religions' fund-raising styles against that standard, they do not measure up very favorably. But then, neither do those of a significant number of conventional, respected charitable organizations. The problem is not nearly as simple as identifying the proverbial wolf in sheep's clothing.

Most Americans do have a real disagreement with the new religions. They do not want to see their hard-earned money support or further the aims of any of these groups, particularly when they are fully aware of their goals. However, because the new religions differ so much in their need for funds, the way in which money is raised, and the purposes for which it is spent, there is no single course of action that would resolve all the public's grievances. Tightening up local laws on public fund-raising or soliciting, for example, would not automatically dry up the financial resources for the groups. In addition, Americans must consider the long-term implications of any policies they support, for other groups whose aims they do support employ many of the same techniques as the new religions.

The People's Temple, for example, received the majority of its money from its members' savings, pensions, social security checks, and personal possessions. It is most unlikely that there would be either public or constitutional support for restrictions on personal donations of this kind, as such contributions are also the lifeblood of mainstream religious groups. How would limits on contributions to unconventional religions, but not on similar contributions to, say, a local Presbyterian church be enforced? Or would donations be limited to one in order to limit them to the other?

All Scientology funds are derived from its classes. Recruits are neither coerced nor deceived. The fact that many outsiders regard the teachings of Scientology as simply quack psychology is not relevant. Americans traditionally have spent large amounts of money on quack remedies, pop therapies of doubtful value, and miracle medicines, and faith healers have always existed at the fringes of medicine and religion. There does not seem to be any effective way of preventing people from purchasing such services when they want them, as the present campaign against Laetrile demonstrates. As long as no definite harm can be proven to result, people have the freedom (we can even say the right) to buy as much "snake oil" as they want. Critics will argue that Scientology has cleverly shielded itself from government agencies and the suits of medical and clinical associations that might expose it as a sham by organizing itself as a church. Regardless of its merits, however, the question is if we close Scientology down should we then prohibit the faith healing that occurs regularly across the nation in many fundamentalist and Christian Science churches (perhaps discouraging many devout Christians from continuing necessary medical treatment) and on religious network television?

The Divine Light Mission finances itself mostly by mission-owned stores and other enterprises. These businesses can be easily identified, yet they continue to be patronized by the public, so clearly there is no consensus about their possible danger. Likewise, the Children of God cannot be prevented on any defensible constitutional grounds from offering its literature for sale to the public. Furthermore, both groups have a limited need for money and probably would not be seriously incapacitated by a boycott of their wares. There are too few members to make it worthwhile for any city or town to enact specific new legislation *in case* they appear.

The two groups that do engage in public solicitation—the Hare Krishnas and the Unification Church—pose a different challenge. Most people are annoyed by the Moonies and Krishnas because of their bald aggressiveness, use of deception, success, and lack of tangible benefits for anyone but themselves. There probably is no solution for that problem except refusing to give. Because large numbers of Americans are willing to give away money with few or no questions asked, under relatively mild pressure (certainly not coercion), the soliciting groups can hardly be blamed. If most Americans truly share the anticultists' hostility toward the Moonies and the Krishnas, they can easily refuse to give. In the end it may be more a problem of consumer education than restrictive laws, which would in the long run hurt the charities most Americans gladly support.

One effective and creative, if zany, attempt at *informal* control over Krishna fund-raisers was devised in 1979 by Californian Mitch Egan. As reported in national newspapers, Egan was enraged at what he termed harassment of his mother at airports by cult members. Egan and several other persons purchased 10,000 metal "clickers" in the shape of frogs, and under the auspices of the Fellowship to Resist Organized Groups Involved in Exploitation (FROGIE) gave them to employees at the San Francisco and Los Angeles International airports. Whenever an employee or airline passenger was approached by a religious fund-raiser, owners of clickers surrounded the fund-raiser and drowned out his pitch in a loud chorus of metallic clicks. Egan reported a noticeable decline in fund-raisers as a result.

There are legal remedies for extreme aggressiveness and outright deceptive practices already on the books in most communities. Many were laws requiring solicitors to wear identification tags or restricting them from certain private places, originally passed as solicitation ordinances designed to thwart peddlers and unscrupulous encyclopedia salesmen. In the past decade, hundreds of communities across the country have passed or revised ordinances to impede fund-raising by the Moonies and Krishnas. Fund-raisers have been refused solicitation or forced to comply with long, time-consuming procedures. Violations have been met with arrests, fines, jailings, and police escorts to the city limits. Local officials have clearly hoped that fund-raisers would go elsewhere rather than deal with a maze of legalities.

Virtually all local ordinances impeding public solicitation have been declared unconstitutional in court. However, ordinances requiring solicitors to wear identification badges with their name and the group's, and prohibiting the blocking of traffic or pedestrians have been declared constitutional.

The conflict over fund-raising probably cannot be completely resolved by existing laws or public habits of charitable giving. The new religions are likely to continue to go after the money that is necessary for their survival and growth. Those groups that need a lot of money have no alternative to public solicitation. Unless memberships in the new religions shrink (which may well happen) or gradually begin to lose their radical flavor (as many earlier groups have done), they are unlikely to change their practices very much, particularly right away.

Therefore, *we* face a choice. We can try either to increase the formal and informal regulation of fund-raising by the new religions *or* choose only to prevent violations of existing laws. The new religions fund-raise in such diverse ways that a variety of laws would have to be passed or changed in order to have any real impact. There is no doubt that laws aimed specifically at the new religions would be discriminatory and unconstitutional. Yet more general laws would not only run into constitutional restrictions on state regulation of religion but would subject conventional groups to all kinds of intolerable and unnecessary scrutiny.

Informal pressures beyond encouraging the public to be more conscious and critical in the way it makes its donations also have undesirable consequences. Several new religions are looking for reasons to condemn and reject conventional society, which make it easier for them to preserve unity and self-sacrifice. Achieving a reduction in their monetary resources at the expense of increasing their isolation could produce greater extremism—something no anticultist would want.

Does this mean there is nothing we can do? No, it means that it is wise to exercise patience, moderation, and tolerance. This country has sanctions it could bring to bear against the new religions, but in the long run its most important interest is the preservation of religious liberty and a free, open society. Democratic societies always are faced with groups that exploit constitutional protection. That we can tolerate and include such groups rather than reject them is a measure of our strength, not our weakness.

7

Deprogramming

Consider the following dramatic instance of conflict from two very distinct points of view:

First, see part of a deprogramming through the eyes of a 23-year-old woman, Pam Fanshier, a college graduate who joined the Unification Church and was later abducted by her parents (and other persons) to be deprogrammed:

> The first part of the deprogramming consisted of three days of very strenuous and continuous verbal attacks. I was mocked, degraded, accused of sexual crimes and prostitution. Bible verses were constantly being hurled at me plus lengthy and boring testimonies of individuals who had been deprogrammed from various other religious groups. Only twice during these entire three days did we carry on even a half-way intelligent conversation. Both of these conversations were quickly terminated by the deprogrammers because various things that individuals said were too supportive of my religious beliefs. Mr. Alexander [Joe Alexander, Sr., a nationally prominent deprogrammer] clearly realized that to talk on any kind of rational vain [sic] only allowed my parents an opportunity to question whether what they were doing was morally right. The remainder of the three days was, therefore, dedicated to developing and maintaining an emotional frenzy within that motel room at all times . . . My brother screamed in

177

my face that I was a prostitute and that I hated my parents and wanted to destroy them. They told me the most outrageous lies about Rev. Moon and other people in our church. They told me that if I ever went back to the church that leaders would make me go to court and sue my father for rape in order to descredit [sic] and bring about the downfall of the "deprogrammers." When one group of "deprogrammers" and body guards got tired they simply called in a fresh group. When I would start to fall asleep someone would kick the bed or poke me to keep me awake. Conversations lasted until very early each morning. I lost track of the hours and no one would tell me what time it was . . . The clothes and all personal possessions which I had were taken from me and my parents were ordered to burn them. For three days the intensive part of the deprogramming continued. I listened to statements and accusations over and over again till I could have screamed. My mind and physical senses were seeking anything other than the monotone of their voices and emptiness of that motel room. On the second day of my captivity I was allowed to go into the restroom alone and take a shower . . .[1]

The Fanshier abduction began a highly publicized series of events during fall 1975. After a number of days of being held against her will, Pam faked a successful deprogramming and, when her family's guard was lowered, escaped into the night and returned to the Unification Church. But she was abducted again — more violently than before — and this time her family tried to have her committed as mentally incompetent to the Menninger Clinic in Topeka, Kansas. Failing, they finally had her successfully committed to the Kansas Medical Center. Thereafter occurred what can only be described as a tragic confrontation: Pam with her lawyers, on the one side, struggling to prove her sane; and her parents with their lawyers, on the other side, seeking to have her declared mentally incompetent. A psychologist and a court-appointed psychiatrist each certified that she appeared to them to be in mentally good health, and ultimately she was legally declared to be so by a judge.

The upshot of the whole court procedure was to frustrate her parents tremendously and further estrange Pam from them. We talked with Pam Fanshier in June 1978, three years later. It was the week before she was to graduate from the Unification Theological Smeiniary in Barrytown, New York. She felt she had made her peace with her parents and that they now appreciated, if not approved of, her right to make her own adult decision in terms of religion and lifestyle. She spoke of her plans to return home several days later for a brief visit before she would return to Barrytown with her parents for graduation. Pam Fanshier never made it back for the graduation ceremony, however. When a lawyer with whom she had prearranged to call twice daily while home (and whom she had not called), arrived at the Fanshier home with a sheriff less than one week later, it was deserted. Pam was elsewhere, locked in a trailer for yet a third attempt at deprogramming. (A robust, resourceful young woman, she was to escape again.)

The Fanshier family saw her involvement with the Unification Church as something other than true commitment and argued that her civil liberties were never involved. According to them her mental processes had been lowered systematically to a child's level through brainwashing. Her father, Robert Fanshier, told a reporter:

> We are positive she has been brainwashed. She was a very happy person with many friends, an education and career ahead of her and now she's given up all those things to follow the church. She has gotten into such a stage that she's threatened three times to take her own life.
>
> We think the brainwashing is very similar to what happened to our prisoners of war in Korea. It's a system of mind control the Orientals know very well, but we know very little about.[2]

Pam portrayed her initial attraction to the Unification Church largely as an intellectual interest in its doctrines:

> The questions the church was dealing with hadn't been in my Christian background. Questions about my purpose, my origin and God's character, things that I'd been asking for a long time, things I'd given up thinking about.

Her mother claimed that such statements only reinforced *her* own belief that Pam had been brainwashed. Mrs. Fanshier commented:

> You just don't believe in God all of a sudden, that's ridiculous. That's something that takes a long time to find and she nevered bothered to go to church and find the answers.

Regarding the statement that one cannot find or believe in God "all of a sudden" (millions of born-again Christians can testify differently), Mrs. Fanshier's skepticism, the suspicions of her husband, and Pam's own claims illustrate the pathos in this conflict. Out of a genuine concern for their maturing or mature children, parents are driven to commit desperate and sometimes violent acts that some courts have declared to be illegal. If abducted adult children are not successfully brought around to their parents' point of view, they experience an acute sense of betrayal, which divides the two generations even further. Sons and daughters may ultimately find themselves suing their own parents for kidnapping and violation of civil liberties, or, as in the case of the Fanshier family, the two parties may sit on opposite sides of a courtroom while the parents seek to have their own daughter labeled mentally ill.

TWO VIEWS OF DEPROGRAMMING

In this chapter we want to show clearly and objectively what is happening in such deprogrammings. Many persons have heard the term deprogramming, yet few have any idea what actually occurs during one. The conflict of interests laid bare in the confrontation atmosphere of a deprogramming is usually soon buried in emotional rhetoric by both anticultists and the defenders of new religions. For example, Ted Patrick in his book *Let Our Children Go!*, claims with magnanimous altruism that his techniques (and intentions) are benevolent: to restore the ability of ex-cult members to think independently and make autonomous decisions. Patrick wrote:

> All I want and all I do is to return them their ability to think for themselves, to exercise their free will, which the cults

have put into cold storage. I thaw them out, and once they're free of the cult, with very few exceptions they begin again to lead productive lives.[3]

In his 1979 *Playboy* magazine interview he described a successful deprogramming in rather exaggerated imagery:

The only way I can describe it is that it's like turning on the light in a dark room or bringing a person back from the dead. It's a beautiful thing, the whole personality changes, it's like seeing a person change from a werewolf into a man.[4]

Alumni of successful deprogrammings are often eager to thank profusely their "liberators" for abducting and deconverting them. Typical of such declarations of gratitude is that of ex-Hare Krishna member Herb Tucker, who announced to the press after his deprogramming: "It's great to be back among the living."[5]

Yet at the same time defenders of civil liberties (for whom the new religions are only one recent issue) and sympathizers with these groups lambaste deprogramming as pseudotherapy for an imaginary problem. They claim it is, ironically, a form of the very brainwashing process that anticult critics purport cult indoctrination to be. Sociologist Thomas Robbins has argued:

Inferring that a person who is not hysterical, violent, drugged, or under physical restraint and who talks coherently albeit dogmatically is a kind of zombie is questionable.[6]

Dean M. Kelley, a civil libertarian employed by the National Council of Churches of Christ in the United States to watchdog infringements of church-state separation, lashed out in stronger language, condemning deprogramming as "spiritual gang-rape":

It should be prosecuted, not just as any other kidnapping, undertaken for mercenary motives would be, but even more vigorously, since it strikes at the most precious and vulnerable portion of the victim's life, religious convictions and commitments.[7]

As we have seen in examining other dimensions of the controversy, the ways in which language has been used by partisans on both sides have often obscured and confused the issues. In order to sort out self-serving rhetoric from precisely what does happen during a deprogramming we first need to examine the term deprogramming itself. Then we shall be in a better position to probe for the basic interests in conflict and clarify the issues associated with deprogramming.

WHAT IS DEPROGRAMMING?

Both anticultists and defenders of the new religions have made sloppy use of the term deprogramming. In reality the word has come to stand for a number of practices and situations. As a result, critics and proponents of deprogramming often talk past each other, doing little to help uninvolved observers understand the real bases of conflict.

Anticultists actually refer to a range of techniques for removing young adults from new religions when they speak of deprogramming. The best-known type assumes that cult members have been brainwashed, that they are incapable of independent critical reasoning, and that they therefore must be physically removed (abducted) from the group, an action that is not "really" against their will as they presumably have no free will anymore. Since they have been programmed to resist attempts to get them to leave, abductions often occur under dramatic, secretive conditions. Parents, friends, and hired deprogrammers stake out the group in question to locate the member and learn his or her schedule. The abduction has to be done swiftly. Frequently there is scuffling, pushing, and shoving, the young member screaming for help or being gagged to stifle protests, and sometimes greater violence, which has occurred when deprogrammers fight off other members of the religion who are trying to help their friend. This is callled *coercive deprogramming* and is what such champions of civil liberties as Robbins and Kelley (as well as the new religions themselves) mean when they criticize deprogramming.

Yet anticultists also use the term deprogramming to refer to arguing, debating, and simply talking persons out of various movements without coercion. For example, parents in telephone conversations make their child feel guilty over the grief and turmoil he or she has caused the family, or a minister talks with a young person, causing doubts and second thoughts about a lifelong commitment to a world-reforming crusade or radically monastic lifestyle. The assumption behind this type of deprogramming is that the young person still has some free will and an ability to reason independently. Otherwise, arguing points of theology or truth claims of the new religion in question would make little sense.

Rabbi Maurice Davis, an outspoken critic of the Unification Church and the Hare Krishna in particular and founder of the early anticult group Citizens Engaged in Reuniting Families, coined the term reevaluation for this technique. Unlike deprogramming, it involves no coercion and violates no one's First Amendment rights. But many anticultists refer to reevaluation as deprogramming, which causes many civil liberties advocates to unfairly lump together persons who abhor coercive tactics with the more radical Ted Patricks of the anticult movement. And many anticultists, perhaps out of a wish to preserve the appearance of unity in an otherwise loosely organized, poorly coordinated movement, have vaguely endorsed deprogramming (with their own private interpretations kept to themselves). In the end, however, not all anticultists mean the same thing by the term.

Promoters of coercive deprogrammings have insisted that no individual can voluntarily walk away from a cultic religious group and that such an individual cannot possibly make independent decisions. They claim that in reevaluation there was never true indoctrination into the group. Simply talking someone into leaving a group without coercively removing him or her casts serious doubts on claims of unilateral brainwashing and zombielike obedience. Deprogramming's defenders must support the brainwashing explanation in order to justify forcible removal of the young person from a new religion, an act that is otherwise repugnant to most Americans. This defense can lead to ludicrous situations, such as the time in 1979 when Ted Patrick was hired by a mother in Oregon to deprogram her 31-year-old daughter who, the mother maintained, was under psychological influence of her fiancée (*no* religious groups or beliefs were involved—the mother simply disapproved of the boyfriend). Another time, in 1978, Patrick was hired by the Greek Orthodox parents of two young women, ages 21 and 23, because the parents were upset that their daughters had resisted the traditional Greek custom of living at home until the parents found them "suitable" husbands. (Patrick confronted the abducted women and told them that their eyes revealed great hate for their parents, like the eyes of the Satan worshippers whom he had previously deprogrammed.)[8] Deprogramming defenses can result in absurd and illogical claims, such as the one that Ford Greene, a deprogrammer who walked away from the Unification Church, had really *deprogrammed himself* through sheer heroic effort.[9]

The defenders of coercive deprogramming have confused the issue because after the abduction is completed and the "deprogrammee" is locked away in a motel room, attic, cellar, or bedroom, the deprogrammers themselves try to talk the cult member out of his or her newfound religious commitment. In other words, they assume a good deal of reasoning ability on the part of the deprogrammees. As Ted Patrick explained his method:

> When I deprogram people, all I do is shoot them challenging questions. I hit them with things they haven't been programmed to respond to. I know what the cults have told them, so I shoot them the right questions and they get frustrated when they can't answer . . . it's just talk. You push the mind through questions until you break through.[10]

Thus, the deprogrammer's fundamental technique of "releasing" the deprogrammee's "mind" is essentially the same as in reevaluation: persuasive argument, laced with emotional appeals. True, coercive deprogramming involves kidnapping, forcible restraint, and the threat of violence (if not actual violence). All this indisputably gives the deprogrammer a psychological advantage over frightened, browbeaten, tired young adults, but ultimately even those who claim that cult members are brainwashed must communicate with them in terms of reason, logic, and ideas. *These are the very things that cult members are supposed to be unable to deal with!* All the rhetoric of "unlocking" minds, "releasing" or "liberating" individual autonomy and self-determination, or forcing reluctant deprogrammees to use their minds again like stiffened, out-of-shape muscles suddenly put to work is merely poetic metaphors that obscure what is really happening. Both reevaluation and coercive deprogramming assume their targets are reasonably intelligent, alert, and able to understand arguments. Thus the very logic of deprogramming and why it should work is hopelessly inconsistent, contradictory, and illogical. The large number of unsuccessful deprogrammings says more about the ineptness of the deprogrammers, who already have the upper hand in being able to force the deprogrammees to listen to their arguments, than it does about the thoroughness of the cults' indoctrination procedures.

But if deprogrammers rely on the very reasoning capabilities of cult members, which they claim in the same breath cannot exist, and if there really is no mysterious process that wipes out the ability to reason, then why *do* some deprogrammed persons make public statements in which *they* claim they were brainwashed? What occurs during a deprogramming that can produce a person who eagerly agrees with the deprogrammer that he or she has been the victim of a fictitious mind control? Critics of deprogramming have suggested that the deprivations, threats, and (from a resisting deprogrammee's perspective) terror of a coercive deprogramming can provide precisely the conditions that resemble what American prisoners of war experienced: fear, prolonged incarceration, continued punishment for voicing ideas and beliefs unacceptable to captors, but also rewards for "collaborating," all mixed with emotional appeals to surrender resistance. What psychoanalyst Sigmund Freud called a "reaction-formation" can occur, i.e., in a desperate psychological attempt to escape the nightmare the captive suddenly flip-flops and identifies with the captor. This is what may have happened to millionairess Patty Hearst: her brutal experiences locked in a closet for days at a time by the Symbionese Liberation Army terrorists could have caused her to join them as a zealous member.

We reject this counterbrainwashing argument for deconversion just as we rejected the brainwashing explanation for conversion. Deprogramming does not warp thought any more than new religions' indoctrination practices do. The remainder of this chapter will show the subtle process of attitude change — call it thought reform — that does occur during a coercive deprogramming, how it relates to the basic conflicts of interests discussed in chapter three, and why some ex-cult members seem so willing to claim they have been victims of brainwashing.

DEPROGRAMMING: THE SEQUENCE OF EVENTS

One curious fact about the deprogramming controversy is that virtually everyone — anticultists and new religions' defenders alike — agree on much of what occurs during a coercive deprogramming. Where they differ is in the interpretation of the motives and actions of those persons involved. A successful coercive deprogramming runs something like this:

After parents have become exasperated from pleading with their adult son or daughter to leave an unconventional religious group that they (the parents) believe is detrimental or even dangerous to their offspring, and after other attempts to bargain or even threaten have met with no success, they consider coercive deprogramming. Why they choose this option rather than becoming resigned to their offspring's activity may be the result of knowing someone else who held a successful deprogramming or reading about a deprogrammer and then contacting him or her. In the past, some anticult groups have operated as referral services for parents seeking deprogrammers. In some cases, ex-members of new religions volunteer their services out of still smoldering anger toward the group or from a desire to help others leave. In cases where a professional deprogrammer is hired, the deprogramming's cost is steep. For example, the now defunct Freedom of Thought Foundation ranch in Tucson, Arizona, used to offer a package deal including extra guards to help with the abduction and later prevent escape during "therapy," writs of temporary conservatorship to lend the whole business what lawyers call " the color of the law" (making it appear legal), plane tickets or cars, and several weeks' room and board at the ranch, all for as much as $25,000.[11]

After locating their offspring, parents arrive unexpectedly and suggest a brief get-together for dinner at a local restaurant, or almost anywhere, to lure their child away from other group members and more easily make an abduction. Early deprogrammers locked deprogrammees in their parents' home or rented rooms in a local hotel for a week or more. Later, as religious groups began to exercise legal protection and organize their own "posses," and as deprogrammers teamed up with lawyers to obtain writs of temporary conservatorship in advance, deprogrammees were transported further distances and sometimes taken on evasive routes to unlikely or remote places.

The procedure of the actual coercive deprogramming itself has been described so often by its recipients (successfully as well as unsuccessfully processed), its practitioners, and its critics that only a general outline needs to be summarized here. The time period for a deprogramming lasts anywhere from several hours to many weeks. The role that actual violence or the threat of violence plays is always a matter of debate. Some unsuccessfully deprogrammed persons have spoken of being struck and of continually feeling in physical danger even when not directly threatened. Walter Robert Taylor, a priest in the conservative Old Catholic Church who was abducted by his family, reported that in addition to threats of bodily harm four persons held him down while his monastic clothes were ripped off.[12] Moonies we interviewed told of frequent shoving and rough treatment. Verbal abuse seems to be common. During one deprogramming, according to a court document in the lawsuit of Unification Church member Wendy Helander against Ted Patrick, Patrick shouted at her that she was a prostitute and "labeled her a vegetable, a dog, a bitch, and maintained that she was out of her mind."[13] Pam Fanshier's description of her deprogramming is similar. Ted Patrick himself has freely admitted that he threatens to strike deprogrammees, and his book, *Let Our Children Go!*, is full of dramatic, violent episodes. But he also has denied that he would ever really hit a client. One could expect that persons who have suffered indignities of abduction and ridicule for their faiths would be prone to paint the worst possible picture of coercive deprogramming, and the episodes in Patrick's book might be brushed aside as incidents embellished to make interesting reading. But the element of violence, planned or spontaneous, cannot be dismissed entirely. A national anticult leader and father of a successfully deprogrammed college graduate bluntly told us about violence in deprogramming:

Leader: It's [deprogramming] a bad thing to go through, because when it's your own child it nearly kills you. You think they're going to ruin your child. They [the child] may commit suicide or you don't know what. It's a horrible thing.

Interviewer: Are the parents usually there at the deprogramming?

Leader.   They ought to be. If they're not, it gets out of hand...it becomes physical. You're encouraged to be there. I always urge people, if they're going to have a deprogramming, to be there. In the beginning they did it physically. They'd pick up a guy and throw him down if he wouldn't talk. They'd say, "You answer! You talk, damn you! You say something!" It was like a gang. They might slap him. It was the only way they knew...but it was very successful. That's all changed, but you still have too much physical abuse. Particularly when you have somebody who doesn't know or understand what they're doing, somebody who has just come out full of hate for the cult and knowing they have to save the kid by making him forcefully listen. You have to force somebody to listen.[14]

The anticult leader's statement that "you have to force somebody to listen" is crucial, for it reinforces that idea that coercive deprogramming, like reevaluation, depends on argument, on the give-and-take exchange of deprogrammer and deprogrammee. What deprogrammers like Ted Patrick really mean when they say they can tell when they're "breaking through" the "walls" around a cult member's mind is that they're getting the person to argue, to fight back. Nothing can stifle the process as much as a deprogrammee who won't talk and refuses to play the game. The deprogrammee must be drawn into a discussion where new or unknown discrediting evidence about the new religion in question can be presented, where seeming inconsistencies between what the group professes and what it does can be confronted, and where the shock/grief/turmoil/concern/desperation that the young member has caused his or her family cannot be denied or easily ignored.

Often the developing of such a dialogue takes time. Since the mid-1970s most groups of any size, such as the Unification Church, The Way International, and the Hare Krishnas, have made absolute demons out of deprogrammers (and families who hire them). Successful resistance to deprogrammers has thus become a test of courage and faith for new religions' members. Those members who resist and return are heroes, so many have a lot of motivation to resist deprogrammings or to fake their deconversions until their captors have relaxed. Then they escape. Reports that groups have drilled their members in emergency antideprogramming resistance measures seem exaggerated or totally fabricated. Shortly after the Jonestown massacre, *New West* magazine published an article in which several ex-Moonies claimed that they and many others had been given systematic suicide instructions by the Unification Church's Oakland Family leaders should members be abducted for coercive deprogrammings. Some anticult spokespersons and authors immediately jumped on the post-Jonestown bandwagon and claimed that a multicult suicide was imminent. Much of this talk was and is sensationalistic exploitation of a freak event. In our extensive examination of both the Unification Church

(Oakland Family and larger national organization), as well as the national anticult movement, we have never found evidence of such training nor of ex-members reporting it. No former Moonie, no matter how hostile and bitter and eager to attack the Church, ever spoke a word about suicide training until after Jonestown. Nor is there evidence from Moonie deprogrammings that any member committed suicide—something that would have happened by now if such training were standard indoctrination. We do know of cases where Moonies have been held captive for a long time and out of desperation cut or injured themselves badly enough to be taken outside the home for medical care where they could call for help, but such cases are rare and cannot be classified (except by persons obsessed with future Jonestowns) as suicide attempts.[15]

DEPROGRAMMING:
THE CONFLICT OF FAMILY INTERESTS

Chapter three outlined the major sources of conflict and strain between the new religions and American society. Foremost is the conflict between a family's expectations for its adult children and the needs of many new religions for total dedication of members. "What a waste!" is the most frequently heard comment of distraught parents. Even more galling to them is the fact that the family's lifestyle is rejected, if not harshly condemned by their own flesh and blood. Authority to manage their lives is sometimes given over by these offspring to gurus and self-proclaimed prophets. As a result, members of such unconventional groups can become alienated from their families, and communications between the two generations shrink severely, if not cease altogether. This is a basic conflict between generations of parental hopes and plans versus youth self-determination. It is this conflict that the deprogramming is meant to resolve.

Why does deprogramming sometimes work? How do Bible readings, tearful pleadings, argument, and threats produce in many new religions' members what seem to be sincere changes of heart and faith? With the above conflict of interests in mind, let's examine the dynamics of the coercive-type deprogramming situation. As in most conflicts of interest, the two parties each believe that they have right on their side and that their own motives are noble, unselfish. Yet beyond that things are not quite so simple. Deprogrammers, for obvious reasons, have a vested interest in claiming that they are dealing with standard situations of mind control and therefore that they follow a routine therapeutic procedure. However, there is much more going on beneath the surface in a deprogramming that can help explain why it does or does not work.

For example, from the new religions' members' standpoint there can be a wide variety of levels of commitment to the new religious faith. As we noted in chapter four, our research found that some Moonies are indeed highly committed to the Unification Church's doctrines, but others may be members mainly because they find tightly controlled, communal lifestyles pleasurable. Some believe every detail of the *Divine Principle* in a highly dogmatic, literal way while others are much more intellectual and abstract in their perspective and do not care about minor doctrinal details. More important, contrary to the zombie image promoted by deprogrammers, many members of new religions *do* have doubts about certain aspects of their faiths and mixed feelings about their group's lifestyles. They do not like talking about these feelings and thoughts with strangers or nonmembers, however. Perhaps they are not excited about their current assigned responsibilities, their future mates (or about the fact that they may be encouraged to remain celibate), or their prospects for advancement up through the structures of their respective movements. In addition, new religions, like any other human organization, cannot escape the development of factions, office politics, and differences of opinion. Anthropologist Francine Daner recounts a clash among Hare Krishna leaders that almost resulted in the fragmentation of the American organization and caused four *sannyasis* (preachers) to be expelled and many members to quit altogether.[16] There are, as well, records of angry confrontations, executive purges, dismissals, resignations, and hostility in the Unification Church, the Church of Scientology, and the Children of God.

The sophistication or naiveté of members about the damaging media reports of their particular groups as well as about such groups' internal politics differs from individual to individual. In sum, members bring to deprogrammings different degrees of commitment, knowledge of their movements, uncertainty, and individual maturity; varying amounts of personal investment of time and energy in the movements; and the tremendous ambivalence that comes from being torn between the obvious emotional uproar they have caused at home and their tentative, youthful idealism. Finally, previous closeness to parents and family may play a greater part in what follows than anything else.

From the family's—particularly the parents'—standpoint, a youth's cult involvement can mean different things. For example, consider a reevaluation versus a coercive deprogramming. In a reevaluation many parents may become only mildly concerned when their son or daughter joins a group and may not try very hard to remove him or her after a reevaluation does not work. They may express confusion, disappointment, and chagrin, even anger—but they stop at that, hoping their offspring is just going through the same phase that other young adults work out differently. Some parents acknowledge their son or daughter as a Moonie, premie, Krishna and resign themselves to it. This does not mean that they do not resent the reality (indeed, it often strains marriages and other relationships), only that they do not take extreme steps to change it. Such parents are least likely to organize coercive deprogrammings, although through the prodding of other relatives or friends they might reluctantly become involved in one.

For those parents whose expectations for their children are most profoundly shattered, however, the offspring's new religious membership carries with it an embarrassing, grating stigma, or shame, that is scarcely bearable but which can be mercifully erased by claiming that their children are brainwashed. In our overpsychologized twentieth-century American society, many persons casually assume that anyone who acts in a culturally different way must be therefore psychologically different as well. This is not a pleasant thought for parents of young adults, many of whom have given their children numerous material advantages and educated them at prestigious colleges and universities. Going off on a wild, idealistic crusade reflects both on those young persons and on their parents. It leads to an unflattering implication: either the children are defective in some way that many others who never join cults are not, or the parents made some grave errors in raising their children. Not wanting to blame themselves or their offspring, families look elsewhere.

It is this train of thought that leads to defensive reasoning something like the following:

> ... my (son, daughter, family member) has embraced a "strange" religion; (2) only inherently "strange" people would be voluntarily attracted to such a religion; (3) my (son, daughter, family member) is obviously not an inherently "strange" person; (4) hence he or she must have been hoodwinked or brainwashed into participating.[17]

Sociologist Hans Toch has called this sort of conclusion "the seduction premise," i.e., such a group (or cult), because of its obvious unsavory aspects, could not attract otherwise reasonable people if they were not "seduced" by some deceptive or beguiling method.[18] This reasoning absolves parents of any blame for their offsprings' erratic, culturally "strange" behavior and keeps the children from being marked as "weird," "overly suggestible," "gullible," or, worse, mentally ill. Thus children do not need a psychiatrist, which would place a stigma on them for their entire lives, but rather a deprogrammer. The explanation also provides young people with a means of being welcomed back into the family fold and "normal society." Both they and their parents have scapegoats to blame for idealistic, youthful mistakes, and general cultural prejudice against minority or unpopular religions will support them.

The mythology that cults possess mysterious, irresistible powers to lure vast numbers of young adults into their ranks is an anticultist myth. To admit otherwise—that new religions really have no such powers or that the actual number of young Americans involved in such groups is grossly exaggerated, is extremely threatening to both ex-members and their families. Sociologically, there is a strong argument that those parents most threatened by their offspring's joining "weird" religions are also those most like to take a hard-line brainwashing/mind-control position. How does one identify "most threatened" persons? Social prestige and wealth are obvious signs. Upper-middle-class and middle-class parents are most likely to suffer "relative deprivation," the shock that their children had turned out so differently from what they had hoped and planned.

Consider the following exercise in such identification:

Among the families who arranged a February 1976 public meeting between anticultists and federal officials in Washington, D.C., we noted a disproportionate number of persons who had superior economic and educational resources, political influence, or access to persons with political influence. Among the eighteen known persons who organized this important public meeting, six had the title "Doctor" before their names (an assistant director of guidance services at a New York State community college, a professor of pharmacology at the University of Kentucky, a dean of the school of education at a New York university, a doctor of divinity, and two others for whom we have no additional information); a rabbi; an assistant director/psychiatric social worker of a prestigious children's clinic at Boston University; a retired colonel in the military; an East Coast state commissioner of insurance; several others of considerable financial means; and the mother of former New York Senator James Buckley's godson and goddaughter (one an ex-member of the Unification Church, the other a current member) who is also the wife of a prominent San Francisco attorney. These people, many of them professionals, are the ones who have promoted the brainwashing explanation most vigorously to the media and public officials.

DEPROGRAMMING: THE RESOLUTION OF FAMILY CONFLICTS

Both reevaluation and coercive deprogramming are best understood as power confrontations, yet many times the self-serving rhetoric of deprogrammers and parents tries to present deprogramming as a new form of mental health therapy for a radically new problem rather than as a clash of interests. As in most power confrontations, *negotiation* is the key to resolving the conflict. This can be most clearly seen in a reevaluation, in which young people enter the dialogue voluntarily. As they are presumed to still have their wits about them, they are accorded dignity as rational human beings. Parents feel freer to admit that the new religion may have some good points in its favor, if only in its ideals. They can discuss alternatives for the future and bargain with their offspring without having to resort to dogmatic condemnations, threats, or name calling. Moreover, if a person can be persuaded to make a decision and yet feel he or she made that decision voluntarily, then the commitment to abide by it is strong. (This is the logic behind thought reform, as discussed in chapter four.)

The young cult member has less room to negotiate in coercive deprogramming. Indeed, the official party line of deprogramming paints a picture of the deprogrammee as totally passive: things are done *to* and *for* him or her. He or she did not decide to be abducted or to be restrained or imprisoned, or to be confronted with negative evidence that discredits his or her new religion, or to be exposed to pleading/weeping/haranguing relatives. This sense of being a passive victim that other people do things to may be one reason that many supposedly successfully deprogrammed persons return to their new religions not long after the deprogramming. Deprogrammers explain their return as "floating," that is, their minds are not yet accustomed to having to make decisions for themselves and so they can easily slide back into cult-regimented mind control. In *Let Our Children Go!* Ted Patrick is always careful to point out that when alumni of his deprogrammings do return to their cults, he is not to blame. The fault is always that of someone who forgot to watch the young person closely enough during the critical "floating" period. However, a more realistic psychological explanation is that there are barely any elements of voluntarism in coercive deprogramming, only the prospect of indefinite imprisonment, intimidation, and the continual pressure to submit—hardly a choice at all. At some level even the success-fully deprogrammed person, i.e., one who sincerely recants, probably knows his real lack of options. Once outside the high-pressure deprogramming situation and returned to the same environment where choice exists, the deprogrammee may reconsider the idealistic new religion and decide to go back.

But what makes a coercive deprogramming work? Media reports show that many persons who enter a deprogramming seemingly totally committed to their new religion leave with about-face views. Are they merely changing their attitudes on religion like hats? There are a number of reasons for successful coercive deprogramming. Perhaps the young person has not been a member long and is shocked by the unsavory evidence of newspaper clippings, television films, and ex-members' testi-monies. Perhaps he or she already had doubts about the group's theology, and a little Bible study convinced him that its beliefs are in error. Perhaps he is burned out by a hectic, demanding lifestyle (this occurs, for example, among Moonie fund-raisers who crisscross the country in vans on a seven-day work-week basis) and is subconsciously looking for an excuse to leave the religion in a way that will not involve having to admit making a colossal mistake. Perhaps there is acute guilt and grief over the turmoil the family has been through. Preoccupied in daily activ-ities for the new religion, a member can easily put aside uncomfortable thoughts. In a coercive deprogramming, intense emotions cannot be ignored.

An experienced deprogrammer develops an intuitive sense of these different motives and learns to manipulate the particular set of dynamics that can affect the offspring the most. Bible quotes may do little to sway a Hare Krishna; however, the sight of his weeping father confessing his inadequacies as a parent, or a younger brother embracing him and saying movingly, "I love you!" may be the hook that has an overwhelming impact. The deprogrammer observes and picks up on such angles of attack, then works with whatever seems best in a given situation. The deprogrammer's ability to manipulate the emotions that arise during this situation (and which he may have generated in the first place) and to seize on which particular strategy to use, i.e., emotional or argumentative, plays a large part in a deprogrammer's success.

This is often a time when latent family problems—from parental religious hypocrisy to marital infidelity to petty jealousies—come out in the open. Buried or ignored previously, these accumulated antagonisms are suddenly laid bare. The offspring may suddenly turn on the offensive, accusing parents and demanding an accounting for *their* past behavior. It is a classic example of "cartharsis": the strains, gripes, and concerns of both sides are aired, perhaps for the first time ever. When the air is cleared, the relief felt by everyone can set up the same conditions for dialogue as a reevaluation does.

Thus, provided that the deprogrammees respond and actively engage in the dialogue the deprogrammers try to provoke, deprogrammings reintegrate and reconcile families. Whether the deprogramming is successful or not in any individual case is not (contrary to deprogrammers' claims) the result of some uniform process of "liberating" the mind so that the deprogrammee can think again. Nor is successful deprogramming, as civil liberties defenders argue, largely the result of the coercion factor. Deprogramming is not brainwashing any more than indoctrination into a new religion is. It is best thought of as a way of resolving conflict. Many different motives and feelings are involved, and they are not the same in every case. At what point in the process a deprogrammee must come to admit consciously or recognize (even if only to himself to herself) doubts and grievances about the new religion, or at what point he or she begins to recognize the rewards of "playing the game" by the deprogrammer's rules *and chooses to play the game* is difficult to pinpoint exactly.

Participation in a new religion is like an economic equation: as long as the rewards outweigh the costs to an individual, he or she stays, and when the costs outweigh the rewards the individual leaves. It is fundamentally a rational decision. Coercive deprogrammings often successfully alter the equation. The promise of better family relations, perhaps based on sharing this traumatic experience, may suddenly outweigh commitments to the new religion. Suddenly, after all the arguing, tears, ambivalence, and emotional drain, the deprogrammee decides that the new religious faith is not worth what it costs. Many deprogrammers liken it to suddenly turning on the light in a darkened room. The mind, they say, is suddenly "free" to think again. This analogy is prosaic and misleading. The mind always was free. It simply makes another decision, one that is now more palatable to the family.

VINDICATION FOR DEPROGRAMMING: THE APOSTATES

Reevaluation does not produce angry ex-members of new religions who are suddenly eager to tell all about the groups. There are some ex-members who walk away from their commitment and write damaging exposés of what they saw and did, but they are rare. Most ex-members made the decision to leave as simply as they made the decision to join.

But for coercively deprogrammed ex-members leaving is not that simple. As we have seen, parents are under strong (if understandable) pressure not to blame either themselves or their children for cult involvement. Once a young person becomes convinced that the new religion is not nearly as lofty, appealing, or benevolent as once thought, he or she too comes under the same pressure: not to blame oneself for misplaced idealism or naivete.

Deprogramming is an option that provides a stigma-free way out of the dilemma: "Yes, my son (or daughter) did become involved in a 'strange' group, but it was not his (her) fault." "Yes, I really did call my parents Satanic and reject them, but I did not know what I was doing—my mind was not my own." Deprogramming provides parents with the potential to remove their children from unconventional groups quickly, but they can only justify such actions on the grounds that the young persons do not know what they are doing. *After* the reconciliation of the family, therefore, pressure on a young person to reinforce the parents for what they did is strong. Once out of the new religion, the ex-member cannot simply admit he or she has made a mistake, then have all forgotten and forgiven. That scenario would not only violate the logic of the brainwashing-deprogramming explanation, it would also ignore several facts:

> that parents had been humiliated and insulted by the offspring's rejection of their lifestyle, values, and past sacrifices
>
> that they had gone to the trouble, potential legal risk, and often considerable expense to stage the deprogramming
>
> that no excuse that the young person had been deprogrammed for his or her own good (thus that violation of the individual's religious freedom was justified) is nearly as convincing to others uninvolved as the ex-member's own testimony.

Thus, some ex-members, or what scholars call "apostates," tell their tales of atrocities that include lurid themes of exploitation, manipulation, and deception.[19] They and their stories, which may be true, false, or embellished, serve several important uses. Aside from justifying the family's desperate and coercive actions and avoiding any public stigma attached to both family and individual, such stories become evidence that other opponents of new religions can point to in seeking laws, police action, and other remedies against the groups. Apostates' claims of what they saw and did have a first-person quality that makes them hard to refute. Since the family and the ex-member appear to be perfectly normal and average in every other respect, their stories deliver a profound impact on listeners and readers. These anecdotes tend to outrage audiences, frighten families of members currently in new religions, and make public officials more willing to consider controlling the so-called cults. For most Americans who know relatively little about new religions, apostates' stories may be their only source of information.

Consider the following excerpts from newspaper articles collected over the past five years (and recall others that we presented earlier in chapter four):

> We were told that if we worked against the movement our grandchildren would dig up our bones and spit on them.

> I was always compelled to sleep on the floor, including the winter. There were no adequate sanitation supplies. For instance, one or two toilets would periodically back up for as many as 100 to 200 males.
>
> I had lost 20 pounds, had pneumonic cough, and was staring into space with a big smile.
>
> We were kept busy 19 to 20 hours a day and restricted to two low-protein diet meals daily.
>
> I would have killed for him. I would have done anything Moon said.
>
> Had I been asked to kill my parents I would not have hesitated.
>
> I pulled in $700 to $800 a week, selling flowers. You go to businesses, commercial places, industrial places. You sneak in. I was pretty good at it . . . I could get money from anyone now. I know how. I got the last penny from a bum on the street.
>
> We went door to door in the poorest section, telling the people we represented an organization called the World Crusade and were selling flowers to raise money to help rehabilitate people who were in trouble. The girl told me, "Any line you can use is a good line."

Anyone who has followed the media's coverage of the cult controversy during the past decade is familiar with such stories. Some apostates have appeared briefly in the public eye to tell their stories, enjoyed a measure of short-lived publicity, and then faded away. A few have sought profit by writing books based on their adventures and/or by going on lecture circuits. (One, Chris Elkins, who appears on Texas campuses annually to speak to evangelical groups, had a movie entitled *Deceived* made from his book.)

A well-known example of this recent apostate phenomenon is ex-Moonie Christopher Edwards, who wrote an autobiographical book of his experiences, *Crazy For God*.[20] Aside from demonstrating a remarkable memory for details and events that allegedly occurred while his brain was being washed, Edwards' account of his indoctrination at the hands of the Unification

Church's Oakland Family is a modern illustration of a literary genre as old as the anti-Mormon and anti-Catholic movements of the early nineteenth century. Edwards portrays himself as a young, idealistic innocent who was reduced by malevolent leaders to a degenerative, zombielike state. He was exploited callously, the reader is told, for their own selfish and fanatical purposes until he was dramatically saved from such an unhappy predicament by his family and hired deprogrammers. With a literary style and deliberate melodramatic construction reminiscent of the script for a made-for-TV movie, *Crazy For God* makes one feel as if the ghost of Maria Monk, that self-proclaimed ex-nun from a nineteenth-century Montreal convent, had reappeared to promote another potboiler tract, this time substituting the Unification Church for the "Papist" Roman Catholics.

In sum, apostates and the horrific stories they tell are necessary, to provide fuel to attack unpopular movements, but, more important, to absolve families (and themselves) of any responsibility for their actions. This can be clearly seen in recent research by British sociologist James Beckford,[21] who went to great efforts to track down examples of that rarely seen but plentiful species: the silent majority of former new religions' members who were not deprogrammed but walked out on the group after deciding it was not for them. Beckford interviewed ex-Moonies and their families in Britain and discovered a telling source of strain remaining in the family even though the son or daughter had returned and resumed a "normal" life. Beckford noted that ex-Moonies continued to be ambivalent about their past participation in the Unification Church. While overall the experience had not worked for them, they still recalled good times and positive aspects. They were also embarrassed, knowing how others regarded the Church, and therefore deliberately avoided publicity concerning their past membership. It was their parents who badgered them to offer outsiders details of their experiences that could be interpreted as manipulative and deceptive. The parents wished to interpret their offspring's participation as the result of brainwashing, but the ex-members knew better. They had voluntarily walked away from the Unification Church.

Psychologist Trudy Solomon's recent study of 100 ex-Moonies, some of whom had been deprogrammed and some of whom had exited voluntarily, also came to the same conclusion. Those who voluntarily left the Unification Church became *less* involved with the anticult movement, as did their parents, and felt *less* pressure to view their past involvement as a totally negative experience. The deprogrammed Moonies, on the other hand, were encouraged to become active anticultists. As one respondent said:

> I felt a compulsion from deprogrammers, family and friends to categorize the Moon experience as bad, negative, what have you, even if unconsciously. I resented this and it made it more difficult to find a balance in my post-Moon thinking.[22]

EVALUATING DEPROGRAMMING

Deprogramming has its passionate defenders, many of whom probably stopped reading this book long before now. Neither can *Strange Gods* please civil libertarians, since the coercion element in deprogramming has been just as overplayed as the manipulation of some new religions' indoctrination procedures. For those less involved, what can be finally said of deprogramming and the issues it raises? Here are some conclusions:

1. *Deprogramming, contrary to the claims of its advocates, is definitely not a new method of mental health therapy.* In fact, a good case can be made that the trauma and psychic conflict it induces can conceivably *cause* mental illness if not exacerbate such problems. Moreover, from a public health perspective it is dangerous to think of deprogramming as anything resembling the psychiatric/clinical psychological professions since deprogrammings' practitioners are, by professional standards, almost always totally untrained in any healing science or profession. For example, Ted Patrick is a high school dropout who served a brief stint as *ad hoc* state social worker in California. Joe Alex-

ander, Sr., his one-time apprentice, is a former used-car sales-man. Another prominent deprogrammer is a private detective, and still another a lawyer. Some claim as credentials the fact that they were once in a cult themselves and were later de-programmed. If this constitutes a legitimate background for tinkering with people's personalities, what does it say about psychiatry and psychology? Does having surgery qualify one to be a surgeon? It is idiotic to think so, yet deprogrammers frequently base their qualifications on similar logic. True, there are many critics of psychiatry and psychology (we are among them), but these professions have codes of ethics and profes-sional standards, including formal education, that at least provide for some systematic supervision of training and prac-tice. Modern deprogrammers remind us of renegade doctors and midwives running backroom abortion clinics before such oper-ations became legal and under state sanction. Caveat emptor: Let the buyer beware.

2. *Deprogramming does not work the way its advocates claim it does.* If it did, we would have to assume first of all a brainwashing process. Chapter four showed that there are no overwhelming mind-numbing powers at the disposal of new religions. What really occurs is family reconciliation, a situa-tion where the conflict of interests is resolved in favor of the parents. Reevaluations, in which cultists decide to stick it out with their new religious commitments, all arguments con-sidered, are no doubt considered failures by parents but are nevertheless resolutions of the conflict. The important feature of such family conflicts is that they can be resolved in a number of ways. Coercive deprogrammings are simply attempts to resolve conflicts of interest in which parents have the upper hand.

3. *The similarities in horror stories told by apostates, or ex-members, of new religions are not the result of their all having experienced the same brainwashing processes; rather, their stories are so similar because the family dynamics—that is, the need of both families and individuals to deflect responsibility for joining a strange religious group away from themselves—are the same for most persons.* Many anticultists claim that brain-

washing and mind control must be real processes because so many deprogrammed ex-members repeat the same accusations and stories. This is specious logic, however. We argue that the family situation puts pressures on ex-members to reinterpret their cult experiences in the same self-serving way, and that after deprogramming became a more widespread practice a folklore of deprogramming developed. Deprogrammers themselves implanted interpretations in the midst of new religions' members. Deprogrammers are like the American colonials who persecuted "witches": a confession, drawn up before the suspect was brought in for torturing and based on the judges' fantasies about witchcraft, was signed under duress and then treated as justification for the torture. In the end, the similarity of ex-members' stories is not the result of similar experiences but rather of artificial and imposed reinterpretations by persons serving their own needs and purposes.

Deprogrammers are self-serving, illegal, and fundamentally immoral. In some cases, despite their protests to the contrary, they have profited handsomely from this practice.[23] The interpretation of deprogramming and cult membership most dear to the parents of young adults caught up in new religious movements is inaccurate. It would take a strong parent indeed who, in the face of resentment and disappointment over an offspring gone off on an exotic, idealistic crusade, could face the facts we have presented with cold logic. But most deprogrammers are not consciously malevolent, and most parents who decide on coercive deprogramming act from sincere motives. One of the tragic elements in this controversy is that parents who risk legal and financial penalties as well as the possible future alienation from their adult children by a deprogramming do so for decent, sincere reasons. These parents have much to gain if the deprogramming works, but also much to lose if it does not. Most people do not risk reputations and more except for causes they believe in. However misguided the critics of deprogramming paint all such parents and friends, they are not simply mindless, knee-jerk bigots. They are basically motivated by love and concern for their children. Neither side can take much comfort in the fact as long as the controversy rages.

8

A Hard Look at the Cult Controversy

Of the three institutions most directly affected by the rise of the new religions—family, church, and government—it is the family that has been the backbone of the anticult crusade. Various government agencies have come into conflict with one or another of the new religions, but there has not been any particular pattern to these disputes. Governmental officials remain wary, as they sense the potential for greater conflict and as they try to balance the demands of new religions for legal protection with the pleas of distraught parents (who are also constituents) for assistance in recovering their children. Churches, particularly the Christian fundamentalists, have regularly attacked all the new religions. They have used the pulpit, Sunday schools, books, and religious tracts to condemn the "heretical" teachings. Churches also have offered moral support to families with young members in new religions, although they have stopped short of approving deprogramming because of the dangerous precedent this would set. The primary goal of the churches has been to warn the faithful of the dangers of cults by condemning the heresy of the new religions and asserting the ultimate truth of orthodox Christianity. Both government and churches, then, have defended their interests, but neither has sensed such a clear and present danger that it has felt compelled to lead the anticult campaign.

It is the family members of converts to the new religions who feel that their interests have been so flagrantly violated that they are willing to band together in groups and fight the cult menace. To parents who feel that their children's love and loyalty have been stolen from them there is sufficient motive to lead the anticult crusade. It is these parent groups who have appealed to the churches for support, petitioned the government for action, and flooded the media with stories of brainwashing and enslavement.

Throughout this book we have attacked what we regard as the myths created and sustained by the leaders of the anticult crusade. We have been more critical of the anticultists than the new religions. Most Americans seem unlikely to be duped by the new religions, particularly after the avalanche of publicity that anticult allegations have received. It seems improbable that many Americans will accept Sun Myung Moon as the new messiah or "Moses" David Berg as a great prophet of the Millennium or Guru Maharaj Ji as the Perfect Master. Nor will many Americans give up their worldly pursuits to chant "Hare Krishna" or retreat to the shores of Europe with the Children of God to await America's ultimate destruction. The charms and appeals of exotic new religions are just not attractive to the vast majority of individuals who encounter them. By contrast, the anticultists have been quite successful in gaining public sympathy and support. Their success has led us to examine their allegations carefully and to be critical of them for three reasons. First, the anticultists have dominated the agenda in terms of which we have discussed and evaluated the new religions. There has been so much allegation and controversy over brainwashing and deprogramming that the question of what, if any, positive or redeeming qualities the new religions may have has been largely ignored. Second, the bulk of available evidence (and it is now considerable) simply does not support the charges made by the anticultists. For example, those professionals who have been the loudest in denouncing alleged mind control and brainwashing practices of new religions are unquestionably in the minority. The groups they unsystematically refer to as cults do not constitute the threat to America they would have us believe. Finally, the implications of granting the anticultists the sanctions against the new religions they seek pose a significant threat to the interests of most Americans in the long run. In closing, let us consider these three points in turn.

EVALUATING THE NEW RELIGIONS

In the preceding chapters we have challenged most of the extreme charges made by the anticultists. At the same time it is also clear that neither the motives nor the actions of the new religions are as pristine as they would like to convey. The question remains, therefore, do they have any positive qualities that make them worth defending? Let us take a step back from the controversy surrounding the new religions and look at their impact on established churches and young adults.

In responding to new religious movements, it is easy to be struck by their instability and disorganization, particularly when they are contrasted with the stable and apparently ageless mainline denominations. Yet a longer historical perspective reveals how dynamic religious belief and organization really are. To the leaders of the Roman Empire, Christianity was a dangerous, subversive movement. Centuries later the Catholic Church regarded Protestantism as organized heresy. The history of Protestantism has been one of denominational rivalry and schism. Such change and conflict have been a persistent feature of religious belief and organization because religion is one of the most important ways in which human beings provide meaning for their activities and relationships. It follows that people will constantly adjust religious beliefs and practices as the social conditions in which they find themselves change. From this perspective the new religions reflect attempts on the part of their founders and members to create new sources of meaning that speak to their needs and aspirations. The disorganization, the seeming strangeness of their beliefs, and the extreme zealousness new religions often exhibit probably are not very useful bases for evaluating their worth. Many of the mainline churches manifested precisely these characteristics during their early histories when they too sought new ways of creating spiritual meaning. So if it is true that religion, like other aspects of social life, requires periodic revitalization, then the new religions should be viewed as normal and as an indication of the strength of the religious impulse rather than as a threat to it.

The strident opposition of the established Christian churches to the new religious movements is a misleading indicator of the real threat posed by the latter. Some new religions have challenged orthodox Christian doctrines; however, it is more likely that on balance the new religions have strengthened Christian solidarity. Every time a new religion appears or there is another sectarian split the question arises whether the new group is *really* Christian. On such occasions the established churches pause in their denominational squabbles and reflect upon what it is that they have in common so that the true Christian churches can be distinguished from the pretenders. Ironically, then, it is exactly the kind of challenge posed by the new religions that creates unity among the established churches. Furthermore, such challenges are a source of revitalization for the major denominations. It has become a virtual cliché among church leaders that "cults are the unpaid bills of the churches." The mainline churches have found it embarrassing that new religions have sparked religious fervor and commitment among young adults while their own memberships have been dwindling. Consequently, these churches have been forced to reassess how well they actually are meeting the spiritual needs of their congregations. To the extent that more vital, responsive churches result from such introspection, the new religions will have the effect of strengthening the Christian tradition.

The new religions have played an important, positive role in the lives of many young adults. For example, one group from which several new religions recruited heavily and successfully was the drug subculture. Many dropouts from conventional society who turned to drugs eventually found that the drug subculture did not offer them a viable lifestyle alternative. The new religions provided a bridge back to more conventional lives.

Social scientists who have studied Meher Baba (which appears on most lists of cults), the Church of Scientology, the Unification Church, the Divine Light Mission, and the Hare Krishna have noted that membership facilitated termination of drug use.[1] Converts to these new religions found alternative sources of meaning that made drug use unnecessary. Mainline denominations made few efforts to reach such youth.

For a much larger group of youth the problem was not drugs but a general disenchantment with their own lives and with American society. A great many young adults have felt that their lives lack discipline, commitment, and goals for which they are willing to make personal sacrifice. Some of those who joined new religions found in these groups a way to realize more of their personal potential. Based on his observations of the Unification Church and Scientology, for example, Dean Kelley concluded:

> It is my contention that a vigorous, dynamic religious movement not only can attract and hold some very impressive and gifted people, but that it can and does attract a great many more people who are *not* visibly impressive or gifted and *instill or bring out in them abilities they did not know they had.*[2]
> . . . because new religious movements make higher demands upon their members than your average church or synagogue, and obtain fuller commitment and investment of self in return, they are able to accomplish far more with even less promising material.

Our own interviews with members of the Unification Church led us to much the same conclusion. Those members who committed themselves, their time, and their energy appeared to us to have received commensurate returns—new skills, time and space in which to grow, or greater personal insight. Most converts to new religions ultimately discover that they do not wish to dedicate their entire lives to the cause, and they simply resume their former lives or start anew. This is not wasted effort; however, it is a discovery that allows these individuals to define a personal course for themselves that holds out a greater potential for personal satisfaction and fulfillment. Were it not for the overwhelmingly negative public judgment of the new religions many converts could look back on that period as a high point of personal growth.

Finally, rather than destroying families as the anticultists contend, in many instances new religions help to solve difficult family problems. Many adolescents have difficulty in breaking away from parental control, and many parents have trouble letting their children go. As a result, even young adults enrolled in college may feel that their lives are not really their own. Instead, they feel they are acting out a role that was planned for them long ago by their families and which leaves little room for them to assert their own needs and aspirations. In such cases, both parents and offspring often agree that family life has been loving and supportive; the sons and daughters merely add that they now wish to make their own decisions, right or wrong. In other cases, family relations were severely strained prior to a son's or daughter's joining one of the new religions. The conversion makes the family conflicts public and parents seek to reassert their control to avoid the consequences of that conflict. In either case the offspring may have a real, legitimate need for self-assertion. Joining a new religion sometimes does result in greater distance between family members, but some separation may well be necessary if the relationship is to be rejoined on a mutually rewarding basis.

EVALUATING THE ANTICULT MOVEMENT

The anticultists contend that there are a number of rapidly growing groups, which they refer to as cults. These cults have common characteristics and pose an unprecedented danger to America. As our description of six of the best-known and most controversial new religions demonstrates, however, they have few characteristics in common and most are no longer attracting large numbers of new members. Many have already peaked and are in decline. Had we included descriptions of other groups routinely labeled as cults (such as Transcendental Meditation; Happy, Healthy, Holy; EST; or The Way International) in this book, the diversity of these presumably uniform groups would have been even more evident. Neither is the present controversy unique except to those with a sense of historical myopia. American history is rich with similar conflicts, each one thought by its participants to be unique. Such groups as the Quakers, Catholics, Mormons, Jehovah's Witnesses, Mennonites, and Christian Scientists have at different times been the targets of allegations strikingly similar to those being made against the new religions. Given the conservative nature of most of these churches today it is hard to believe that earlier generations of Americans burned and looted Catholic convents, assassinated Joseph Smith and mobilized the United States Army against the Mormons, and sentenced Quakers to death for their refusal to serve in the armed forces. The fact that Americans have exaggerated the danger posed by new religions in the past does not mean that current warnings should be dismissed out of hand. The lessons of our own history, however, do suggest that we should be cautious and skeptical.

The centerpiece of the anticultists' allegations is that cults brainwash their members through some combination of drugging, hypnosis, self-hypnosis, chanting or lecturing, and deprivation of food, sleep, and freedom of thought. If this argument were true, the new religions would not have such a sorry recruitment record, the defection rate among those who do join would not be as high as it is, individual members could not be counted on to work with the zeal they do, and ex-members would not be able to recall in such exquisite detail how they were brainwashed. Social scientists have largely repudiated the concept of brainwashing as the anticultists have used it. Certainly it is possible to break people down physically and psychologically through coercive techniques. But there is no evidence that people so abused will show the kind of positive motivation and commitment that converts to the new religions manifest.

Although the brainwashing argument is false, there is no doubt that the demands of those new religions that are organized communally can be total and consuming. Such groups require that converts cut off ties with the outside world and their former lives, demand total discipline and commitment, and provide for virtually all members' personal and social needs within the self-contained community. To distraught parents it might seem that only coercive measures could produce the personal sacrifice and the apparent single-mindedness with which converts to the new religions pursue the groups' goals. However, many young Americans are seeking out idealistic groups that demand a high level of discipline and commitment, even if most eventually tire of it and return to their former lives. For parents this distinction may not matter since in either case they lose the capacity to exert any significant influence over their offspring. For the rest of us, however, this distinction is a vital one. Evidence of coercive, destructive brainwashing probably would gain the anticultists many supporters. Yet revelations of intensive socialization tactics like those used by convents, monasteries, military academies, and Marine Corps boot camps arouse much less indignation, despite the similarities.

Once the brainwashing, or programming, explanation for conversion to the new religions falls, so does the justification of deprogramming as a remedy. What is called deprogramming sometimes *does* result in new religious converts' renouncing their memberships. But, as we have shown, there are many possible explanations for these "successes." Some individuals cannot tolerate the stress and anguish their parents are experiencing. Some have relied on the solidarity of the communal group for their strength and are unable to sustain their commitment without support from their peers. Some may have already experienced doubts and conflicts and find parental insistence a convenient way of avoiding having to make the choice themselves. Some probably are intimidated by deprogrammers or parents. The point is that anticultists resist these more varied and complex explanations because it would be much more difficult to justify deprogramming or persecution of the new religions if they were accepted. And some full-time deprogrammers have an actual financial interest in furthering the simplistic deprogramming interpretation. For them it has proved too profitable to do otherwise.

The other issues are much less significant beside the brain-washing and deprogramming controversies. It is true that Moonies and Krishnas have sometimes utilized deception in their fund-raising activities and are generally regarded as public nuisances. Both groups have major alternative sources of funding, however, and the other new religions do not rely on street solicitation. The spiritual leaders seem no more or less sincere than leaders of other religious groups in America. Several, such as L. Ron Hubbard and Sun Myung Moon, amassed considerable wealth before founding churches in this country. Most, like Jones and Berg, labored for years or even decades before attracting substantial numbers of converts and some, like Moon, experienced considerable persecution. In short, founding a new religion is not an attractive get-rich-quick scheme, despite beliefs to the contrary. It is also true that some of these leaders have enormous influence over their followers. Moon has chosen marriage partners for many of his followers as well as three-piece suits for his lieutenants. Berg persuaded virtually his entire flock to migrate to Europe and even some of his married female followers to offer themselves to outsiders in hopes of converting them. Jim Jones, of course, is almost a caricature of the power of such spiritual leaders as a result of convincing at least some of his followers to join in revolutionary suicide. Yet each of these leaders has been confronted by factions, divisions, and challenges to his leadership. It is not at all clear that the power of these gurus is or was as absolute as the anticultists contend nor that these leaders confront(ed) their organizational problems in the same way.

In the final analysis the campaign against the new religions is better understood as the product of the anticultists' interests rather than as a civic crusade to save the rest of us from a dark, evil conspiracy. The anticultists have two primary goals. First, they are determined to extricate their sons and daughters from the new religions they have joined. Second, they seek an explanation for what they believe to be a disastrous turn of events that will minimize their social embarrassment and relieve personal feelings that range from sorrow and disappointment to guilt and anger. Much of the mythology surrounding the cult controversy must be understood in this light. Anticultists' contentions that there are a large number of rapidly growing and highly dangerous cults have the effect of creating an image of a critical problem that warrants the deep concern of the public-at-large and clear targets against which to direct actions. Parents who allege that their adult children have been brainwashed place full blame for their troubles on the new religions. Parents do not have to wonder whether family problems might be part of the explanation for their offspring's decision to join a new religion and to limit communication. And parents do not have to make excuses for their offspring's embarrassing behavior since brainwashing implies capture, not conversion. Furthermore, the brainwashing charge gains allies. After all, if cults can snatch innocent youth off the streets and turn them into robots, no one is safe. The unscrupulous quest for power and wealth by fraudulent gurus supplies the missing motive for this conspiracy.

The anticultists are forced to use simplistic stereotypes precisely because they seek to arouse righteous indignation in others that will provide confirmation of their own indignation and gain supporters. So for the diversity of new religions they substitute cults; for the diversity of motives individuals have for converting they substitute brainwashing; and for the diversity of tactics used to pressure their offspring to leave new religions they substitute deprogramming. Inflamed rhetoric and stereotyping are typical of groups engaged in all-out conflict, and there is no doubt that the anticultists see this struggle in exactly those terms. The anticultists have to reject more complex explanations, which would undermine their efforts to justify the extreme actions they wish to undertake against the new religions.

This indictment of the anticultists' motives and allegations may seem harsh, but it is not intended to demean their feelings. It is easy to understand that parents are deeply disturbed when carefully made lifelong plans are upset and their children choose a course that seems to imply permanent disruption of established family relationships. There is genuine grief and anguish for both parents and children. Nevertheless, we must separate our personal sympathy for others undergoing a very difficult experience from the more serious implications of joining with them in their campaign against the new religions. As citizens we must consider where our own interests lie in this conflict.

IMPLICATIONS OF THE ANTICULT CRUSADE

It is not easy to know how to proceed in a conflict in which well-meaning, respectable parents genuinely feel they and their children have been victimized. Even if readers accept all the arguments in this book, they still may be left with the uncomfortable feeling that something is wrong and that something should be done. As one clergyman exclaimed after hearing our conclusions at a symposium: "But *something* is going on there!" From another point of view, the position of the new religions that find little merit in conventional society—the means-justify-the-ends mentality and the holier-than-thou stance—is hardly reassuring. Is their attitude rhetoric or a genuine threat? Let us carefully consider some of the implications of siding with the anticultists.

There is a real danger in treating all the new religions as cults. Since the new religions are extremely diverse, it is really the communal organizations of such groups as the Moonies and Krishnas that are the primary sources of contention. To lump all new religions together is to create unnecessary conflict and confrontation. If the conflict with all new religions intensifies, some of them will be forced into a more combative stance than they would otherwise assume. One result is that it will be more difficult for those who join a new religion to leave. Whenever groups engage in conflict they draw together more tightly for commitment, loyalty, and discipline. A "we-versus-they" mentality emerges in which each side views the other as the enemy. Each side is then likely to employ more extreme rhetoric and engage in more hostile, provocative actions. Under such circumstances members of both sides become locked into their positions, and the only ways to cross group lines are defection and surrender. Withdrawal and compromise are obviously more difficult under such circumstances. To support the anticultists' present position is to run the risks associated with the escalation of conflicts. Such a course probably will not help parents of converts to the new religions who wish to reestablish family love and trust.

In considering punitive actions against the new religions, it is important to recall the history of new religions in this country. Most new religions never achieved substantial size and simply disappeared after a brief period. Scholars who have studied those groups with longer histories have found that they resemble mainline denominations more and more closely with the passage of time. They accommodate, or become more like the very society from which they originally sought to be different. Groups such as the Mormons, Jehovah's Witnesses, and Christian Scientists, for example, are much less radical in their beliefs and organizations than they were during their early histories (and the general public perceives them as less threatening). There are a variety of reasons for this gradual evolution. Members gain a greater stake in the "establishment" world as they get jobs, form families, and experience the rewards of stability and comfort. Furthermore, second-generation members lack the zeal of church pioneers. Since they were not part of the early fight for survival and the issues of those times have declined in importance, second-generation members often feel less fervor. Finally, new groups may moderate doctrines and organization both to reduce friction with conventional society and to attract a larger membership. Whatever the reasons, this evolutionary process has been quite common. Therefore, unless total repression or destruction of a new religion can be justified and carried out—an improbable outcome in a democracy such as the United States—there is considerable wisdom in accommodation and compromise rather than persecution and confrontation.

While there are real costs associated with stereotyping and needlessly escalating conflict, the greater danger is that of allowing the anticultists to give their interests the force of law. Since the anticultists organized early in the 1970s, they have consistently sought legislation at the local, state, and federal levels that would allow sanctions to be imposed on the new religions. Somewhat surprisingly (and ironically), efforts to secure passage of such legislation have intensified even as the growth of the new religions was visible falling off. There have been attempts to pass local ordinances that limit or eliminate street solicitation by some new religions. Such ordinances have been overturned upon appeal in virtually every case when challenged as violations of freedom of speech and religion. There have been other bills that attempt to define fraudulent religions and treat formation of such groups as a criminal violation, but these bills have not received much legislative support.

The most significant kind of legislation for both the new religions and the anticultists allows parents to gain legal custody over an adult son or daughter who has joined one of the new religions. These bills usually are introduced as extensions of conservatorship powers, which were originally intended to permit protective custody by family members of elderly, senile individuals in danger of self-injury or of being defrauded of money or property. Such bills allow parents to become legal guardians on the premise that converts to the new religions have been subjected to coercive mind control techniques, which leave them unable to conduct independently their own affairs or to make rational, free choices. Parents become guardians for periods ranging from a few weeks to a few months, and often deprogramming is allowable under these bills. Such legislation has been introduced in nearly a dozen states in recent years and passed both legislative houses in New York during 1980 and 1981 before being vetoed by the governor. These laws, if passed, obviously would represent a considerable victory for the anticultists. Not only would they allow parents to enlist the courts and police in their efforts to extricate their offspring from a new religion, but they would also grant legitimacy to the brainwashing allegation. The government would essentially be allied with the anticultists.

We would argue that it is not in the public interest to support the passage of such legislation for two reasons. First, this legislation creates a great potential for discrimination and violation of religious liberty. All pious talk about respect for religious freedom aside, these bills *are* aimed at religious groups. However, due to constitutional prohibitions on legislation in the area of religion the bills refer only to recruitment tactics and do not mention religion or churches. Naturally such bills rely heavily on the brainwashing theme. Since brainwashing as the anticultists describe it is a myth, the criteria by which the presence or absence of mind control is established must logically be false. The criteria by which brainwashing is demonstrated are based partly on simplistic stereotypes or gross exaggerations, such as allegedly dilated pupils, wooden masklike expressions, inability to think for oneself, cessation of facial hair growth in men and of menstruation in women. There is no evidence to support the presence of such bizarre, vague, and unmeasurable characteristics in converts to most new religions. Such telltale marks, therefore, invite discrimination. Other criteria refer to qualities possessed by almost any group that is organized communally, from monks to Marines. If passed, such legislation could be used in conflicts involving groups of no particular interest to the anticultists or in future disputes long after the current cult controversy has subsided. In essence the public — through its elected representatives in government — is being asked to risk discriminatory treatment of a wide range of present and future groups so that the anticultists can resolve their current family problems. It is a bad gamble if there is to be justice under law. Futhermore, under at least some of these legislative bills, deprogramming is permissible once custody has been granted. At this point, the government — acting in the name of all its citizens — may well be in the position of supporting individuals who are paid a fee to find a way of inducing converts to the new religions to repudiate their faiths. No matter how one feels about the new religions, this seems to be a dangerous precedent to set if freedom of religion is to be preserved. From a democratic as well as a scientific point of view, it would be nothing less than a pernicious travesty.

The second reason for not supporting such legislation is that there are real dangers for a democratic society in trying to legislate morality. These sorts of problems have been repeated throughout American history, beginning in the earliest colonies. Perhaps the classic case was the ill-fated Prohibition Movement of the 1920s and early 1930s. A small, vocal, well-organized group managed to get prohibition legislation passed in Washington, D.C. Not only did this legislation fail to stop the sale and consumption of alcohol, it created a flourishing black market that served as a primary revenue source for organized crime. Prohibition legislation represented an attempt to give the moral preferences of some American Protestants the force of law at a time when the lifestyles and customs of European immigrant Catholics were seen as a threat to traditional values. The problem with such legislation is that there is no limit to the moral preferences that various groups within our society would like to see enacted into law. As Americans we put ourselves in the same position as nations that attempt to protect domestic markets through tariffs. There is no limit to the number of interest groups in every nation that would seek such protection and justify their petition on the basis of protection granted to others. If groups representing moral and lifestyle interests are allowed to use law in this fashion, these laws will collapse under their own weight. Just as tariffs destroy free markets, the legislation of morality erodes cultural diversity and basic individual freedoms.

There is one further danger associated with the legislation of morality: we deny and reject a part of the very essence of our society. The *public face* of religion in America is the mainline denominations that are both large and visible: Methodists, Episcopalians, Presbyterians, Roman Catholics. The *reality* of religious life in America is that there are literally thousands of religious groups, most of which are so small that we are generally unaware of their presence. Only a tiny fraction of these groups ever achieves the size of the six groups we have considered in this book, and even fewer become large, stable churches as have the Mormons, Christian Scientists, Jehovah's Witnesses, and Quakers. Nevertheless, these small religious groups are just as much a part of the reality of American religious life as are the mainline denominations. To the extent that legislatures create laws rejecting the legitimacy of certain forms of religious organization and expression, for whatever excuse, they are essentially declaring that these groups are alien to *us*. The closer we as citizens move toward considering only the beliefs and practices of certain dominant, established segments of our society as legitimate, the closer we move toward the destruction of democratic pluralism. Diversity, tolerance, and openness are not easily created and sustained, and democracy is a continuing quest, not a stable condition or some finished end. There are very real costs attached to pluralism and democracy, and one of these is allowing lifestyles and values to exist while we simultaneously disagree with or even despise them. In the case of the new religions the costs to those most affected have been made very visible to us.

For our part, we have concluded that the new religions of this era do not pose a great danger to American society. To some the costs might seem large when they experience the anguish of families struggling through a difficult life crisis. However, these short-run costs pale beside the long-term cost of diminishing in any way democratic freedoms, cultural diversity, and protection of the weak against the strong in the best American tradition. Americans will probably always be beset by calls for a rush to judgment in one conflict or another by groups who seek to defend their immediate interests at the expense of collective, long-term interests. Whenever cries are raised to abridge basic values and freedoms, that is the time we need to consider our course most carefully, for far-reaching consequences will surely follow. Whenever we are warned that the enemy is at the gates and that we cannot pause lest we be destroyed, that is the time that we must be most certain they know the true face of their presumed enemy. In the cult controversy, we Americans cannot join in the anticult crusade without at the same time violating our own most fundamental interests. And that is too high a price.

Notes

Bibliography

Index

Notes

PREFACE

1. This quote appeared in Jim Siegelman and Flo Conway, "Snapping: Welcome to the Eighties," *Playboy* (March 1979), p. 59. Their thesis is presented in longer form in *Snapping: America's Epidemic of Sudden Personality Change* (New York: Lippincott, 1978).

1. THE HEART OF THE ISSUE

1. Ted Patrick's quote appeared in his now defunct newsletter, "Lightning News," which appeared as often as he could type and Xerox it in 1976. Dean M. Kelley's quote is taken from his widely read article, "Deprogramming and Religious Liberty," in *The Civil Liberties Review*, Vol. 4 (July/August 1977), pp. 23-33.

2. One historian has illustrated this point by comparing the similar rumors, propaganda, and hysteria that fueled persecution of such dissimilar groups as the Roman Catholics, the fraternal order of Freemasons, and the Mormons. See David Brion Davis, "Some Themes of Counter-Subversion: An Analysis of Anti-Masonic, Anti-Catholic, and Anti-Mormon Literature." *The Mississippi Valley Historical Review*, Vol. 47 (September 1960), pp. 205-24.

3. Martin E. Marty, *Righteous Empire: The Protestant Experience in America* (New York: Harper & Row, 1970), p. 128.

4. James Stuart Olson, *The Ethnic Dimension in American History* (New York: St. Martin's, 1979), pp. 80-81.

5. The analogy between wartime propaganda, or "atrocity tales," and media treatments of Sun Myung Moon's Unification Church (the best publicized of the cults) has been explicitly developed in David G. Bromley, Anson D. Shupe, Jr., and Joseph C. Ventimiglia, in "Atrocity Tales, the Unification Church, and the Social Construction of Evil," in *Journal of Communication*, Vol. 29 (Summer 1979), pp. 42-53.

6. Cited in Donna L. Oliver, "The Role of Apostates in the Mobilization of Counter-Movements" (Master's thesis, The University of Texas, 1980), p. 112.

7. Davis, "Some Themes of Counter-Subversion: An Analysis of Anti-Masonic, Anti-Catholic, and Anti-Mormon Literature," p. 219.
8. Cited in Ray Allen Billington, *The Origins of Nativism in the United States, 1800-1844* (New York: Arno Press, 1974), p. 359.
9. Maria Monk, *Awful Disclosures of the Hotel Dieu Nunnery* (Harden: Archer Books, 1962), and Rebecca Reed, *Six Months in a Convent* (New York: Arno Press).
10. J. P. Chaplin, *Rumor, Fear and the Madness of Crowds* (New York: Ballantine), p. 17.

2. WHO ARE THE CULTS?

1. Ted Patrick and Tom Dulack, *Let Our Children Go!* (New York: Ballantine, 1977), p. 11.
2. The definitive statements of clarifying the concept of cult have been made by British sociologist Geoffrey K. Nelson in a pair of journal articles: "The Spiritualist Movement and the Need for a Redefinition of Cult," *Journal for the Scientific Study of Religion*, Vol. 8 (Spring 1960), pp. 152-60, and "The Membership of a Cult: The Spiritualists National Union," *Review of Religious Research*, Vol. 13 (Spring 1972), pp. 170-77.
3. A. James Rudin and Marcia R. Rudin, *Prison or Paradise? The New Religious Cults* (Philadelphia: Fortress Press, 1980), pp. 15-16. The Rudins' book is one of the most recent popular works promoting the cult stereotype.
4. Patrick shot from the hip on a number of other topics besides cult size. See Jim Siegelman and Flo Conway, "*Playboy* Interview: Ted Patrick," *Playboy* (March 1979), p. 56.
5. One of the earliest examples of evangelical criticism of Christian heresies is Wm. C. Irvine's *Heresies Exposed* (Neptune, N.J.: Loizeaux Brothers, 1970), first printed in 1917 with the title *Timely Warnings*. This and other works such as Horton Davies' *Christian Deviations*, third revised edition (Philadelphia: Westminster Press, 1972), continue to be best-selling reading for conservative Protestants. Undoubtedly the most widely read book refuting sects and nonmainline Christian groups (reprinted 24 times) has been Walter R. Martin's *The Kingdom of the Cults* (Minneapolis: Bethany Fellowship, 1977).
6. Pat Means, *The Mystical Maze* (Downers Grove, Ill.: Campus

Crusade for Christ, 1976), pp. 121-23.

7. Siegelman and Conway, *"Playboy* Interview: Ted Patrick," p. 220.

8. Roy Wallis, "Observations On the Children of God," *The Sociological Review*, Vol. 24 (November 1976), p. 811.

9. For further details on size and organization of the Children of God as well as "Moses" David Berg's links to the late 1960s Jesus Movement, see Wallis, "Observations On the Children of God," and Rex Davis and James T. Richardson, "The Organization and Functioning of the Children of God," *Sociological Analysis* Vol. 37 (Winter 1976), pp. 321-39. Davis and Richardson do a very good job of summarizing the complex structure of the international Children of God and give illustrations of the organizational problems with which the movement has had to deal.

10. Wallis, "Observations On the Children of God," p. 819.

11. There are a number of popular books available on Sun Myung Moon and the Unification Church. Most have been written by evangelical Christians or Jewish spokespersons whose main interest lies in portraying the movement as heretical/anti-Christian/anti-Semitic, or by angry ex-Moonies who feel they were exploited, manipulated, and misled while Unificationist members. Both camps are more caught up in condemning Moon's group than in understanding the conflict it has precipitated. A few reasonably nonpartisan sources exist, however. Sociologist John Lofland's *Doomsday Cult*, revised edition (New York: Irvington Press, 1977) is the earliest serious study of the Unification Church in the United States. Lofland studied the first missionaries in the San Francisco Bay area with the purpose of developing a scientific model of conversion. He succeeded sociologically, but his portrayal of the individual Moonies (with pseudonyms), many of whom went on to become important leaders in America and internationally, as misfits and bunglers earned him the unremitting wrath of the Unification Church. Our own more recent study, which took the Church from its Korean origins up to events in 1979, was particularly concerned with analyzing the Church as an organization and how it overcame certain standard problems common to all social movements. Readers are referred to David G. Bromley and Anson D. Shupe, Jr., *"Moonies" in America: Cult, Church and Crusade* (Beverly Hills, Calif.: SAGE Publications, 1979), from which much of the material in this section is taken. Finally, the respected sociologist Irving Louis Horowitz, who has

been an outspoken critic of Moon's movement, edited a volume of papers and articles largely addressed to the theology of the movement with only a feeble attempt at balance. See Irving Louis Horowitz (ed.) *Science, Sin and Scholarship: The Politics of Reverend Moon and the Unification Church* (Cambridge: M.I.T. Press, 1978).

12. Sun Myung Moon, "On Bible Understanding," *The Master Speaks* (Washington, D.C.: Unification Church, 1965).

13. See *Investigation of Korean-American Relations. Report of the Subcommittee on International Organizations of the Subcommittee on International Organizations of the Committee on International Relations.* U.S. House of Representatives (Washington, D.C.: U.S. Government Printing Office, 1978).

14. See Gregory Johnson, "The Hare Krishna in San Francisco," in Charles Y. Glock and Robert N. Bellah (eds.), *The New Religious Consciousness* (Berkeley: University of California Press, 1976), pp. 33, 36. The best source of details on daily life among American Krishnas as well as on the movement's organizational structure is Francine Jeanne Daner, *The American Children of KRSNA* (Chicago: Holt, Rinehart & Winston, 1976). A more theological picture of the movement and its relation to the 1960s youth counterculture can be found in J. Stillson Juday, *Hare Krishna and the Counterculture* (New York: John Wiley, 1974).

15. Daner, *The American Children of KRSNA*, p. 34.

16. Daner, *The American Children of KRSNA*, p. 52.

17. Carroll Stoner and Jo Anne Parke, *All Gods Children: The Cult Experience* (Radnor, Penn.: Chilton, 1977), p. 68.

18. See James V. Downton, Jr., *Sacred Journeys* (New York: Columbia University Press, 1979), p. 2. As Downton points out, *Mahatma* means "great soul" and "premie" refers to members of the Divine Light Mission.

19. As in the other movements we have described in this chapter, high turnover rates and inadequate means of keeping track of membership result in "foggy" membership estimates in the Divine Light Mission. For two separate attempts at counts, see Downton, *Sacred Journeys*, p. 5, and Thomas Pilarzyk, "The Origin, Development, and Decline of a Youth Culture Religion: An Application of Sectarianization Theory," *Review of Religious Research*, Vol. 20 (Fall 1978), p. 30.

20. Downton, *Sacred Journeys*, p. 3.

21. Pilarzyk, "The Origin, Development, and Decline of a Youth Culture Religion: An Application of Sectarianization Theory," p. 32.

22. Downton, *Sacred Journeys*, p. 5.

23. Pilarzyk, "The Origin, Development, and Decline of a Youth Culture Religion: An Application of Sectarianization Theory," p. 38.

24. Scientology has been observed in its evolution during the past three decades by various persons largely unsympathetic to, or at least unenthusiastic with, the movement's claim of being a significant new form of psychospiritual therapy. Two older sources that attempt to debunk Hubbard's claims are popular science writer Martin Gardner, *Fads and Fallacies in the Name of Science*, revised edition (New York: Dover, 1957), pp. 263-80, and British psychologist Christopher Evans, *Cults of Unreason* (New York: Dell, 1973), pp. 17-134. Two recent studies by sociologists are William Sims Bainbridge and Rodney Stark, "Scientology: To Be Perfectly Clear," *Sociological Analysis*, Vol. 41 (Summer 1980), pp. 128-36, and (undoubtedly the most comprehensive) Roy Wallis, *The Road to Total Freedom: A Sociological Analysis of Scientology* (New York: Columbia University Press, 1976).

25. Evans, *Cults of Unreason*, p. 33.

26. Wallis, *The Road to Total Freedom*, 1976.

27. Evans, *Cults of Unreason*, p. 17. See, for a discussion of the linkages between Hubbard's theory and science fiction literature, Harriet Whitehead, "Reasonably Fantastic: Some Perspectives on Scientology, Science Fiction, and Occultism," in Irving I. Zaretsky and Mark P. Leone (eds.), *Religious Movements in Contemporary America* (Princeton, N.J.: Princeton University Press, pp. 547-48).

28. Evans, *Cults of Unreason*, p. 35.

29. Evans, *Cults of Unreason*, p. 36. The patently unhealthy obsession of Dianetics (whatever it reflects on Hubbard) with incompetently self-induced abortions *via* coathangers and sewing needles by mothers and with their alleged repeated adulterous affairs carried on into late pregnancy are not simply the exaggerations of anti-Scientological authors. See also, for what is apparently a pro-Scientology popular source, Walter Braddeson, *Scientology for the Millions* (Los Angeles: Sherbourne Press, 1969).

30. Wallis, *The Road to Total Freedom*, p. 128.

31. James T. Richardson, "People's Temple and Jonestown: A Correc-

tive Comparison and Critique," *Journal for the Scientific Study of Religion* Vol. 19 (September 1980), p. 248.

32. J. Gordon Melton, "Jim Jones, Charles Manson and the Process of Religious Group Disintegration." Paper presented at the annual meeting of the Society for the Scientific Study of Religion (October 1979), San Antonio, Texas, p. 5.

33. Statement of Wayne Pietila, quoted in Mel Whilte, *Deceived* (Old Tappan, N.J.: Spire Books, 1979), p. 57.

34. Richardson, "People's Temple and Jonestown," p. 251.

35. Richardson, "People's Temple and Jonestown," p. 242. See also Archie Smith, Jr., "An Interpretation of the People's Temple and Jonestown: Implications for the Black Church." Paper presented at the annual meeting of the Association for the Sociology of Religion (August 1979), Boston, Mass.

3.   THE CULTS' CHALLENGE TO AMERICA

1. The allegations by ex-Moonies that they had received suicide instructions from Unification Church leaders can be found in J. Carroll and B. Bauer, "Suicide Training in the Moon Cult," *New West* (January 29, 1979), pp. 62-63.

2. See our discussion in David G. Bromley and Anson D. Shupe, Jr., *"Moonies" in America: Cult, Church and Crusade* (Beverly Hills, Calif.: SAGE Publications, 1979), pp. 127, 131-32.

3. These incidents were widely reported in the media. Our sources are syndicated newspaper accounts, for example, Linda S. Herskowitz, "Krishna Consciousness: Chanting of Peace Comes More Easily in a Mansion Filled with Weapons," Fort Worth *Star-Telegram* (February 4, 1979).

4. Two accounts of the federal investigation—one a government document, the other a book written by a staff member who helped produce the government report—are *Investigation of Korean-American Relations* (Report of the Subcommittee on International Organizations of the Committee on International Relations, U.S. House of Representatives; Washington, D.C.: U.S. Government Printing Office, 1978), and Robert Boettcher and Gordon L. Freedman, *Gifts of Deceit* (New York: Holt, Rinehart & Winston, 1980).

5. We found this widely reported incident as a syndicated story reprinted locally as "9 Scientologists Convicted in Plot," Dallas

Morning News (October 27, 1979).

6. Jack Sparks, *The Mind Benders* (New York: Thomas Nelson, 1977), pp. 261-62.
7. R. D. Clements, *God and the Gurus* (Downer's Grove, Ill.: Inter-Varsity Press), pp. 36-37.
8. Sparks, *The Mind Benders*, p. 177.
9. Jerry I. Yamamoto, *The Puppet Master* (Downer's Grove, Ill.: Inter-Varsity Press), p. 129.
10. The classic work on the subject of communal lifestyles and what it takes to make them work for members is Rosabeth Moss Kanter, *Commitment and Community* (Cambridge, Mass.: Harvard University Press, 1972).
11. Bromley and Shupe, Jr., *"Moonies" in America: Cult, Church and Crusade*, p. 184.
12. Gregory Johnson, "The Hare Krishna in San Francisco," pp. 31-51, in Charles Y. Glock and Robert N. Bellah (eds.), *The New Religious Consciousness* (Berkeley: University of California Press, 1976), p. 40.
13. These quotes are taken from field notes and interviews with Unification Church members in 1978.
14. Bromley and Shupe, Jr., *"Moonies" in America: Cult, Church and Crusade*, p. 176.
15. Johnson, "The Hare Krishna in San Francisco," p. 45.
16. Johnson, "The Hare Krishna in San Francisco," p. 43.
17. Johnson, "The Hare Krishna in San Francisco," p. 41.
18. Johnson, "The Hare Krishna in San Francisco," p. 45.
19. Anson D. Shupe, Jr., and David G. Bromley, *The New Vigilantes: Deprogrammers, Anti-Cultists and the New Religions* (Beverly Hills, Calif.: SAGE Publications, 1980), p. 42.
20. This quote was taken from a transcript of a public meeting between parents involved in the anticult movement and various federal officials sponsored by Senator Robert Dole. See National Ad Hoc Committee Engaged in Freeing Minds, *A Special Report, The Unification Church: Its Activities and Practices*, Vol. I and II, Arlington, Tex.: National Ad Hoc Committee, A Day of Affirmation and Protest, 1976, Vol. II, p. 60.
21. National Ad Hoc Committee, p. 52.
22. National Ad Hoc Committee, p. 35.
23. *The Home News* (New Brunswick, N.J.: November 12, 1975).

4. JOINING THE NEW RELIGIONS

1. Ted Patrick and Tom Dulack, *Let Our Children Go!* (New York: Ballantine, 1977).
2. See Anson D. Shupe, Jr., and David G. Bromley, *The New Vigilantes: Deprogrammers, Anti-Cultists and the New Religions* (Beverly Hills, Calif.: SAGE Publications, 1980), p. 252, Fitzpatrick reference.
3. See Jim Siegelman and Flo Conway, "*Playboy* Interview: Ted Patrick," *Playboy* (March 1979), pp. 53ff.
4. These and other atrocity stories told by deprogrammed ex-members of the Unification Church and other groups are taken from our analysis of how such stories are used by countermovements to discredit their opponents. See David G. Bromley, Anson D. Shupe, Jr., and Joseph C. Ventimiglia, "Atrocity Tales, the Unification Church, and the Social Construction of Evil," *Journal of Communication*, Vol. 29 (Summer 1979), pp. 42-53.
5. The term "brainwashing" is a misleading translation of the Chinese *hsi nao*, which means "to cleanse the mind" (that is, of non-Maoist communist thoughts). Its popular adoption is primarily due to Edward Hunter's book *Brainwashing in Red China. The Calculated Destruction of Men's Minds*, Enlarged Edition (New York: Vanguard, 1953). Hunter, in 1950s cold-war fashion, portrays the process as a distinctly communist, un-American one. Psychiatrist Robert J. Lifton, in *Thought Reform and the Psychology of Totalism* (New York: Norton, 1961), p. 4, has rejected the term brainwashing because its "loose usage makes the word a rallying point for fear, resentment, urges toward submission, justification for failure, irresponsible accusation, and for a wide gamut of emotional extremism." Likewise, psychologist Edgar H. Schein rejects Hunter's sensationalistic translation and speaks of the more extreme (and infrequent) attempts at *hsi nao* as "coercive persuasion." See Edgar H. Schein, with Inge Schneier and Curtis H. Backer, *Coercive Persuasion* (New York: Norton, 1961).
6. Robert Jay Lifton, "Thought Reform of Chinese Intellectuals: A Psychiatric Evaluation." *Journal of Social Issues*, Vol. 13 (1967), pp. 5-19.
7. Kurt Lewin, "Group Dynamics and Social Change," in Amitai Etzioni and Eva Etzioni-Halevy, *Social Change: Sources, Patterns,*

    and Consequences, Second Edition (New York: Basic Books, 1973), p. 377.

8. Seymour Lieberman, "The Effects of Changes in Role on the Attitudes of Role Occupants," *Human Relations,* Vol. 9 (1956), pp. 385-407.

9. Sanford N. Dornbusch, "The Military Academy As an Assimilating Institution," *Social Forces,* Vol. 33 (1955), pp. 316-21. See also, for a caricature of a Catholic convent and its indoctrination techniques, David G. Bromley and Anson D. Shupe, Jr., "The Tnevnoc Cult," *Sociological Analysis,* Vol. 40 (Winter 1979), pp. 361-66.

10. Alan Scheflin and Edward Opton, *The Mind Manipulators* (New York: Paddington, 1978), p. 89.

11. Edgar H. Schein, "The Chinese Indoctrination Program for Prisoners of War: A Study of Attempted 'Brainwashing,' in Eleanor E. Maccoby, Theodore M. Newcomb, and Eugene L. Hartley (eds.), *Readings in Social Psychology,* Third Edition (New York: Holt, Rinehart & Winston, 1958), p. 332.

12. Thomas Robbins and Dick Anthony, "The Limits of Coercive Persuasion as an Explanation for Conversion to Authoritarian Sects." Paper presented to the International Society of Political Psychologists, (May 1979), Washington, D.C., p. 6.

13. Two very readable analyses of flirty fishing can be found in articles by British sociologist Roy Wallis. See "Fishing for Men," *The Humanist,* Vol. 38 (January/February 1978), pp. 14-16, and "Recruiting Christian Manpower," *Society,* Vol. 15 (May/June 1978), pp. 72-74.

14. The official public denial is similar to this: "Our only link with the Unification Church is through the Reverend Moon, who initially inspired us." However, the Unification Church of America owns the deeds to much NEDS property, most recruits taken in by the Oakland Family's staff are soon assigned to work elsewhere for the Church, the Oakland Family's staff are *all* long-time Church members, and its former director Martin Irwin "Mose" Durst is now President of the Unification Church of America. In our own fieldwork in San Francisco we encountered the same pious denials of any connection with the Unification Church by the group's street missionaries, though once we were recognized as less than naive researchers of the movement the ruse was immediately dropped. A complete analysis of this West Coast

wing, or faction, of the Unification Church and its relation to the latter can be found in David G. Bromley and Anson D. Shupe, Jr., *"Moonies" in America: Cult, Church and Crusade* (Beverly Hills, Calif.: SAGE Publications, 1979) pp. 138-42.

15. In 1976, at the first of two public meetings between Senator Robert Dole and various other federal officials and angry parents of cult members, a coalition of regional anticult organizations decided to limit their complaints and call for investigations of Moon and the Unification Church. This seemed to them a reasonable strategy since Moon and his movement have been so highly publicized through numerous financial investments, possible political skull-duggery in the Koreagate scandal, and outspoken support of President Richard Nixon during the Watergate/impeachment scandal. Their reasoning was that successful repression of Moon's large and wealthy movement would serve as a precedent for attacking other cults. Further details on how and why the Unification Church was singled out by the anticult movement to be its arch-nemesis can be found in Shupe and Bromley, *The New Vigilantes: Deprogrammers, Anti-Cultists and the New Religions*.

16. A clear example of the dynamics of how rumors and outright conjecture can be repeated often enough by journalists until these are assumed without doubt to be fact is provided by Edward Jay Epstein in his book *Between Fact and Fiction: The Problem of Journalism* (New York: Vintage, 1975), pp. 33-77. Epstein meticulously analyzed the widespread and repeated accusation that the shooting of several Black Panther leaders by police in 1969 was part of a national law enforcement pattern that had resulted in the deaths of a total of 28 Panthers. Taking the cases one by one, Epstein ultimately found this charge, despite its frequent uncritical repetition by many journalists, to be largely fabrication and/or gross exaggeration.

17. Carroll Stoner and Jo Anne Parke, *All Gods Children: The Cult Experience* (Radnor, Penn.: Chilton, 1977), p. 68. Stoner and Parke's book, despite its attempts to maintain journalistic neutrality, nevertheless takes for granted many anticult assumptions. Therefore it unavoidably propogates a misleading picture of the extent of cult influence.

18. See Bromley and Shupe, *"Moonies" in America: Cult, Church and Crusade*, pp. 169-96.

19. Personal Interviews at Unification Theological Seminary, Barrytown, New York, 1978.

20. Two sources that discuss these research findings in more theoretical terms are Bromley and Shupe, *"Moonies" in America: Cult, Church and Crusade,* pp. 169-96, and David G. Bromley and Anson D. Shupe, Jr., " 'Just a Few Years Seem Like a Lifetime': A Role Theory Approach to Participation in Religious Movements," in Louis Kriesberg (ed.), *Research in Social Movements, Conflicts and Change* (Greenwich, Conn.: JAI Press, 1979), pp. 159-85.

21. James V. Downton, Jr., *Sacred Journeys: The Conversion of Young Americans to Divine Light Mission* (New York: Columbia University Press, 1979), p. 75.

22. Francine J. Daner, *The American Children of Krishna* (New York: Holt, Rinehart & Winston, 1976), p. 64. Another researcher of the Hare Krishna movement has mentioned an affiliate status conferred by the movement on those persons interested in the doctrines and goals but unable (or unwilling) for whatever reason to live in strict communal fashion. See J. Stillson Judah, "The Hare Krishna Movement," in Irving I. Zaretsky and Mark P. Leone, *Religious Movements in Contemporary America* (Princeton, N.J.: Princeton University Press, 1974), pp. 463-78. ·

23. Robert Balch, "Looking Behind the Scenes in a Religious Cult: Implications for the Study of Conversion," *Sociological Analysis,* Vol. 41 (Summer 1980), pp. 137-43.

24. Saul V. Levine and Nancy E. Salter, "Youth and Contemporary Religious Movements: Psychosocial Findings," *Canadian Psychiatric Association Journal,* Vol. 21 (1976), p. 414.

25. J. Thomas Ungerleider and David K. Wellisch, "Coercive Persuasion (Brainwashing), Religious Cults, and Deprogramming," *American Journal of Psychiatry,* Vol. 136 (March 1979), p. 281.

26. J. Thomas Ungerleider and David K. Wellisch, "Psychologists' Involvement in Cultism, Thought Control and Deprogramming," *Psychiatric Opinion,* Vol. 16 (January 1979), p. 15. Another source on this subject, using a greater number of subjects, is Mark Galanter, Richard Rabkin, Judith Rabkin, and Alexander Deutsch, "The Moonies: A Psychological Study of Conversion and Membership in a Contemporary Religious Sect," *American Journal of Psychiatry,* Vol. 136 (February 1979), pp. 165-70.

27. For examples of these researchers' claims that brainwashing does occur in a variety of new religious groups, see John G. Clark, Jr., "Cults," *Journal of the American Medical Association,* Vol. 242 (July 20, 1979), pp. 279-81, and Margaret Singer, "Coming Out of the Cults," *Psychology Today,* Vol. 12 (January 1979), pp. 72-82.

28. For additional scholarly descriptions and analyses of the Oakland Family's recruitment tactics, see Bromley and Shupe, Jr., *"Moonies" in America: Cult, Church and Crusade,* pp. 169-96, and John Lofland, "'Becoming a World-Saver' Revisited," *American Behavioral Scientist* Vol. 20 (July/August 1977), pp. 805-18.

29. There are competing versions of a general psychological theory that says human beings have a need to make their attitudes consistent with their actions. Since actions are often affected by immediate social pressure, attitudes about these actions are usually formed to explain them in ways that are plausible to the actor-thinker. In other words, we infer our attitudes about specific things and events from observing our own actions regarding them. For general statements of such well-established theory, see Leon A. Festinger, *A Theory of Cognitive Dissonance* (Stanford, Calif.: Stanford University Press, 1957), and Darrel J. Bem, "Inducing Belief in False Confessions," *Journal of Personality and Social Psychology,* Vol. 3 (1966), pp. 707-10.

30. See David L. Altheide and John M. Johnson, "Counting Souls: A Study of Counseling at Evangelical Crusades," *Pacific Sociological Review,* Vol. 20 (July 1977), pp. 331-32.

5. THE LEADERS

1. "An Interview with Reverend Sun Myung Moon," reprinted from *Newsweek International,* June 14, 1976, by the Unification Church of America.

2. See David G. Bromley and Anson D. Shupe, Jr., *"Moonies" in America: Cult, Church and Crusade* (Beverly Hills, Calif.: SAGE Publications, 1970), pp. 149-67.

3. John Lofland, *Doomsday Cult* (New York: Irvington, 1977), pp. 341-42.

4. Carroll Stoner and Jo Ann Parke, *All Gods Children* (Radnor, Penn.: Chilton, 1977), p. 112.

5. Jeffrey K. Hadden and Charles E. Swann, *Prime Time Preachers: The Rising Power of Televangelism* (Reading, Mass.: Addison-Wesley, 1981), pp. 2-3.

6. John Cotter, "Rev. Moon Seeks Power Through 'Gospel,'" Chicago *Tribune,* December 14, 1975, p. 12.

7. Maharaj Ji, "You Are Disciples Now." Speech given at Satsang at Hampstead Town Hall, England, October 31, 1971.

8. Rex Davis and James Richardson, "The Organization and Functioning of the Children of God," *Sociological Analysis*, Vol. 37 (Winter 1976), p. 326.
9. Bromley and Shupe, Jr., *"Moonies" in America: Cult, Church and Crusade*, pp. 97-105.
   Religious Group Disintegration." Paper presented at the annual meeting of the Society for the Scientific Study of Religion (October 1979), San Antonio, Texas, p. 13.

6. FUND-RAISING AND THE NEW RELIGIONS

1. Harvey Katz, *Give! Who Gets Your Charity Dollar?* (Garden City, N.Y.: Doubleday, 1973), p. 4.
2. Katz, *Give! Who Gets Your Charity Dollar?*, p. 20.
3. Katz, *Give! Who Gets Your Charity Dollar?*, p. 80.
4. F. E. Andrews, *Attitudes Toward Giving* (New York: Russell Sage Foundation, 1953), pp. 14-65.
5. David Sills, *Means and Ends in a National Organization* (Glencoe, Ill.: The Free Press, 1957), p. 157.
6. National Broadcasting Corporation, "Prime Time with Tom Snyder" (New York: National Broadcasting Corporation, July 1, 1979).
7. Sun Myung Moon, "God's Hope for America," in Bo Hi Pak (ed.), *Christianity in Crisis: New Hope* (New York: Holy Spirit Association for the Unification of World Christianity, 1974), p. 58. Moon's theology of charitable solicitations, as one example of gathering necessary resources in new religions, is discussed at length in David G. Bromley and Anson D. Shupe, Jr., "Financing the New Religions," *Journal for the Scientific Study of Religion* Vol. 19 (September 1980), pp. 227-39.
8. Quoted in Bromley and Shupe, "Financing the New Religions," p. 233.

7. DEPROGRAMMING

1. Pam Fanshier's testimony, and that of other unsuccessfully deprogrammed members of new religions, can be found in *Deprogramming: Documenting the Issue* (New York: Alliance for the Preservation of Religious Liberty, 1977).
2. For this quote and the following excerpts see the *Tribune*, Great

Bend, Kansas, October 15, 1975, for only one example of a series of newspaper articles.

3. Ted Patrick and Tom Dulack, *Let Our Children Go!* (New York: Dutton, 1976), p. 71.

· 4. Jim Siegelman and Flo Conway, "*Playboy* Interview: Ted Patrick," *Playboy* (March 1979), pp. 70-74.

5. "Ex-Krishna Glad He Was Kidnapped," *Dallas Morning News*, October 11, 1980.

6. Thomas Robbins, "Cults and the Therapeutic State," *Social Policy* (May/June 1979), p. 44.

7. Dean M. Kelley, "Deprogramming and Religious Liberty," *The Civil Liberties Review* Vol. 4 (July/August 1977), p. 32.

8. This case is described in Robert J. Moore, "Terror in Denver," *Liberty* (March/April 1979), pp. 8-13.

9. See Josh Freed, *Moonwebs: Journey in to the Mind of a Cult* (Toronto: Dorset Publishing Company, 1980), p. 122. Freed's account of a deprogramming, originally published in installments in the Montreal *Star* in 1978, provides a good example of how journalism can descend into sensational melodrama and how the conflicts of interest inherent in this controversy, with some skillful literary embellishments, can be exploited to make dramatic reading.

10. Siegelman and Conway, "*Playboy* Interview: Ted Patrick," p. 70.

11. Writs of temporary conservatorship were originally enacted by states to permit one adult to become the legal guardian, or conservator, of another (usually a family member) and his or her estate in the event that the second person became not legally responsible for his or her actions. Such writs can be granted by a judge on short notice without a formal hearing and without the person in question present. They can be granted for 30- , 40- , or 60-day periods, allowing emergency action if a senile or mentally unstable person is about to do something irreparably injurious, such as elderly Aunt Tilly intending to sign over her mortgage to a 25-year-old gigolo with whom she has become infatuated. Customarily the person seeking to become the legal guardian appears before a judge with a psychiatrist, family physician, or some other professional who can testify to Aunt Tilly's erratic, possibly harmful behavior. During the temporary period Aunt Tilly loses the right to conduct legal transactions and essentially assumes the legal status of a child.

Members of new religions are rarely present at these preliminary hearings. Indeed, almost all judges who have granted such conservatorships have never seen the person for whom they issue such writs. Writs of temporary conservatorship have become less frequently used in recent years as higher courts have ruled that they were not designed to be used for cases involving possible violations of religious freedom. The Freedom of Thought Foundation ran into trouble not only on those grounds but also because it often obtained through its lawyers writs of temporary conservatorship granted in one state and served them in another state, which is illegal. For a discussion of these writs and other legal tactics used by deprogrammers, as well as for more information on the money involved in deprogrammings, see Anson D. Shupe, Jr., and David G. Bromley, *The New Vigilantes: Deprogrammers, Anti-Cultists and the New Religions* (Beverly Hills, Calif.: SAGE Publications, 1980), pp. 130-36.

12. See Walter Robert Taylor's affidavit of his deprogramming in *Deprogramming: Documenting the Issue*, pp. 65-67.
13. Taken from W. J. Helander v. Ted Patrick, Jr., et al. "Memorandum of decision in re Helander vs. Patrick, Jr." (Fairfield, N.Y.: Superior Court, No. 15-90-62, September 8, 1979).
14. This excerpt from an interview transcript made in 1976 was published in Anson D. Shupe, Jr., Roger Spielmann, and Sam Stigall, "Deprogramming: the New Exorcism," *American Behavioral Scientist* Vol. 20 (July/August 1977), p. 950.
15. For the original article claiming suicide training in the Unification Church (and nowhere else), see J. Carroll and B. Bauer, "Suicide Training in the Moon Cult," *New West* (January 29, 1979), pp. 62-63. For our critical analysis of such claims, see Shupe, Jr., and Bromley, *The New Vigilantes: Deprogrammers, Anti-Cultists and the New Religions*, pp. 214-17.
16. See Francine Jeanne Daner, *The American Children of KRSNA* (New York: Holt, Rinehart & Winston, 1976), pp. 55-56.
17. Shupe, Jr., Spielmann, and Stigall, "Deprogramming: the New Exorcism," p. 951.
18. Hans Toch, *The Social Psychology of Social Movements* (Indianapolis: Bobbs-Merrill, 1965), p. 226.
19. For a more complete analysis of this type of story, and of the category of people who tells it, see David G. Bromley, Anson D. Shupe, Jr., and Joseph C. Ventimiglia, "Atrocity Tales, the Unifi-

cation Church, and the Social Construction of Evil," *Journal of Communication* Vol. 29 (Summer 1979), pp. 42-53.

20. Christopher Edwards, *Crazy for God* (Englewood Cliffs, N.J.: Prentice-Hall, 1979).

21. See James Beckford, " 'Brainwashing' and 'Deprogramming' in Britain: The Social Sources of Anti-Cult Sentiment," forthcoming in James T. Richardson (ed.), *The Deprogramming Controversy: Sociological, Psychological, Legal, and Historical Perspectives* (New Brunswick, N.J.: Transaction Books), and "Politics and 'The Anti-Cult Movement,'" *Annual Review of the Social Sciences*, Vol. 3, pp. 169-90.

22. This quotation appeared in Trudy Solomon, "Integrating the 'Moonie' Experience: A Survey of Ex-Members of the Unification Church," in Thomas Robbins and Dick Anthony (eds.), *In Gods We Trust. New Patterns of Religious Pluralism in America* (New Brunswick, N.J.: Transaction Books, 1981), p. 288.

23. For example, in its one and only real year of operation, the Freedom of Thought Foundation deprogramming ranch cleared an estimated $195,000. Likewise, there is convincing evidence that Ted Patrick did not do badly himself during the mid-1970s. See Shupe, Jr., and Bromley, *The New Vigilantes: Deprogrammers, Anti-Cultists and the New Religions*, pp. 135-41, for further details on available profit figures from deprogramming.

8.   A HARD LOOK AT THE CULT CONTROVERSY

1. For a discussion of this issue see, for example, J. Stillson Judah, "The Hare Krishna Movement," in Irving Zaretsky and Mark Leone (eds.), *Religious Movements in Contemporary America* (Princeton: Princeton University Press), pp. 463-78; Dick Anthony and Thomas Robbins, "The Meher Baba Movement: Its Effect on Post-Adolescent Social Alienation" in Zaretsky and Leone (eds.), *Religious Movements in Contemporary America*, pp. 479-514.

2. Dean Kelley, "The 'Redeeming' Qualities of New Religious Movements," Paper presented at the Conference on Conversion, Coercion and Commitment in New Religious Movements, Center for Study of New Religious Movements, Berkeley, Calif., June 1981, pp. 11-12.

Bibliography

FURTHER SCIENTIFIC READING

Bainbridge, William Sims, and Stark, Rodney. "Scientology: To Be Perfectly Clear." *Sociological Analysis*, Vol. 41, Summer 1980: 128-36.

Balch, Robert, and Taylor, David. "Seekers and Saucers: The Role of the Cultic Milieu in Joining a UFO Cult." *American Behavioral Scientist*, Vol. 20, July/August 1977: 839-60.

_____. "Salvation in a UFO." *Psychology Today*, Vol. 10, October 1976: 361-66.

Billington, Ray Allen. *The Origins of Nativism in the United States, 1800-1844*. New York: Arno Press, 1974.

Bromley, David G., and Shupe, Jr., Anson D. "The Tnevnoc Cult." *Sociological Analysis*, Vol. 40, Winter 1980: 361-66.

_____. *"Moonies" in America: Cult, Church and Crusade*. Beverly Hills, Calif.: SAGE Publications, 1979.

Cantril, Hadley. *The Psychology of Social Movements*. London: Chapman and Hall, 1941.

Clark, Jr., John G. "Cults." *Journal of the American Medical Association*, Vol. 242, July 20, 1979: 279-81.

Cox, Harvey. *Turning East*. New York: Simon & Schuster, 1977.

Damrell, Joseph. *Seeking Spiritual Meaning: The World of Vedanta*. Beverly Hills, Calif.: SAGE Publications, 1977.

Davis, David Brion. "Some Themes of Counter-Subversion: An Analysis of Anti-Masonic, Anti-Catholic, and Anti-Mormon Literature." *The Mississippi Historical Review*, Vol. 47, September 1960: 205-24.

Downton, Jr., James V. *Sacred Journeys: The Conversion of Young Americans to Divine Light Mission*. New York: Columbia University Press, 1979.

Ellwood, Jr., Robert S. *Alternative Altars: Unconventional and Eastern Spirituality in America.* Chicago: University of Chicago Press, 1979.

————. *The Eagle and the Rising Sun: Americans and the New Religions of Japan.* Philadelphia: The Westminster Press, 1974.

Enroth, Ronald. *The Lure of the Cults.* Chappaqua, N.Y.: Christian Herald Books, 1979.

————. *Youth, Brainwashing, and the Extremist Cuts.* Kentwood, Mich.: Zondervan, 1977.

Evans, Christopher. *Cults of Unreason.* New York: Dell, 1973.

Festinger, Leon; Riecken, Henry W.; and Schachter, Stanley. *When Prophecy Fails.* New York: Harper & Row, 1956.

Galanter, Marc; Rabkin, Richard; Rabkin, Judith; and Deutsch, Alexander. "The Moonies: A Psychological Study of Conversion and Membership in a Contemporary Religious Sect." *American Journal of Psychiatry,* Vol. 136, February 1979: 165-70.

Glock, Charles Y., and Bellah, Robert N., eds. *The New Religious Consciousness.* Berkeley, Calif.: University of California Press, 1976.

Greeley, Andrew M. *The Denominational Society.* Glencoe, Ill: Scott, Foresman, 1972.

Harris, Sara. *Father Divine.* Rev. ed. New York: Collier Books, 1971.

Heirich, Max. "Change of Heart: A Test of Some Widely Held Theories About Religious Conversion." *American Journal of Sociology,* Vol. 83, November 1977: 653-80.

Hennan, Edward F. *Mystery, Magic and Miracle: Religion in a Post-Aquarian Age.* Englewood Cliffs, N.J.: Prentice-Hall, 1973.

Hoge, Dean R., and Roozen, David A., eds. *Understanding Church Growth and Decline 1950-1978.* Philadelphia: Pilgrim Press, 1979.

Kelley, Dean M. *Why Conservative Churches Are Growing.* 2nd ed. San Francisco: Harper & Row, 1977

————. "Deprogramming and Religious Liberty." *The Civil Liberties Review,* Vol. 4, July/August 1977: 23-33.

Kephart, William M. *Extraordinary Groups: The Sociology of Unconventional Lifestyles.* New York: St. Martin's Press, 1976.

Krinsky, Fred. *The Politics of Religion in America.* Beverly Hills, Calif.: Glencoe Press, 1968.

Levine, Saul V., and Salter, Nancy E. "Youth and Contemporary Religious Movements: Psychosocial Findings," *Canadian Psychiatric Association Journal,* Vol. 21, No. 6, 1976: 411-20.

Lifton, Robert J. *Chinese Thought Reform and the Psychology of Totalism.* New York: Norton, 1961.

_____. "Thought Reform of Western Civilians in Chinese Communist Prisons." *Psychiatry,* Vol. 9, 1957: 385-402.

Lofland, John. *Doomsday Cult.* New York: Irvington Press, 1977.

Meerloo, J. *The Rape of the Mind.* New York: World, 1956.

Morgan, Richard E. *The Politics of Religious Conflict.* New York: Pegasus, 1968.

Needleman, Jacob. *The New Religions.* New York: Pocket Books, 1972.

Needleman, Jacob, and Baker, George, eds. *Understanding the New Religions.* New York: Seabury Press, 1979.

Nelson, Geoffrey K. "The Spiritualist Movement and the Need for a Redefinition of Cult." *Journal for the Scientific Study of Religion,* Vol. 8, Spring 152-60.

Richardson, James T.; Stewart, Mary W.; and Simmonds, Robert B. *Organized Miracles: A Study of a Contemporary, Youth, Communal, Fundamentalist Organization.* New Brunswick, N.J.: Transaction Books, 1979.

Robbins, Thomas, and Anthony, Dick, eds. *In Gods We Trust: New Patterns of Religious Pluralism in America.* New Brunswick, N.J.: Transaction Books, 1981.

Sargent, William, *Battle for the Mind.* Garden City, N.Y.: Doubleday, 1957.

Scheflin, Alan, and Opton, Edward. *The Mind Manipulators.* New York: Paddington, 1978.

Shupe, Jr., Anson D. *Six Alternative Perspectives on New Religions: A Case Study Approach.* New York: The Edwin Mellen Press, 1981.

Shupe, Jr., Anson D., and Bromley, David G. *A Documentary History of the American Anti-Cult Movement.* New York: The Edwin Mellen Press, 1981.

_____. *The New Vigilantes: Deprogrammers, Anti-Cultists and the New Religions.* Beverly Hills, Calif.: SAGE Publications, 1980.

Shupe, Jr., Anson D.; Spielmann, Roger; and Stigall, Sam. "Deprogramming: The New Exorcism." *American Behavioral Scientist,* Vol. 20, July/August 1977: 941-56.

Singer, Margaret T. "Coming Out of the Cults." *Psychology Today,* Vol. 12, January 1979: 72-82.

Ungerleider, J. Thomas. *The New Religions: Insights into the Cult Phenomenon.* New York: Merck, Sharp and Dohme, 1979.

Ungerleider, J. Thomas, and Wellisch, David. "Psychiatrists' Involvement in Cultism, Thought Control and Deprogramming." *Psychiatric Opinion*, Vol. 16, January 1979: 10-15.

_____. "Coercive Persuasion (Brainwashing), Religious Cults, and Deprogramming." *American Journal of Psychiatry*, Vol. 136, March 1979: 279-82.

Verdier, Paul A. *Brainwashing and the Cults*. Hollywood, Calif.: Institute of Behavioral Conditioning, 1977.

Wallis, Roy. *The Road to Total Freedom: A Sociological Analysis of Scientology*. New York: Columbia University Press, 1977.

Washington, Jr., Joseph R. *Black Sects and Cults*. Garden City, N.Y.: Doubleday, 1973.

Wilson, Bryan, ed. *The Social Impact of New Religious Movements*. New York: The Rose of Sharon Press, 1981.

Wilson, John. *Religion in American Society: The Effective Presence*. Englewood Cliffs, N.J.: Prentice-Hall, 1978.

Wuthnow, Robert. *Experimentation in American Religion*. Berkeley: University of California Press, 1978.

Zaretsky, Irving I., and Leone, Mark P., eds. *Religious Movements in Contemporary America*. Princeton, N.J.: Princeton University Press, 1974.

FURTHER RELIGIOUS READING

Bjornstad, James. *Counterfeits at Your Door*. Glendale, Calif.: Regal Books, 1979.

_____. *The Transcendental Mirage*. Minneapolis: Dimension Books, 1976.

_____. *The Moon is Not the Son*. Minneapolis: Bethany Fellowship, 1976.

Breese, David. *Know the Marks of Cults*. Wheaton, Ill.: Victor Books, 1979.

Clements, R. D. *God and the Gurus*. Downers Grove, Ill.: Inter-Varsity Press, 1975.

Davies, Horton. *Christian Deviations*. 3rd rev. ed. Philadelphia: Westminster Press, 1972.

Langford, H. *Traps: A Probe of Those Strange New Cults*. Montgomery,

Ala.: Committee for Christian Education and Publications, Presbyterian Church in America, 1977.

Levitt, Zola. *The Spirit of Sun Myung Moon*. Irvine, Calif.: Harvest House, 1976.

MacCollum, Joel. *The Way of Victor Paul Wierwille*. New York: Seabury Press, 1979.

McBeth, L. *Strange New Religions*. Rev. ed. Nashville: Broadman Press, 1977.

Martin, Walter R. *The New Cults*. Santa Ana, Calif.: Vision House, 1980.

———. *The Kingdom of the Cults*. Rev. ed. Minneapolis: Bethany Fellowship, 1977.

Means, Pat. *The Mystical Maze*. Downers Grove, Ill: Inter-Varsity Press, 1976.

Newport, John P. *Christ and the New Consciousness*. Nashville: Broadman Press, 1978.

Robertson, Irvine. *What the Cults Believe*. 2nd ed. Chicago: Moody Press, 1979.

Sparks, Jack. *The Mind Benders*. New York: Thomas Nelson, 1977.

Starkes, M. Thomas. *Confronting Popular Cults*. Nashville: Broadman Press, 1972.

Streiker, Lowell D. *The Cults Are Coming!* Nashville: Abingdon Press, 1978.

Yamamoto, J. I. *The Puppet Master*. Downers Grove, Ill.: Inter-Varsity Press, 1977.

OTHER POPULAR CRITICISMS OF NEW RELIGIONS

Boettcher, Robert, and Freedman, Gordon L. *Gifts of Deceit: Sun Myung Moon, Tongsun Park, and the Korean Scandal*. New York: Holt, Rinehart & Winston, 1980.

Cohen, Daniel, *The New Believers*. New York: Ballantine Books, 1975.

Conway, Flo, and Sielgeman, Jim. *Snapping*. New York: Lippincott, 1978.

Cooper, Paulette. *The Scandal of Scientology*. New York: Tower, 1971.

Edwards, Christopher. *Crazy for God.* Englewood Cliffs, N.J.: Prentice-Hall, 1979.

Freed, Josh. *Moonwebs: Journey into the Mind of a Cult.* Toronto: Dorset, 1980.

Hunter, Evan. *Brainwashing: From Pavlov to Powers.* New York: The Bookmailer, 1962.

_____. *Brainwashing in Red China: The Calculated Destruction of Men's Minds.* New York: Vanguard, 1953.

Martin, Rachel. *Escape.* Denver: Accent Books, 1979.

Mills, Jeannie, *Six Years With God.* New York: A & W Publishers, 1979.

Patrick, Ted, and Dulack, Tom. *Let Our Children Go!* New York: Ballantine Books, 1976.

Rudin, James, and Rudin, Marcia. *Prison or Paradise? The New Religious Cults.* Philadelphia: Fortress Press, 1980.

Stoner, Carroll, and Parke, Jo Anne. *All Gods Children.* Radnor, Penn.: Chilton, 1977.

Thielmann, Bonnie. *The Broken God.* Elgin, Ill: David C. Cook, 1979.

Underwood, Barbara, and Underwood, Betty. *Hostage to Heaven.* New York: Clarkson N. Potter, 1979.

Wood, Allen T., and Vitek, J. *Moonstruck.* New York: Morrow, 1979.

Index

David G. Bromley, chairman of sociology at the University of Hartford, Connecticut, and Anson D. Shupe, Jr., associate professor of sociology at the University of Texas, Arlington, have been collaborating on studies of the cult controversy for over five years. Both authors have written extensively about the cults and anticultist movement. They travel and speak widely on this uniquely American concern.